# LOCOMOTIVES OF THE DULUTH MISSABE & IRON RANGE

## By Frank A. King

Published by;
## Pacific Fast Mail
P.O. Box 57, Edmonds
Washington, 98020

Other books by Frank King:
THE MISSABE ROAD, 1972
MINNESOTA LOGGING RAILROADS, 1981

© Copyright 1984 by Pacific Fast Mail.
All rights reserved, including those to
reproduce this book, or parts thereof, in any
form without written permission of the
publisher, PFM Publications.

Library of Congress #83-061456

ISBN #0-915713-11-X

Book Design/Cover Illustration, Mike Pearsall

Illustrations, Jim Finnell, Mike Pearsall

Lithographed in Canada by:
Evergreen Press, Ltd.
Vancouver, B.C.

Typography by:
The Type Merchant
Everett, Washington

## BIBLIOGRAPHY
**Books**

Beaver, Roy C., *The Bessemer and Lake Erie Railroad 1869-1969*. San Marino, Golden West Books, 1969.

Bruce, Alfred W., *The Steam Locomotive in America*, New York, W. W. Norton & Co., Inc., 1952.

King, Frank A., *The Missabe Road*, San Marino, Golden West Books, 1972.

**Periodicals**

*Baldwin Locomotives*, Baldwin Locomotive Works Quarterly Publication, 1923 1943, various issues.

*Locomotives of Recent Construction*, Locomotive Catalogs Published by the Baldwin Locomotive Works, 1906-1923.

*Locomotive Cyclopedia*, Simmons-Boardman, various editions.

Various Publications published over the years by the D&IR, DM&N and the DM&IR.

*Trains*, November, 1980

*Railway Age*, June 5, 1943.

## DEDICATION
**To:** Patrick M. Sullivan who rose from engine wiper to Superintendent of Motive Power and Cars of the Missabe Road. During his half century with the road, which began in 1902 on the DM&N, "Paddy," as he was known to all and sundry, also served as locomotive fireman, engineer and general road foreman of engines. He was a steam man of the old school, a colorful character, much loved and respected by his associates.

Pacific Fast Mail and the author wish to thank the Editors and Publishers of *Trains* magazine and *Railway Age* for graciously allowing us to reprint portions of the November, 1980 issue of *Trains*, and the June 5th, 1943 issue of *Railway Age*.

Bruce E. Meyer

# TABLE OF CONTENTS

| | | |
|---|---|---:|
| 1. | D&IR Motive Power 1883-1900 | 11 |
| 2. | DM&N Motive Power 1892-1903 | 27 |
| 3. | Consolidations Everywhere! | 39 |
| 4. | Mikados and Santa Fes | 79 |
| 5. | Articulateds — Mallets to Yellowstones | 107 |
| 6. | Passenger Power | 173 |
| 7. | Switchers | 207 |
| 8. | Postwar Power | 225 |
| 9. | The Diesels | 245 |
| | Servicing Facilities | 271 |
| | Rolling Stock | 286 |
| | Mining Locomotives | 289 |
| | Rosters | 297 |
| | Index | 314 |

# PREFACE/ACKNOWLEDGEMENTS

From 1883 until the present time the Missabe Road and its predecessor companies, the Duluth and Iron Range and the Duluth, Missabe and Northern, have owned and operated 352 steam locomotives and 136 diesel units. During the past century this motive power fleet has moved a mountain of iron ore totaling 2,002,923,927 tons (as of December 31, 1982).

Few roads of this size have owned such a variety of steam locomotives. Among them were the D&IR's fleet of 30 big, clean-lined 4-8-0's, one of which was exhibited by Schenectady at the 1893 World's Fair in Chicago as an outstanding example of the builder's art. The DM&N's big Baldwin 2-8-8-2 Mallets were rated among the world's largest and most powerful locomotives when they were placed in service on Proctor Hill in 1910. During 1938 the DM&N received its big 0-10-0 switchers from Baldwin. Initially assigned to the Proctor Yard ore-sorting service, they were the heaviest of their type in the age of steam. The 18 superb Yellowstones, received during World War II, were acclaimed the finest articulated locomotives built by Baldwin. These great engines handled 17,000 plus ton trains 40 years ago, a feat equaled by few roads today in spite of diesels and other advanced technology. Lastly, the big 0-10-2's and 2-10-4's received after World War II each represented the most powerful examples of their respective types.

**Conversion to diesel power was completed during 1960. Yellowstone #222 made the last steam powered ore run on July 5th of that year. Two years later, on September 29, 1962, USRA Santa Fe locomotive 514 handled the farewell trip for steam over the Missabe Road. This special train, carrying 325 passengers, commemorated the construction of the DM&N Railway and the first shipment of ore from the Mesabi Range 70 years before.**

Delaying dieselization had its benefits. The Missabe avoided acquiring a polyglot assortment of diesel locomotive makes and types, a problem encountered by so many roads that dieselized early. The Missabe, always noted for its well-maintained steam power, continues this practice with its diesel fleet. Early in dieselization, the company elected to standardize on units of the six-motor, C-C, road switcher type. This fleet, consisting of EMD SD 9, SD 18, SD 38 and SD 38-2 locomotives, has performed well for the Missabe, where high tractive effort and moderate horsepower are the primary considerations.

This book has been compiled to fill the need for a detailed look at the locomotives of the Missabe. The writer's first book, entitled *The Missabe Road*, was a company history, and for this reason motive power was not given the attention it richly deserves.

Appreciation is expressed to the Duluth, Missabe and Iron Range Ry Co. from whose files considerable information used in this book was obtained. Appreciation is also due to Donald B. Shank, recently retired Vice President and General Manager of the Missabe Road, for his valued suggestions and critique concerning this project. Recognition is expressed to the St. Louis County, Lake County and Minnesota Historical Societies who have made photographic material available. Also to Gerald M. Best for his previous assistance with the locomotive roster. A book requires a publisher. Donald Drew and Mike Pearsall of Pacific Fast Mail, Publishers, must be recognized for their valuable support and talents without which this book would never have become a reality.

Frank A. King

Bruce E. Meyer

# INTRODUCTION

Culture has been defined as the accumulation of knowledge; in this sense, one of its higher forms is the preservation and interpretation of history. The railroad industry and its millions of enthusiastic devotees are indebted to those individuals who spend a lifetime researching and recording the fascinating world of railroading and sharing that knowledge with us through their writings.

It has been my unique privilege to know and to work with Frank King, a leading authority on state and local history, who has made a substantial contribution to our knowledge of railroading through his two important books, *The Missabe Road* (1972) and *Minnesota Logging Railroads* (1981). This skilled historian has also written numerous articles for national and state publications, one of which appeared in the November, 1980 issue of *Trains* magazine and which has been included in this publication.

Although this book is his latest in a long line of important historical contributions, it is embryonic in nature in that it represents the beginning of his lifetime love of railroading — the steam locomotive!

I have reviewed Frank King's manuscript with a critical eye, because I, too, have spent the greater part of my life with Missabe's locomotives — as a locomotive fireman and engineer during the heyday of steam power on the Duluth, Missabe and Iron Range Railway and as the chief operating officer when the last steam train ran on the railroad, an eventful day which ended a nostalgic period and which heralded the most significant change in power generation in the industrial world. So it is because of this past experience that I can say that Frank King has done a splendid job in writing a factual and interesting story of the locomotives on the Missabe Road; in doing so, he has contributed substantially to the preservation of our important history and to the enrichment of our culture.

*Donald B. Shank* (retired)
Vice-President & General Manager
Duluth, Missabe and Iron Range Railway
Duluth, Minnesota

Bruce E. Meyer

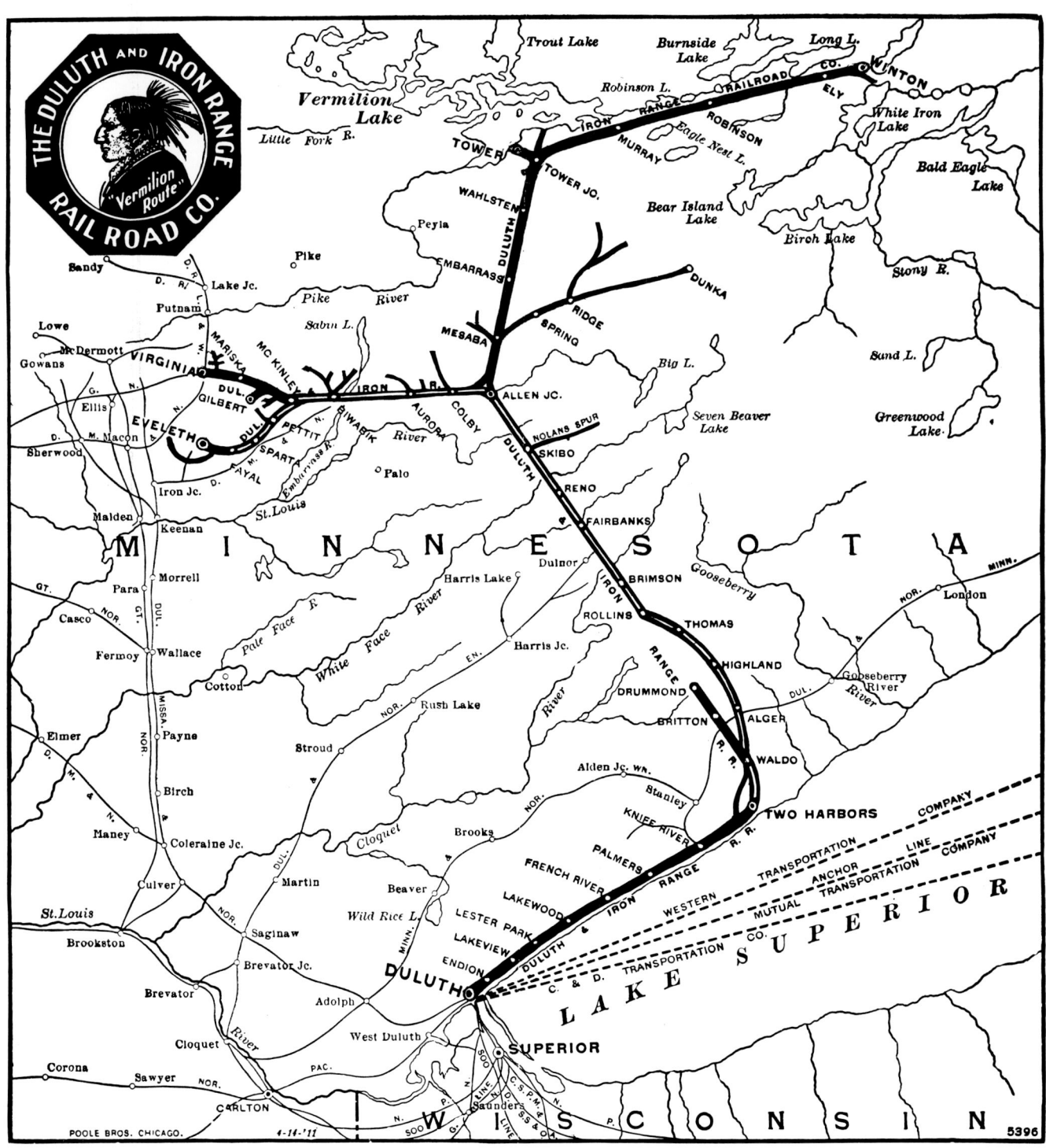

# 1. D&IR MOTIVE POWER-1883 to 1900

During the summer of 1883 construction began on the Duluth and Iron Range Railroad, which was to run from Agate Bay on Lake Superior to the newly developed iron mines near Tower on the Vermilion iron range. The contract called for the 68-mile line to be completed by August 1, 1884, approximately 12 months.

During August, 1883 the first track (laid with sixty-pound rail rolled by the Pennsylvania Steel Company) was put in place on the merchandise dock at Agate Bay, shortly to be known as Two Harbors. A locomotive was soon needed to assist with rail laying; the company had placed an order with the Baldwin Locomotive Works for a wood-burning Mogul on July 10. This locomotive, which was assigned number 3 rather than number 1, was available for immediate shipment, because it was built originally for a railroad in Brazil, the San Juan and Vera Cruz, which had refused her for technical reasons. Purchase price of the little engine was $9,750 to be paid in cash even though the financier of the entire railroad and mining venture was Charlemagne Tower, a prominent and respected citizen of Philadelphia, where the locomotive was built.

Because there was no rail connection between Two Harbors and Duluth, it was necessary to ship the engine by barge. Transporting No. 3, later affectionately known as the Three Spot, seemed like a routine job. It was a beautiful summer day and the big lake was calm when the company tug, the Ella G. Stone, left Duluth pulling the scow with the precious locomotive. About 20 miles up the lake a moderate north-easter began to blow and soon increased to gale proportions. The tug captain ordered the crew to stand by and be ready to take an ax to the lines securing the tug to the scow, but fortunately this was not necessary, as the tug found refuge in the peaceful waters of Agate Bay and safely delivered its cargo to the dock.

A wood-burner, the little locomotive literally lived off the land as she pushed north with the rail train, consuming wood from the nearby forests and syphoning water from the streams. The Three Spot was the only wood-burning locomotive on the D&IR, as all subsequent engines were fired with eastern bituminous coal shipped to Two Harbors on lake steamers. Interestingly, the first seven locomotives (Nos. 1-7) were equipped with diamond stacks and some old-timers on the D&IR erroneously referred to them as wood-burners.

By mid-July of 1884 there were eleven new Baldwin locomotives and 350 ore cars on hand. All of this equipment was shipped from Duluth to Two Harbors by water, because there was no rail connection until 1886. The locomotives were as follows:

| No. | Type | Built | Construction Number | Engine Weight | Cylinders | Driver Diameter |
|---|---|---|---|---|---|---|
| 1 | 4-4-0 | 1884 | 7258 | 83,900 lbs. | 17 × 24″ | 63″ |
| 2 | 4-4-0 | 1884 | 7259 | 83,900 lbs. | 17 × 24″ | 63″ |
| 3 | 2-6-0 | 1883 | 6649 | 75,000 lbs. | 16 × 24″ | 52″ |
| 4 | 0-4-0 | 1884 | 7252 | 69,000 lbs. | 16 × 24″ | 51″ |
| 5 | 0-4-0 | 1884 | 7358 | 69,000 lbs. | 16 × 24″ | 51″ |
| 5 | 2-8-0 | 1883 | 6874 | 110,000 lbs. | 20 × 24″ | 51″ |
| 7 | 2-8-0 | 1883 | 6937 | 110,000 lbs. | 20 × 24″ | 51″ |
| 8 | 2-8-0 | 1884 | 7347 | 110,000 lbs. | 20 × 24″ | 51″ |
| 9 | 2-8-0 | 1884 | 7354 | 110,000 lbs. | 20 × 24″ | 51″ |
| 10 | 2-8-0 | 1884 | 7374 | 110,000 lbs. | 20 × 24″ | 51″ |
| 11 | 2-8-0 | 1884 | 7381 | 110,000 lbs. | 20 × 24″ | 51″ |

By this time the track had been pushed to within ten miles of the mines. Contractor Wolf was at the end of the line, driving his men to complete the road on time. By superstition, Friday was considered an unfavorable day, so plans were revised to have the first ore train move on Thursday, July 31. Only by working his crews round the clock was the contractor able to meet his new deadline. Early that morning, a train consisting of ten empty ore cars was spotted for loading.

Meanwhile, Consolidation No. 8 steamed out of Two Harbors at 7 a.m. with a train consisting of ten empty ore cars and trailing caboose No. 21, which served as the private car for President Tower and his special guests. Snorting up the three percent grade leading from Lake Superior, the little train climbed some 1,100 feet in the first 12 miles. The engineer in charge of No. 8 was Thomas Owens, later to become Superintendent and Vice President of the road. The cars were of 20-ton capacity and 28 feet in length. (These cars soon proved incompatible with the newly established 12 foot vessel hatch and dock pocket spacing. They were rebuilt to standard 24 foot length within a short time.)

The residents of Tower and the nearby mining community of Soudan turned out in force that morning to celebrate the arrival of the train, which would depart with the first shipment of Minnesota iron ore. (Even though everyone present was aware of the symbolic importance of the event, few would have predicted that ore shipments from the Vermilion and the soon-to-be-discovered giant Mesabi Range would total over three billion tons by the following century.

Finally, around 11 a.m., No. 8 emerged from the pine forest and rolled to a stop near the ore loading pocket at Soudan. The schedule called for a 2 p.m. departure in order to arrive at Two Harbors before nightfall. However, the ensuing celebration and program consumed much more time than anticipated, and the train did not pull out until 4 p.m.

Engineer Owens moved more cautiously on the southbound trip, as he was uncertain of the new roadbed. More important, Owens was not sure he would be able to control the train on the downgrades, because he felt that the cars were grossly overloaded. The ten-car train actually contained 220 long tons of ore, which was not a serious overload.

As no water tanks had been constructed along the route, it was necessary to stop occasionally to syphon water from streams. Owens was also slow and cautious because of the top officials and their wives riding in the caboose. The train finally reached Two Harbors at about 11 p.m. with everyone aboard contented with their great day. Before the 1884 shipping season was over, 62,122 tons of rich Vermilion lump was loaded into vessels at Two Harbors — a good start, even though there was some difficulty in selling the new ore.

Passenger service between Two Harbors and Tower began on August 11. The two Baldwin 4-4-0's, Nos. 1 and 2, were assigned to handle this run. D&IR timetable No. 1 showed trains 1 and 2 running daily except Sunday, with 5 hours and 10 minutes required for the 68 mile run in either direction. No one complained of the length of the trip though, for before the railroad the trip had required several days.

No new locomotives were acquired during 1885. The fleet of 11 Baldwins was adequate to handle 227,075 tons of ore as well as the general freight and passenger business. Work on a second ore dock was well under way to handle the increase in business anticipated for the coming year.

Only two new locomotives, both Baldwins, were received during 1886, even though the ore business increased substantially. No. 12, a Consolidation, was the last locomotive to be shipped by barge from Duluth, for during December, 1886, the line between Duluth and Two Harbors was completed. Engine No. 12 was the pride of the road. While previous engines had come with unbalanced (d) valves with Stephensen Link motion and a crosshead-actuated feedwater pump, No. 12 sported Robinson balanced valves, injectors, Westinghouse air brake equipment and a hydrostatic lubricator. The other engine, No. 13, an 0-4-0 switcher, also came equipped with Westinghouse air brakes. By this time the average tonnage for the Baldwin Consolidations, based on 20 wooden ore cars per train, was 457.4 tons of ore and 706 tons gross train weight, including the four-wheel caboose. This required the assistance of a Consolidation pusher from Tower Junction to Rivers and from Embarrass to Hinsdale. The annual report for that year listed a $300,000 surplus from mining and railroad operations. The future, indeed, looked most promising.

This prosperity was not to last, however, because the newly formed Illinois Steel Company had acquired a rich ore deposit at Ely, 20 miles east of the Tower property. In order to have an outlet for their ore, Illinois Steel was determined to buy the D&IR or bring in a competing trunk line to the Vermilion Range if necessary. Rather than fight it out, in 1887 the Tower group sold their Minnesota Iron Company and its subsidiary, D&IR, to Illinois Steel for $6,400,000. Although unhappy about losing control of the Minnesota mining and railroad empire, Tower was probably solaced by almost doubling his money within five years. That year the road acquired two 0-4-0 switchers, Nos. 14 and 15, and Consolidations 16 and 17 from Baldwin.

Author's Collection

Mogul No. 3 was the first locomotive owned by the D&IR. It was purchased in 1883 for $9750 . . . cash! At right is the original voucher to Baldwin, signed by Charlemagne Tower Jr. (above), President of the D&IR from 1883 to 1887. In 1899 the little engine, no longer needed, was sold off to a lumber road. About the time of the photograph at right, No. 3 had been reacquired by the railroad and used for various historical functions before being placed on display at Two Harbors.

Engine 3, rebuilt and "back dated," poses alongside D&IR Mikado 308 during dedication ceremonies. The legend on the lower photo tells the story . . .

Both photos, author's collection

During 1887 the D&IR, with the St. Paul and Duluth Railroad, began a commuter train service between downtown Duluth and Lester Park (located at the eastern end of the city). The service ran 15 round trips daily. Motive power, provided by the D&IR, was an old shotgun-stacked 4-4-0, equipped with 54" drivers and 16 × 24 inch cylinders, purchased from the Chicago and Eastern Illinois, which was controlled by Illinois Steel. This engine, numbered 99 by the D&IR, was built by Hinckley in 1871 for a road which later became part of the C&EI. With the extension of the Duluth Street Railway to Lester Park in 1892, the D&IR's suburban service was discontinued. Old No. 99, no longer needed, sat derelict at Two Harbors until it was scrapped in about 1911.

During May, 1888 the new management approved construction of a 21 mile extension from Tower Junction to Ely to serve the Chandler Mine, which was expected to produce 300,000 tons of ore per year. In anticipation of this added traffic, the road bought five Consolidations, Nos. 18-22 and three 4-4-0 passenger locomotives, Nos. 23-25. The latter were heavier and more powerful than the two previous 4-4-0's, weighing 96,600 pounds vs. 83,900 pounds for the 1884 machines. These engines were equipped with 18 × 24 inch cylinders and 63" drivers. In addition, one 0-4-0 switcher, No. 26, was acquired. These locomotives were all built by Baldwin and would be the last received from this builder for nearly a decade, as the new owners had no strong allegiance to Philadelphia. The road also received 426 freight cars that year, including 200 ore cars of the new standard 24' length. These ore cars were constructed in the company shops at Two Harbors. Ore traffic totaled slightly over one half million tons during 1888, the first full year under the new regime.

One six-wheel switcher, No. 27, weighing 94,400 pounds, and six Consolidations, were received from the Schenectady Locomotive Works in 1889. The Consolidations, Nos. 28-33, were short-lived on the D&IR, for they were sold to affiliate Chicago and Eastern Illinois three years later. These Consolidations weighed 120,400 pounds and carried 20 × 24 inch cylinders. That year the quick-action triple valve was adopted for use on passenger equipment in place of the plain triple. This triple valve was also adopted for freight cars, and the 8" Westinghouse air pump was made standard for locomotives. At this time air brakes were applied to engines 6-13, 16-22 and 26. It is interesting that the D&IR was the first railroad in the United States to have its locomotives and rolling stock completely equipped with air brakes. The road was also listed later as the first to be completely equipped with MCB automatic couplers.

Discovery of soft, high grade hematite iron ore on the Mesabi Range, first at Mountain Iron and shortly afterwards at Biwabik, a little distance to the east, posed both a threat and a challenge to the Illinois Steel Company and its railroad subsidiary, the D&IR. The first reaction was negative. It was felt that opening any sizeable body of ore on the Mesabi would decrease the value of the high grade ore on the Vermilion, which was harder to mine.

The decision was wisely made, however, to construct a branch in 1892 from the main line at Allen Junction to McKinley (18 miles to the west) in order to compete with the Duluth, Missabe and Northern, whose line was rapidly being extended eastward to Biwabik. In anticipation of increased tonnage from the Mesabi Range, ten Consolidation type locomotives, Nos. 50-59, were received in 1892 from Schenectady. These engines were practically identical to the six 1889 Consolidations, Nos. 28-33, which were then sold to the Chicago and Eastern Illinois Railroad. During 1893 the 1892 Consolidations averaged 21 loaded, wooden ore cars per train, carrying 517 tons of ore, for a total gross weight of 777 tons.

In 1893 the road made a radical departure from the two previous classes of freight power and purchased ten 4-8-0 Twelve-Wheelers from Schenectady. Costing $11,792.96 each, these engines were given numbers 60-69. Totaling 174,800 pounds in working order, equipped with 22 × 26-inch cylinders and carrying 144,800 pounds on their 54" drivers, they were among the largest engines of their time. No. 68 had the distinction of being placed on exhibition at the World's Fair in Chicago that year. (The 4-8-0 was then receiving considerable attention from a number of trunk lines; the Great Northern and Southern Pacific roads bought them in substantial numbers.) During 1893 the 4-8-0's averaged 26 loaded, wooden ore cars per train, carrying 639 tons of ore. The average gross weight of the loaded trains, including caboose, was 960 tons.

The 4-8-0's were to reign during the nineties. Four more, Nos. 70-73 were acquired from Schenectady in 1895, allowing the road to handle a peak ore volume of over two million tons. The following year the road acquired ten additional Twelve Wheelers, Nos. 74-83, this time returning to Baldwin in Philadelphia.

By 1899, "Three Spot," the little Mogul that helped build the railroad, was no longer needed. She was sold to the nearby Duluth and Northern Minnesota Railway at Knife River, renumbered 2, and was immediately put to work hauling trains of white pine logs. In addition, for some unknown reason, Consolidation 56 was sold to the far away El Paso and Northeastern Railroad.

On October 30, 1899 the road placed an order with Schenectady for six Twelve Wheelers, Nos. 84-89, at a cost of $15,000 each, F.O.B. Chicago. Included in the same order were four Ten Wheel (4-6-0) locomotives, Nos. 101-104, at a cost of $13,350 each, F.O.B. Chicago. On November 21, D&IR President J. L. Greatsinger wired Schenectady . . . "Would like to add two more Ten Wheelers to my order for May delivery." Schenectady Vice President and General Manager, A. J. Pitkin, responded . . . "Can offer you two additional Ten Wheelers in June. Find that the cost of these engines has advanced $500 since closing last contract. Are desirous to meet your wishes so far as possible and will divide the difference in increased cost of material, making price of engines $13,600 each at Chicago. When I tell you that we have been obliged to decline to bid on some 50 engines within the last week or ten days, not being able to offer delivery before the Fall of 1900, you will appreciate something of the condition of the locomotive business; but we are extremely anxious to build the two additional locomotives you require and hope that we may have your proposal." The offer was quickly accepted by the D&IR. The Ten Wheelers weighed 150,800 pounds and had 19 × 26 inch cylinders and 58" drivers.

All 12 locomotives included in this order were received during 1900. Thus, the beginning of the new century found the D&IR with 75 locomotives. That year there was little rest for these engines, with ore tonnage booming at slightly over four million, and general freight and passenger business also attaining new highs.

Lake County Historical Society

D&IR No. 1, 1 4-4-0, was the first passenger engine on the road. She is shown soon after delivery, with her original lettering and builders stripes.

State Historical Society of Wisconsin

The D&IR's second passenger engine, aptly numbered 2, is seen after being rebuilt with an extended smokebox and straight stack. The road's first switcher was the little No. 4, a 0-4-0. It had the distinction of being the smallest locomotive owned by the road. She is shown here in two views: At the Soudan mine loading pocket in 1884 and, below, in ore dock service.

Tower-Soudan Historical Society

Author's Collection

17

H.L. Broadbelt collection

The first heavy freight engines on the D&IR were the G class Consolidations. Seven engines, numbers 6 to 12, were delivered by Baldwin between 1883 and 1886. Above, engine No. 7 was a sister to the No. 8, the locomotive that hauled the first train of iron ore in 1884. Left, No. 9 is shown at Ely, Minnesota around 1890 while, below, the No. 10 sits at Two Harbors in 1884. The little 4-4-0, No. 1, is in the background.

Author's Collection

Minnesota Historical Society

Grace Lee Nute collection, from Northeast Minnesota Historical Center

Above, G class 2-8-0 No. 12 heads an ore train at Ely, Minnesota in the 1880's. Below, an unknown G class and B class 0-4-0 stand before the ornate depot at Biwabik.

Author's Collection

Author's Collection

(Minnesota Historical Society)

The little B class 0-4-0 switchers served the D&IR for many years. Above, No. 4 and train loading ore at the open pit Fayal mine, in the heart of the Mesabi range. 0-4-0 No. 14 has a cut of wooden ore cars in stockpile loading service at the Canton mine, near Biwabik, Minnesota, in 1895. Below, in later years, No. 14 was used as the shop switcher at Two Harbors.

Author's Collection

Right, class H 2-8-0 No. 51, assisted by another 2-8-0 on the rear, heads a 16-car special. The trip was sponsored by the Minnesota Iron Company in 1895, and included such notables as Chicago meat packer P.D. Armour, Marshall Field, and west coast banker, Darius Ogden Mills. Mills, you may recall, was one of the principal backers of the fabled narrow gauge, the Carson & Colorado.

Engine 51 is shown again in 1901 on another special. Note the unusual headlight . . . it didn't last long!

Below, D&IR No. 24 was a beautiful example of the "C" class 4-4-0's. With its 63" drivers it was prime passenger power in the 90's.

All photos, author's collection

Both photos, author's collection

Like so many railroads, the D&IR turned to the 4-8-0 type to haul heavy tonnage in the 1890's. Above, two views class "J" of No. 60, the first of its type delivered to the road: one in a typical locomotive photograph of that era; the other on the turntable at the Two Harbors roundhouse. At right, Schenectady-built 4-8-0 No. 66 heads a long train of empty ore cars, while No. 67 thaws cars of frozen iron ore. The problem of thawing the ore plagued the Lake Superior district during the early spring and late fall shipping periods. Steam generated by the locomotives was fed to lances inserted into the tops and sides of the cars, thereby thawing the frozen ore.

Both photos, author's collection

23

Author's Collection

During the early years of the century, the D&IR moved more logs into Duluth than any other railroad serving the city. Above, No. 69, in this view taken in 1910, heads a log train near west Duluth.
Below, another example of the 4-8-0 wheel arrangement was No. 83, in this photo taken at Two Harbors. The engine was built by Baldwin in 1899.

Author's Collection

Engine 99, a 4-4-0, was the former No. 12 of the Chicago & Eastern Illinois. The D&IR acquired the locomotive in 1887 and used it in suburban train service.

Author's Collection

Not too much is known about this "cornfield meet" except it involved two 4-8-0's in ore train service sometime in the 1890's.

Jerry K. Nichols collection, from Larry Easton

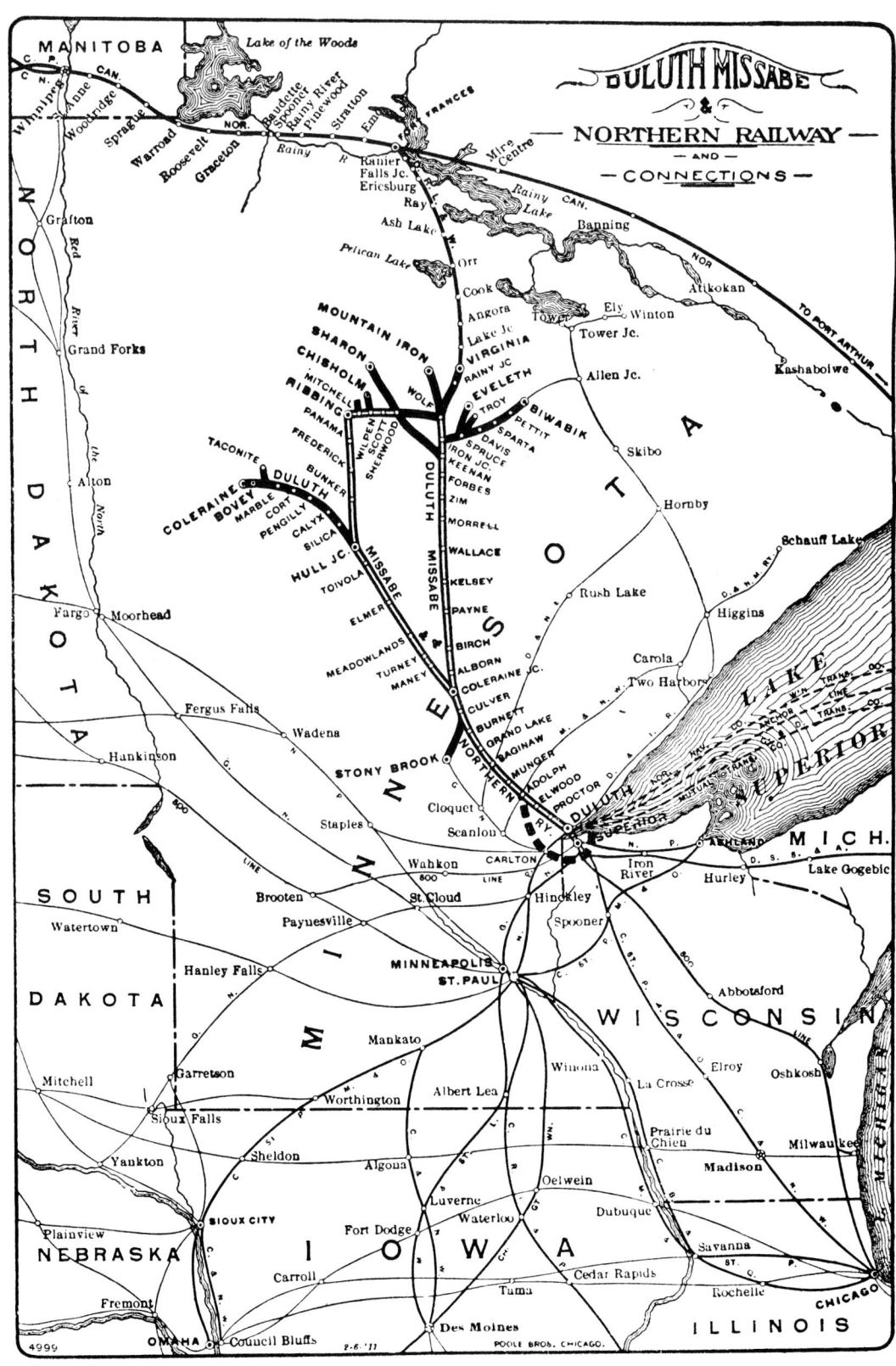

# 11. DM&N MOTIVE POWER-1892 to 1900

A 100 mile ridge of granite slashes diagonally across Northern Minnesota. The Mesabi range lies on the south side of that granite ridge. At its closest point the range is about 60 miles north of Duluth. Mesabi, sometimes spelled Mesaba, Missabe (as with the DM&N) or Missabay, means giant in the Chippewa Indian language, and the range is sometimes referred to as the Giant's Ridge. To date, over three billion tons of iron ore have been extracated from it.

After 15 years of searching, Duluth's famed Merritt Brothers discovered rich, soft hematite iron ore at a location now known as Mountain Iron on November 16, 1890. But the closest railroad was the Duluth and Iron Range, some 30 miles to the east. To the south, 48 miles distant, ran the Canadian Pacific-backed Duluth and Winnipeg. The Merritts were primarily interested in developing the ore bodies and did not want to construct and operate a railroad. They first asked the Duluth and Iron Range to construct a branch from their main line west to Mountain Iron, but the D&IR was unreceptive. Then the Merritts approached the Northern Pacific and the St. Paul and Duluth railroads, but neither was interested because of the high investment and risk involved. The Merritts were forced to build a railroad of their own.

The Duluth, Missabe and Northern Railway Company was incorporated by the Merritt group on June 23, 1891, and on January 28, 1892 a contract was let for construction of a railroad extending from the Duluth and Winnipeg road at Stony Brook Junction 48 miles north to Mt. Iron. Separate contracts called for a 16.5 mile branch from Iron Junction to Biwabik on the east and a five mile branch from Wolf to Virginia.

Operating headquarters were located at Iron Junction, where both an enginehouse and a rip track for repairs were provided. At Stony Brook Junction a two-stall enginehouse, a 60' turntable, and fuel and water facilities were constructed. These facilities, while minimal, were adequate for the early operations.

Throughout the summer and early fall of 1892, construction of the railroad moved ahead rapidly with 60 pound rail being laid at rates as high as two miles per day. The line was completed to Mountain Iron by mid-October, and on October 15 the Merritts ran a special train from Duluth to Mt. Iron to celebrate the occasion.

Although the DM&N had placed orders for two 4-4-0 and three 4-6-0 locomotives during 1892, they did not receive them until the following year. During 1892, the contractor leased a number of ex-New York Central Moguls (2-6-0's) from the New York Construction Company. In addition, the DM&N leased 4-4-0 engines from both the Northern Pacific and the St. Paul and Duluth on an occasional basis.

On October 17 the first train of iron ore from the Mesabi Range was dispatched to the Duluth and Winnipeg ore dock at Allouez (Superior, Wisconsin). The consist included 10 cars of rich hematite assaying better than 63 percent iron. Between Mountain Iron and Stony Brook Junction, the train was pulled by an ex-NYC Mogul. At Stony Brook Junction it was picked up by the D&W local freight and hauled the remainder of the way to Allouez.

Ore then began moving in solid trains of 40 cars between Mountain Iron and Allouez. It was necessary to doublehead these trains over the Duluth and Winnipeg, because the only locomotives available were small American 4-4-0's. A total of 394 cars were on order and in service, of which 200 were 25 ton capacity ore cars. First year shipments totaled only 4,245 tons due to difficulty experienced with frozen ore, both in the cars and in dock pockets. This total constituted two vessel loads and required running one ten-car train and five trains of 40 cars each.

During 1893, the first full year of operation, DM&N motive power consisted of 18 locomotives. Ore and general freight traffic was handled by 10 Ten-Wheeler (4-6-0) locomotives, Nos. 5-14, developing 24,000 pounds of tractive effort, weighing 123,000 pounds, and purchased at a contract price of $9,928.75 each. They had 19 × 26 inch cylinders and 56" drivers. Two American (4-4-0) passenger engines, Nos. 1 and 2, each costing $7,855 and weighing 89,800

DM&N engine No. 2, built by Pittsburgh Locomotive Works in 1893, softly steams next to the road's first operating headquarters at Iron Junction. Pittsburgh was the DM&N's favorite builder in the early days. Engine 2 was later sold to the Cazenovia Southern Ry., a Wisconsin shortline.

pounds made up the remainder of the original motive power along with six 0-6-0 switchers, Nos. 50-55, weighing 84,000 pounds and with a price tag of $8,035 apiece. All of these locomotives were constructed by the Pittsburgh Locomotive Works. Rolling stock consisted of 1,001 ore cars, 35 boxcars, 210 flatcars, 50 logging bunks, 13 cabooses, eight miscellaneous passenger and head-end cars and the business car "Missabe." Interestingly, the logging bunks were received without trucks, inasmuch as they were in service only during the winter, or non-ore season, and could use trucks removed from idle ore cars. Extension of the DM&N into Duluth, along with construction of a large wooden ore dock on St. Louis Bay, was completed by July, 1893.

In early 1894, the road received six additional Ten-Wheelers, Nos. 15-20, from Pittsburgh. In addition, engine No. 300, a Consolidation, was received from the same works for service on the 5.5 mile 2.2 percent grade between Proctor Yard and the ore dock at West Duluth. This engine developed 36,800 pounds of tractive effort and weighed 160,000 pounds. Her cylinders were 22 × 28 inches and her drivers were 50" in diameter. She was advertised by the builder as the most powerful locomotive in the world and contained several unusual features, such as both air and water brakes (a feature also incorporated on Denver and Rio Grande locomotives because of heavy grade service), a clerestory cab, a slope-backed tender to afford a clear view while backing down the hill, blind tires on the two middle pairs of drivers, and an air-operated bell ringer. No. 300 proved very satisfactory on the Hill and in 1895 was joined by a duplicate, No. 301, also built by Pittsburgh. The contract price of these engines was $10,350 each.

With the rapidly expanding ore business expected to top three million tons in 1899, it became apparent that heavier and more powerful road engines would have to be placed into service. To determine future motive power requirements a test train of 65 loads of ore was made up and set out on Grand Lake Siding, and on October 24, 1898, Consolidation locomotive No. 301 pulled this train of 3,182 tons into Proctor. This was by far the heaviest train yet handled by the DM&N, and it contained 2,060 long tons (2,240 pounds) of ore.

Thirteen additional Ten-Wheelers, identical to those in the initial order, were received during the next three years. Engines 21 and 22 arrived in 1898, Nos. 23-26 in 1899 and 27-33 in 1900. Automatic hose couplings were placed on engines 5, 23, 25, 27 and 33 to enable use in passenger service. (Upon completion of the line into Duluth all main line passenger service was handled by the Class F Ten-Wheelers.) During 1900, two heavier 0-6-0 switchers were received from Pittsburgh. Weighing 120,450 pounds and costing $11,900 each, these engines were assigned Nos. 56 and 57. They were assigned to Proctor Yard for switching and ore sorting service. In addition, two road service Consolidations, Nos. 302 and 303, arrived from the same builder that year. Costing $12,279 and $14,500 respectively, these engines weighed 180,000 pounds and developed 36,900 pounds tractive effort. Equipped with long, narrow fireboxes (121 × 14¼ inches), these two Consolidations were difficult to fire in heavy ore service, for it was almost impossible to throw coal to the forward end of the grates. Much of the time, the fireman had to push the coal forward with a fire hoe. On long, heavy grades, the firedoor was often open, and the firemen wore heavy leather aprons to keep from being burned. These engines were equipped with 22 × 28 inch cylinders and 56" drivers.

During 1900 the DM&N's fleet of 43 locomotives transported a record 3.9 million tons of ore. This tonnage fell short of the D&IR's record by only 139,868 tons. Within two years the DM&N's ore tonnage would eclipse that handled by the D&IR and remain higher thereafter.

At left, ten-wheeler No. 15 arrives at the newly built DM&N ore dock at Duluth with the first train of iron ore to Duluth from the Mesabi range. The 15 was built in 1893 and retired in 1933.

Author's Collection

The DM&N favored the ten-wheeler type for ore hauling and engines 7 and 9 are typical examples. No. 9 is on the head of an ore train sometime after delivery. Sister engine No. 7 weighed 123,000 pounds and was capable of handling 35 wooden ore cars, with each car containing 25 tons of ore.

Author's Collection

It seems everything was worth a picture in the 90's . . . even wrecks. Here a DM&N wrecking crew pauses for the camera while in the process of cleaning up a nasty ore train spill.

DM&N No. 300, one of two Consolidations equipped with slope-back tenders heads up the 2% grade to Proctor with a train of empties. Ten-wheeler No. 31, built by Pittsburgh in 1900, was used as a switcher on Duluth ore dock No. 1.

Heavy traffic in the 90's — especially the Hibbing district — meant replacing the older and lighter wood trestles with steel structures. Here, a DM&N ten-wheeler crosses a new steel span on the Superior branch.

A group of hearty Duluth citizens and railroad personnel pose before the first carload of Mesabi ore in 1892. The car was on display at Duluth Union Depot. The pine tree on top of the car signified that this was the first load of ore from a new mine . . . a tradition on the iron range.

This photograph illustrates the enormous size of the Duluth ore docks. These massive structures, originally employing millions of feet of lumber in construction, were replaced in later years with steel. On the left is 2-8-0 No. 300 and at right, one of the interesting whaleback ore boats that were in vogue on the Lakes at the time.

Three photos, author's collection

Jim Kaysen collection

The Cazenovia Southern was a tiny midwest shortline that operated between Cazenovia and Lavalle, Wisconsin, where it connected with the C&NW. It ran two trains a day east and west between the two towns — a distance of only six miles. Power on the line was the ex-DM&N 4-4-0 No. 2. As it says on the photo, service on the line was leisurely.

Author's collection

John B. Allen

The early roster of the DM&N was loaded with ten-wheelers . . . some lasting until the DM&IR era, while others were sold off to various shortlines. At left DM&N No. 17 is nearing the end of her days at Proctor. Above DM&N No. 19, built by Pittsburgh in 1893, kept her same number on the DM&IR. Her boiler was later used to provide steam at the Virginia, Minnesota engine house. Engine No. 20 is shown at Virginia on a snowy day in 1918. Speaking of snow, No. 22 is practically covered with the white stuff while on plowing duty at some unnamed yard.

Both photos, author's collection

John B. Allen

Both photos, author's collection

Another shortline that bought surplus DM&N ten-wheelers was the Detroit, Caro & Sandusky, a 48-mile freight-only line that ran from Caro to Roseburg, Michigan. Above, one of the engines sold to the DC&S was DM&N No. 5, the first of the class F 10-wheelers and a Pittsburgh product of 1893. Another was the No. 15, that originally was No. 31 on the DM&N. It was sold to the DC&S in 1940. At right, two views of DM&N No. 21, both taken at Proctor. Also at Proctor is DM&N No. 30 in May, 1930. All the class F's had 56-inch drivers with 23,000 pounds of tractive effort. The little engines served the DM&N and the before-mentioned shortlines for many years.

Author's collection

John B. Allen

37

Baldwin-built D&IR G class Consolidation No. 46 pauses at Endion Station in Duluth with a train of sawlogs bound for West Duluth sawmills. The little engine was sold for scrap in 1933.

# III. CONSOLIDATIONS EVERYWHERE!

In the first year of the twentieth century, the D&IR and DM&N handled just short of eight million tons — a record. Most of this ore came from the booming Mesabi Range. By 1901 the D&IR had 75 locomotives and 3,635 freight cars, of which 2,974 were for ore service. Though not as well situated with respect to the Mesabi ore deposits as the DM&N, the D&IR was a close knit, well managed little road with a bright future.

By this time the future of the DM&N was even more promising, with its much more strategic access to the vast Mesabi. In addition, the DM&N had a ruling grade southbound of only 0.30 of one percent compared to adverse grades of 0.62 of one percent on the D&IR. With only 43 locomotives the DM&N was handling approximately the same ore tonnage as the D&IR, which had 75 engines on its roster. This statistic alone illustrates the grade and distance advantages enjoyed by the DM&N. That road's ore car fleet then comprised 3,480 cars.

During 1901 the D&IR and the DM&N were acquired by the newly formed United States Steel Corporation. Although now under common control, they continued to operate side by side as separate entities until in 1930 depressed business required the DM&N to lease the D&IR. The motive power policies of the two roads would be quite different, however, with the D&IR generally being more conservative than the DM&N.

By 1901 most of the ore tonnage over the D&IR was handled by its fleet of 30 sturdy Class J 4-8-0's, assisted as required by 23 older and smaller Consolidations. On the DM&N the ore was moved by 29 Class F 4-6-0's, and four Class C1 2-8-0's. The motive power fleets changed, however, when both roads invested heavily in new Consolidations in the next decade.

The DM&N chose the Consolidation type for road ore service in 1899 with the purchase of No. 302 from the Pittsburgh Locomotive Works and a duplicate, No. 303, from the same builder a year later. By this time management had established that 55 all-steel cars carrying 2,750 tons of ore would constitute the standard train. The Ten-Wheelers were unable to handle trains of this weight and, in 1901, six of them, Nos. 7, 8, 9, 10, 14 and 18, were judged surplus and sold to the Indiana, Illinois and Iowa Railroad.

To replace these engines the DM&N received three additional Class C1 Consolidations, Nos. 304 through 306, costing $14,315 each. Received from the Dickson Works of the American Locomotive Company in 1902, these engines, with their 22" × 26" cylinders and 56" drivers, developed a tractive effort of 36,900 pounds and weighed 180,000 pounds. In 1903 they were followed by six engines of the same class, Nos. 307 through 312, from the Cooke Works of the American Locomotive Company. Six similar Consolidations, Nos. 313 through 318, designated as Class C2, were received from the Pittsburgh Works of the American Locomotive Company during 1904. By then, the price tag had risen to $16,840 apiece.

By this time the D&IR was also shopping for heavier and more powerful motive power. Increased ore traffic and heavier trains — made possible by 50-ton capacity steel ore cars — severely taxed the stalwart 4-8-0's. The motive power department decided to revert back to the Consolidation rather than opt for more 4-8-0's. The 2-8-0 carried a higher percentage of its total weight on drivers and for this reason was better suited for heavy-duty, slow-speed road service. During 1905 the road received nine Class K Consolidation locomotives. They weighed 194,000 pounds, which was almost double the weight of the earlier Class G Consolidations, and had 22" × 28" cylinders and 54" drivers. Tractive effort was pegged at 42,553 pounds vs. 37,600 for the 4-8-0's. The 4-8-0, or Twelve-Wheeler, was never a popular locomotive when compared to the 2-8-0. Only about 600 4-8-0's were built for service in the United States, most of them between 1890 and 1900. By contrast, the Consolidation became the workhorse on most railroads in this country. About 21,000 Consolidations were ultimately used in the United States.

Ore tonnage over the D&IR for 1905, a record year, came to almost eight million tons. The next year promised to be even greater and, accordingly, the road placed an order with Baldwin for nine additional Consolidations, Nos. 200 through 208, for early March delivery at a cost of $14,750 each. This was a bargain, for the road had paid $15,000 for smaller 4-8-0's six years earlier. These locomotives, like the first Class K Consolidations, were equipped with short tenders in order to keep their overall length within the 60-foot turntable at Two Harbors. The size of the doors at the Two Harbors roundhouse, rather than clearances along the line, also limited the locomotives to 15'6" in height and 10'3" in width.

Meanwhile, the DM&N was also investing in additional Consolidations, receiving 12 engines of this type, Nos. 319 through 330, during 1905. Costing approximately $15,000 each, these engines weighed 185,500 pounds and exerted a tractive effort of 39,080 pounds. Designated Class C3, these locomotives had 22" × 28" cylinders and 56" drivers. They and the D&IR Class K Consolidations were the first engines for either road to come equipped with wide fireboxes. The DM&N was still in the market for additional Consolidations, receiving six engines numbered 331 through 336 in 1906, and 14 numbered 337 through 350 in 1907, from the Pittsburgh Works of the American Locomotive Company. The Missabe's fleet of 51 sturdy Consolidation locomotives were now sufficient to handle all ore traffic over the road as well as on Proctor Hill.

The Consolidation proved to be a real workhorse for both roads. Both the D&IR Class K and the DM&N Class C3 Consolidations were built as "saturated" engines. By 1915 the advantages of superheating steam were well understood in motive power circles, so the D&IR decided as an experiment to superheat No. 219, one of its Class K Consolidations. The greater boiler output increased the rating of this engine from 2,250 to 2,650 tons. During the years 1920 and 1921, all engines of this class were superheated and the old slide-valve cylinders were removed and replaced with new piston-valve cylinders. The older Class Ks, which came equipped with Stephenson valve motion, were fitted out with the modern Baker gear at this time. For a while, the superheated Class K Consolidations were designated as Class Ks, a symbol also used on the Pennsylvania Railroad to denote superheating. About this time the DM&N similarly upgraded its 32 Class C3 Consolidations by equipping them with type A superheaters and piston valve cylinders, upping their rating from 2,850 to 3,250 tons.

Little was done to upgrade the earlier D&IR Class G and H Consolidations, as by then they were assigned to switching, mine-servicing, and logging operations not requiring high boiler output. All of these engines received minor improvements, such as air-operated fire doors and electric headlights. These small Consolidations proved especially useful for service on the many logging spurs, for their light weight enabled them to operate safely over the jerry-built, temporary trackage encountered in the woods. Most of these engines were disposed of by the mid-thirties. The last Class G Consolidation to operate was DM&IR No. 141, formerly D&IR No. 41 and originally D&IR No. 11. She was kept specifically for operation on the Wales Branch during the spring months when the roadbed was soft and the rails were sometimes covered with water in swampy locations. Roadbed and track improvements made on this branch finally allowed the line to scrap her in 1939. The last Class H Consolidation, DM&IR No. 155 (originally D&IR No. 55), had been scrapped the previous year.

Superheating the D&IR Class K Consolidations increased their weight from 194,000 to 214,650 pounds; mechanical stokers brought the weight to 221,900 pounds. Tractive effort was then increased to 50,800 pounds. Likewise, the weight of the DM&N Class C3 Consolidations increased from 185,500 to 204,800 pounds with superheating, which raised the tractive effort to 42,750 pounds. Because the C3 engines carried less than 200,000 pounds on their drivers, they were not later required by I.C.C. rule to be equipped with stokers. A study was made during the early 1920s to determine the advantages of superheating the smaller DM&N Class C2 Consolidations, but none of them was modified, as by then they had been relegated to switching and branch line service. A number of the C2's were later sold to the Oliver Iron Mining Company and superheated by them, however.

The C3 and K class Consolidations continued to provide yeoman service well beyond World War II, many of them surviving until almost the end of steam during the late 1950s. They were the all-around workhorse in their later years, handling switching, mine run, and local freight assignments. Some were even equipped with steam line connections for passenger service.

Author's Collection

John T. Granfors

"Before" and "after" photographs of the D&IR's G class 2-8-0's. Above, No. 38 is shown in stockpile loading service in the Vermilion range early in her career. She was eventually renumbered 138 and was retired in 1933.
Below, No. 141 depicts the G class in later years. Except for a few modern appliances and a rebuilt tender, very little has been changed. This engine was the last of its class, and finally was scrapped in 1939.

Above, an unknown D&IR G class 2-8-0 spots a boxcar for loading frozen fish at the Two Harbors coal unloading dock. Note the fishing boat alongside the dock and the fire tug "Torrent" at right. Several engines (below) in the G class, like No. 37, received slope back tenders from scrapped 0-4-0's for improved vision by their crews. No. 37 was the former D&IR No. 7 and is shown in ore stockpile loading service.

Both photos, author's collection

D&IR No. 45, the former 18, seems to have a rough time of it in mine switching service . . . notice the damaged footboards. This engine was later renumbered 145.

Author's collection

The little G class engines were preferred power on the D&IR's logging spurs because of their light weight (55 tons). Here, No. 49, formerly the 22, is with a train of logs somewhere along the Eastern Mesaba branch.

John Carr collection

Author's collection

Here is another view of the 49 with a mixed train, also on the Eastern Mesaba branch. While below, the same 2-8-0 is shown leased to the Kileen and Gillis logging RR in January, 1923. Below, another log train on the D&IR with a 2-8-0 on the head end. The trains were important enough to warrant a caboose on the rear.

Douglas County Historical Society

44

Wayne Olsen collection

Author's collection

Above, an unknown 2-8-0 spots cars for loading at the Pioneer mine stockpile in Ely during 1901.

Below, No. 50, the first of the H class engines, pauses while on a caboose hop in the early 1900's. She was Schenectacy-built in 1892 and was later renumbered 150. The four-wheel caboose is similar to the caboose on the previous page.

Lake County Historical Society

D&IR No. 52, later the 152, poses for a typical turn-of-the-century portrait, while below, as the 152, the locomotives sits at Two Harbors in 1934, just two years away from retirement.

All photos, author's collection

D&IR Schenectady-built H class 2-8-0 No. 53 passes milepost one at Duluth with a train of logs received from the Duluth & Northern Minnesota Ry. at Knife River. The engine has already seen some rebuilding . . . notice the metal paneled cab. By the time this picture was taken in 1913, log hauling into Duluth was on the decline. Below, sister engine No. 54 waits for log-loading operations to be completed on some unknown logging branch.

By 1910, when this photo was taken, the new Baldwin-built K class 2-8-0's had taken over the majority of main line ore hauling. Here is a "K" rounding "Port City Hill" at Two Harbors with a long train of empties bound for Biwabik on the Mesabi range.

The K class went through several changes during its long years of service. Notice the differences, even in the same locomotive. Above right, No. 191, the former 91, at Virginia, Minnesota in 1939, and in contrast at Proctor in the mid-fifties show the difference in piping and air pumps. Below, D&IR 197 looks well kept as she awaits a new mine run assignment, also at Virginia in the late thirties. This engine was originally D&IR No. 97.

All photos, author's collection

Above, builders photo of No. 92 at the Baldwin plant in 1905, while below, sister engine No. 196 at Proctor, presents quite a different appearance. Note the Baker valve gear.

The K class were versatile, popular engines and all lasted well into the DM&IR era. No. 208 depicts a typical "K" as built by Baldwin in 1906. No.'s 1200 and 1201, the former 200 and 201 respectively, show the "modern" version of the K class. Note the interesting octagonal D&IR herald on the tender of the 1200 and the large sand dome for added capacity on the 1201.

Both photos, author's collection

Frank A. King

The right side of D&IR No. 1209, shown at Virginia, Minnesota in mine run service, also sports the larger sand dome, like her sister engine 1201, on the previous page. K1 No. 1212, at Mitchell, Minnesota in September, 1952 shows off an interesting maze of piping, pumps and air tanks. The apparatus just before the pumps is a radiator for trapping moisture in the air tanks.

Both photos, author's collection

Frank A. King

Here is DM&IR No. 1213 at Biwabik with practically the same amount of plumbing as the 1212. No. 1213 is equipped with an interesting cinder-catcher and fin-tube type air cooler below the running board. The cinder-catcher was dictated by forestry regulations as the locomotive often ran into the Superior National Forest. At left, two views of 1213 after she ran off the end of the track in service on the familiar Eastern Mesaba branch at Babbitt, Minnesota.

Both photos, author's collection

Below, Engine 1214 at Proctor in September 1952 is practically a twin to No. 1217 on the next page. Right and left views of D&IR No. 216, the first engine of its class to be superheated at the Two Harbors shops, are shown to the left.

Three photos, author's collection

Two views of K-1 class No. 1217. Above, in a familiar rods-down pose at Proctor, while the other picture shows her on the Wales branch in 1948 with a short freight. The wood reefer (second car) was for L.C.L. service. Note cinder screen on stack.

Both photos, Frank A. King

Frank A. King

Another view of the same freight with 2-8-0 No. 1217 up front, near Sawbill Landing on the Wales Branch, under a beautiful dramatic sky.

DM&IR No. 1218 in service, and on display. At right, at Proctor on a cold overcast day, and below, at Tower, Minnesota, the birthplace of the iron ore industry in Minnesota.

Both photos, author's collection

Author's collection

At Virginia, Minnesota in 1938, engine 1223 presents a conventional appearance, while below, on the shop "jitney" run at Proctor in 1949, the 1223, with her added piping and air reservoirs atop the boiler, looks quite different. She was cut up for scrap soon after with over 49 years of service.

Frank A. King

In 1913, two D&IR ore trains collided head-on at Colby, Minnesota in what turned out to be the most serious wreck in the history of both the D&IR and DM&N in terms of lives lost — four. Both engines were K class Consolidations.

DM&N No. 301 was built by Pittsburgh in 1895 for service on Proctor Hill. The engine was originally equipped with a slope-back tender for better visibility in backing down the hill. She later went to the Duluth & Northeastern as their No. 23.

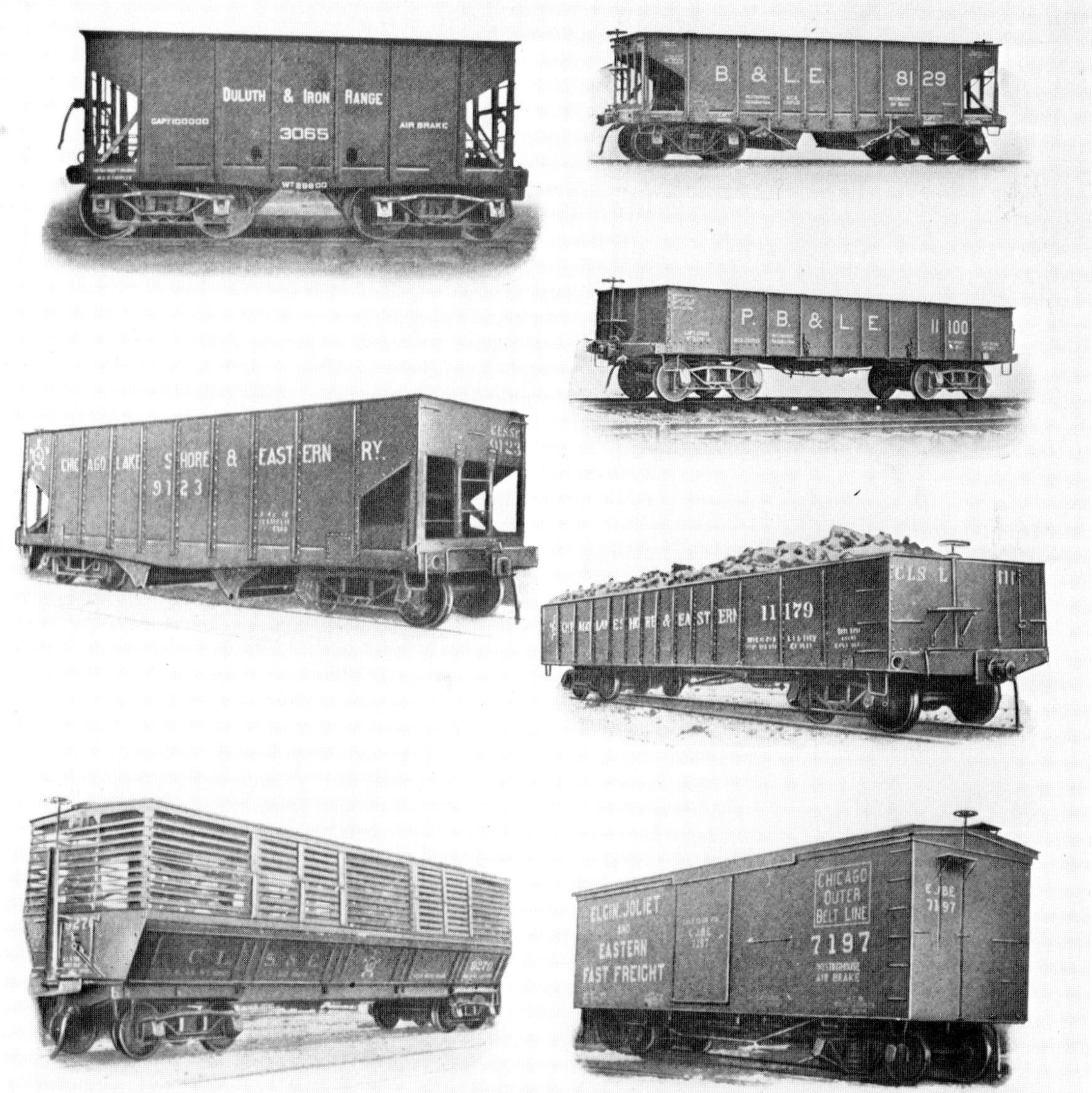

DM&N No. 302, fresh from delivery, poses at Proctor in 1899.
The engine featured a back-up pilot on the tender rear, since backing down
Proctor Hill was common. The parent U.S. Steel Corp. thought enough of the
302 that it was included in a company brochure in 1901.

All photos, author's collection

The life and times of DM&N No. 306. It began with a builders photo at the Dickson plant in 1902. Soon after delivery the 306 blew up near Alborn, killing the head brakeman and seriously injuring the fireman and engineer. Then a few years later, the engine was involved in a runaway on Proctor Hill. This view shows a wrecking crane placing her back on the rails on the approach to the Duluth ore docks. Note the tender frame in the foreground and the tender tank under the dock approach. The next photo shows her after rebuilding, backing down the hill with an ore train. While the 306 may have been jinxed during her early career, she lasted another 46 years. The last photograph, taken at Proctor, was just a few years away from retirement in 1948.

Three photos, author's collection

Both photos, Douglas County Historical Society

C.T. Felstead

Two photos, C.T. Felstead

The C-1's in their final configuration. Both the 307 and 308 were built by Cooke in 1903 for the DM&N. Both engines were sold to American Steel and Wire Corp. in 1948. Note the pair of cross-compound pumps on 307 ... an unusual feature for an engine of such small size.

The engine cab was a favorite place to pose for pictures. Here are several photographs of various DM&N C-1 class 2-8-0's with their crews featured prominently.

Two photos, author's collection

Above, a builder view of 311. While below, the 309 and 311 in several pictures taken soon after shopping, shows them with two cross-compound pumps. The headlight has been converted to electricity.

Three photos, author's collection

Engine No. 315, one of the first of the DM&N's C-2 class 2-8-0's. Above, as built, while below, in service with a different tender. The C-2's could handle a 65-car train of 50-ton ore cars.

Left, built by Pittsburgh in 1904 for the DM&N as their No. 313, it was sold in 1919 to the Oliver Iron Mining Co., and renumbered 513. The engine was superheated and equipped with piston valves by the O.I.M. and used in mining service. They must have needed plenty of "air" . . . note the combination of single-stage and cross-compound air pumps. Above left, the 513 shoves an interesting mix of loaded ore cars out of the company's mine pit in 1920.

All photos, author's collection

A grand panoramic view of the massive wooden ore docks at West Duluth around 1910. At left, dock No. 1 is being dismantled. Note the coal train coming up the hill with a 2-8-0 on the head end.

Author's collection

(Minnesota Historical Society)

Two photos, author's collection

**DM&IR No. 324 in 1951 at Proctor. Three years later the engine was scrapped.**

Author's collection

The C-3's had 56-inch drivers with 42,750 pounds of tractive effort. Above, C-3, No. 328, switches the washing plant at Coleraine, Minnesota during the 1950's.

Left above, DM&N No. 325 was involved in a nasty spill and two wrecking cranes had to be used to get her back on the rails. While below, a builder portrait of sister engine No. 327.

Author's collection

John T. Granfors

Engine 332 enjoyed a long and varied career. In 1910 she pauses while on the Biwabik local at Iron Junction. The long ladder on the pilot deck aided in servicing the headlight. Eventually all the slide valve C-3's were superheated. Left, the 332 is on the Coleraine Branch passenger train at Bovey, in the late 1930's. Just below, a left side view taken in June 1953. The 332 was sold to the Duluth & Northeastern and renumbered 28. Here she is shown drifting downgrade from Saginaw toward Cloquet with a trainload of pulpwood. The 28 was used on several excursions and is now on display at the Lake Superior Museum of Transportation in Duluth.

Author's collection

All photos Frank A. King

The DM&N sold off several of its surplus 2-8-0's, with two going
to the Minneapolis Northfield & Southern.
MN&S No. 404 and 405 were formerly DM&N 329 and 337.

Two views of C-3 No. 333. Above at Proctor in her final years
and below, working the ore steaming plant at Proctor.

All photos, author's collection

DM&IR C-3 class 2-8-0 No. 335 and an unknown K class Consolidation switching at Steelton yards in 1950.

Two views of C-3 No. 340, one taken at Proctor, the other on an ore train passing Saginaw around 1915. The Duluth & Northeastern crossing is just in front of the young lady and her family.

All photos, author's collection

Author's collection

Frank A. King

The C-3 class were certainly handsome, trim locomotives in their later years.
No. 346 was built in 1907 and scrapped by the Missabe in 1949.
No. 347 is now on display at the Museum of Mining at Chisholm, Minnesota.
No. 348 was sold to the Duluth & Northeastern as their No. 27 in 1955.
The last C-3, No. 350, was finally scrapped in 1955.

H. Van Horn collection

Two photos, author's collection

Lima-built Mike No. 1304 running light at 45 m.p.h. between Duluth and Two Harbors on May 11, 1960.

Frank A. King

# IV. MIKADOS AND SANTA FES

In 1912, with ore traffic reaching new highs, the two railways began to look for more powerful locomotives. The problem was especially acute on the D&IR, whose fleet of 35 Class K Consolidations struggled to transport a record 9.4 million tons of ore to Two Harbors that year. Traffic density was becoming troublesome, too, because these engines could handle only 2,250 gross tons (35 loads of ore plus weight of cars) per train.

Breaking with tradition, in January 1913, the D&IR placed an order with Baldwin for six Mikado (2-8-2) locomotives. The road asked for an engine that would best the tonnage rating of the Consolidations by 50 percent! This figure meant raising the tonnage per train from 2,250 (35 loads) to 3,400 (52 loads). Specifications called for 58" drivers, 27" × 30" cylinders, 287,600 pounds total engine weight, and a tractive force of 59,250 pounds. The engines were to be equipped with Vanderbilt tenders weighing 166,000 pounds (loaded) for a total engine and tender weight of 456,600 pounds. Strangely, oil-burning headlights were specified. (The following year, electric headlights were applied to all six Mikados, as well as to 90 other D&IR locomotives.) During February, 1913, the January Baldwin order was reduced from six to four locomotives, Nos. 300 through 303, and the Lima Locomotive Corporation received the contract for the other two engines, Nos. 304 and 305. The Lima locomotives were identical to those built by Baldwin with one exception — they were equipped with an old-style, box-type oil headlight instead of the more conventional round-case light supplied by Baldwin. The base price of all six locomotives was $26,150 each.

The onset of World War I had little immediate impact on the operations of the D&IR and DM&N. It became apparent, however, that even if the United States did not become directly involved, the demand for steel would increase sharply. The impact of the war in Europe became real in 1915, with combined DM&N-D&IR ore tonnages reaching a new high of 24,212,801 tons — a figure double that attained only the previous year.

Indications pointed to even higher tonnages for 1916! Something had to be done to improve the performance of the Consolidation-powered road trains. The DM&N, deciding that a much larger locomotive was needed, bypassed the popular Mikado and placed an order with Baldwin for six Santa Fe (2-10-2) locomotives capable of handling 135 carloads of ore between the Mesabi Range and Proctor, compared with 65 loads for the C3 Consolidations.

The Class E Santa Fes, costing $30,753 each, carried 55,000 pounds per driving axle, and their 28" × 32" cylinders exerted a tractive force of 65,800 pounds — approximately 50 percent more than the heaviest Consolidations. The boiler was equipped with a deep firebox placed back of the driving wheels. The grate area was 80 square feet. Specialties included a brick arch in the firebox, a power reverse mechanism, and a mechanical stoker. (Firemen with sufficient seniority naturally preferred the stoker-fired Santa Fes over the back-breaking, hand-fired Consolidations. In addition, the pay was better, as the Santa Fes had a higher weight on drivers.) Total engine weight was 346,600 pounds, and total weight, including tender, was 537,000 pounds. Overall height and width were 16 and 11 feet, respectively. Until arrival of the first Yellowstones in 1941, the diameter of the drivers (60") was the largest for any Missabe Road freight power.

The D&IR was again in the marketplace for heavier and more powerful locomotives to cope with the anticipated 1916 tonnage. (The combined DM&N-D&IR 1916 tonnages peaked at 33.3 million . . . 11 million carried by the D&IR . . . a figure not to be exceeded until 1941, a quarter century later.) Consequently, during early 1916, preliminary specifications were prepared for a heavy Santa Fe locomotive with a 67,000-pound axle loading, weighing 335,000 pounds on drivers and 400,000 pounds total engine weight. Specifications included 58" drivers, and the engine would have produced 84,000 pounds of tractive effort. The design was based largely on the Bessemer and Lake Erie's Vanderbilt tender-equipped Class D-1-A 2-10-2's, which were received from Baldwin in 1916.. The proposed Santa Fe engines would obviously have been much heavier and more powerful than the Santa Fes received by the DM&N during 1916. After considering the added cost of upgrading track and bridges to carry a 67,000-pound axle loading, plus lengthening the roundhouse stalls at Two Harbors, as well as other considerations, the decision was made to stay with the Mikado. Accordingly, during July, 1916, an order was placed with Baldwin for three additional Mikados, Nos. 306 through 308. These engines were identical to the Mikados received in 1913, with two exceptions: Pyle National electric headlights in place of oil-burning lights, and coal-pushers on the tenders.

During 1919, the DM&N received ten additional Santa Fe locomotives, Nos. 506 through 515, designated as Class E1. The Santa Fes now pulled most of the ore on the road. Built by the Brooks Works of the American Locomotive Company to United States Railway Administration (USRA) specifications for the light 2-10-2 type, these engines, costing $56,795 each, were similar to the Baldwin Santa Fes in size, weight, and power. In most respects, however, they were a much better design. Cylinders and driving wheels were slightly smaller (27" × 32" and 57"), an improved valve gear (Southern) was applied, and a notable improvement in most details was effected. Also, the stoker was far superior, frames and machinery parts better proportioned, and auxiliary devices increased in number. A cast-steel tender frame, as well as cast-steel truck sideframes, were included for the first time. That the USRA design was good was evidenced by the improved performance of the Class E1 engines compared to the earlier Class E Santa Fes.

Overall, the 16 Santa Fe locomotives were judged the most versatile ever operated by the Missabe. Originally built for main-line ore service, they were later used effectively for heavy switching, ore-sorting, transfer, and local freight service. During the late 1920s, all engines of this type were equipped with Franklin trailing truck boosters, a modification that increased tractive effort by 11,000 pounds. At the same time, the majority of the Santa Fes received feedwater heaters as follows:
No. 500 - Coffin
Nos. 501, 502, 503, 504, 506, 507, 590, 513 -Elesco
Nos. 505, 511 - Worthington

Other improvements made to these engines included Delta trailing trucks, coal-pushers, Nicholson firebox syphons, speed recorders, and power reverse with automatic cut-off feature. After these improvements, the weight on drivers for both classes was listed at 296,760 pounds, and the total engine weight at 376,710 pounds. Tractive effort without booster was 71,200 pounds for Class E and 69,600 pounds for the E1's. In addition, tender water capacity was increased from 10,000 to 12,000 gallons. Twelve-thousand-gallon auxiliary water cars were also added, enabling these engines to run non-stop in either direction between Proctor and the Mesabi Range.

During the fall of 1927, the DM&N instituted a new locomotive repair and maintenance policy which placed an emphasis on improved daily inspection procedures. The old policy, in which each locomotive was scheduled to go through the backshop every winter, was discontinued. Instead, locomotives were shopped on a mileage basis, with the exception of flue replacement and air-brake work, which was dictated by I.C.C. regulations. The new policy almost doubled the average locomotive mileage between shoppings for heavy repairs, and allowed a substantial reduction in the shop force. For example, mileage between heavy repairs for Class E and E1 Santa Fes rose from 19,985 per locomotive in 1925 to 51,140 in 1929. The improvement in overall locomotive performance was astonishing, with locomotive miles between failures rising from an average of only 34,178 in 1921 to 227,870 by 1929!

One shortcoming of the E1 Santa Fes was that their main driving wheels (only 57") were not counterbalanced for operation at speeds much in excess of 40 miles per hour. While this was not a limitation in ore service, where maximum speeds were restricted to 35 miles per hour or less, the lack of counterbalancing did pose problems occasionally. One such incident recalled by this writer occurred during the late 1930s, when the 1100 class Pacific on passenger train No. 6 broke down near Highland, about 11 miles north of Two Harbors. An ore train pulled by an E1 Santa Fe was weighing at Highland, and the dispatcher instructed its crew to leave their train and bring No. 6 into Two Harbors; the company was concerned to protect its mail contract. Attempting to make up lost time, the engineer unleashed his Santa Fe, attaining speeds of 55 to 60 miles per hour. While No. 6 arrived at Two Harbors almost on schedule, the price paid was a high one. Several miles of rail were severely kinked by the hammer blows of the main drivers and had to be replaced with new steel.

The last new locomotives purchased by the D&IR were three Mikados, Nos. 309 through 311 (Class N2), received from Baldwin in 1923. They were the first engines on the road to come equipped with stokers, feedwater heaters (Elesco), and Franklin trailing truck boosters which raised the total tractive effort to 70,250 pounds. These Mikados, weighing 321,400 pounds, were among the most powerful of their type and were well-suited for heavy "drag" service. Like the previous Mikados, they had 27" × 30" cylinders and 58" drivers. On the southbound run from Biwabik, they were rated to handle trains grossing 3,600 tons over maximum grades of 0.62 percent. With later grade reduction, train tonnage was increased to 3,825 (59 loads).

During 1922, D&IR Mikados Nos. 300 through 308 were equipped with stokers and Coffin feedwater heaters, and the coal-pushers were removed. Franklin trailing truck boosters were applied in 1926, enabling these engines to pull the same tonnage as the newer N2 Mikados. Tractive effort was increased to 64,000 pounds, and to 75,775 pounds with boosters. These improvements resulted in increasing the weight on drivers to 251,270 pounds, and total engine weight to 338,320 pounds, for all classes of Mikados.

Introduction of the big Yellowstones during 1941 and 1943 forecast the end of both the Mikados and Santa Fes as main-line road power. Both types, however, remained useful in lesser duties, and saw service up to the end of the steam era.

In this magnificent photograph Mikado 1303 is being serviced at Endion before making a night run with the Ely local.

Frank A. King

The N class Mikados enjoyed a long and varied career on both the D&IR and DM&IR. Engines 300 through 303 were built by Baldwin in 1913, while the last two, 304 and 305, were built by Lima. On this page, the 300 and sister engine 301 show the locomotives in their original configuration. No. 301 is seen at Two Harbors, a few years after delivery, while the 300 is snowbound at the same location, during the winter of 1923. Over the years, the N class were rebuilt and modernized until they bore little resemblance to the original engines. At right are several views of the rebuilt 300 and 301. Renumbered 1300 and 1301, the engines show off their Coffin feedwater heaters, sport model cabs, added piping, top-mounted tanks, and cast Delta trailing trucks. Even the tenders came in for their share of modification with added coal boards and Andrews trucks replacing the original archbar.

Two photos, author's collection

Two photos, author's collection

Wayne Olsen collection

Author's Collection

Frank A. King

Engines 302 (later 1302) and 1303, the former D&IR No. 303, were the road's third and fourth Mikados, respectively. Above, the 302 sits for her builders portrait at the Baldwin plant in 1913; while below the rebuilt 1303 is a plumber's nightmare at Biwabik, Minnesota quite a few years later. To avoid contamination by ore dust, the air pump filters were placed on top of the boiler, directly behind the sand dome.

Author's Collection

Frank A. King

Mike 1304 (and the 1305), built by Lima in 1913, were practically duplicates of the Baldwin engines. The builders photo of 304 is interesting in that the photo-retoucher did not finish "whiting out" the background. Like all the Missabe's Mikes, the 304, renumbered to 1304, was much rebuilt.

Author's collection

Frank A. King

No. 305 was the second Lima-built 2-8-2.
Above, fresh and shiney at Two Harbors in 1913, and below,
as DM&IR No. 1305, at Two Harbors.

Two photos, author's collection

D&IR 306-308 were the second group of 2-8-2's on the road. They were built by Baldwin in 1916 and classed N-1. The 307 shows her original appearance in a builders photo while below, as DM&IR No. 1307, at Two Harbors, the locomotive has quite a different look. No. 306, the first N-1, has just been freshly shopped in this photo, also at Two Harbors. The locomotive has been equipped with a Coffin feedwater heater.

Frank A. King

309
309

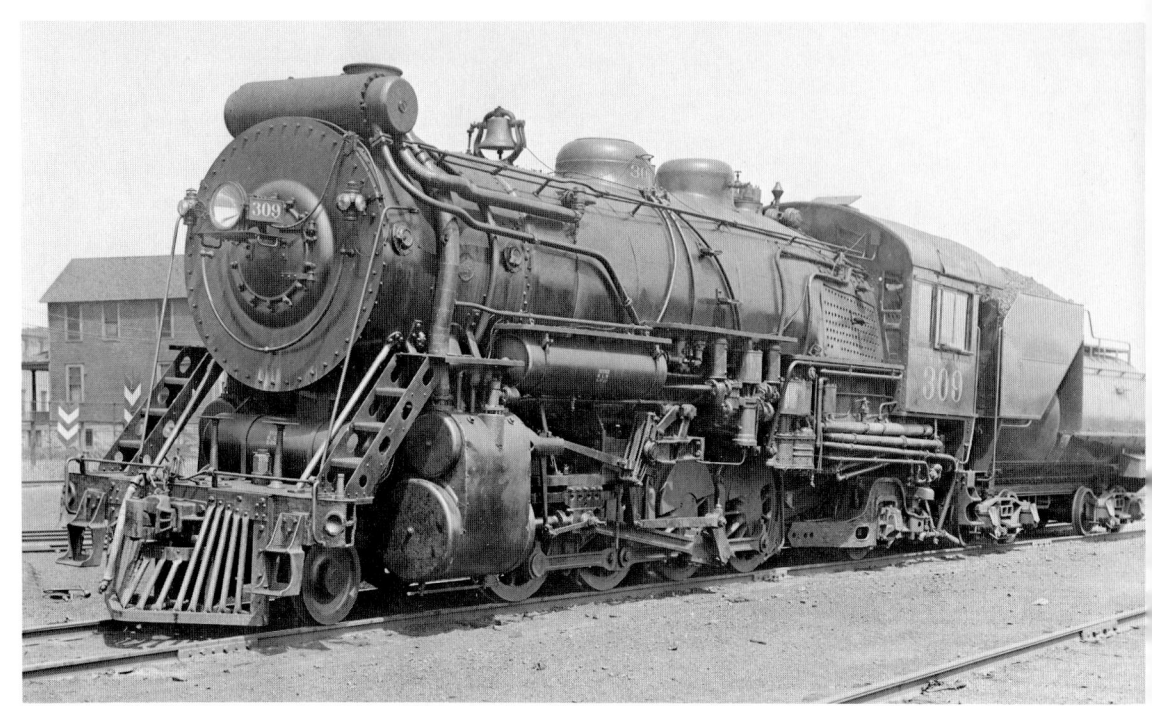

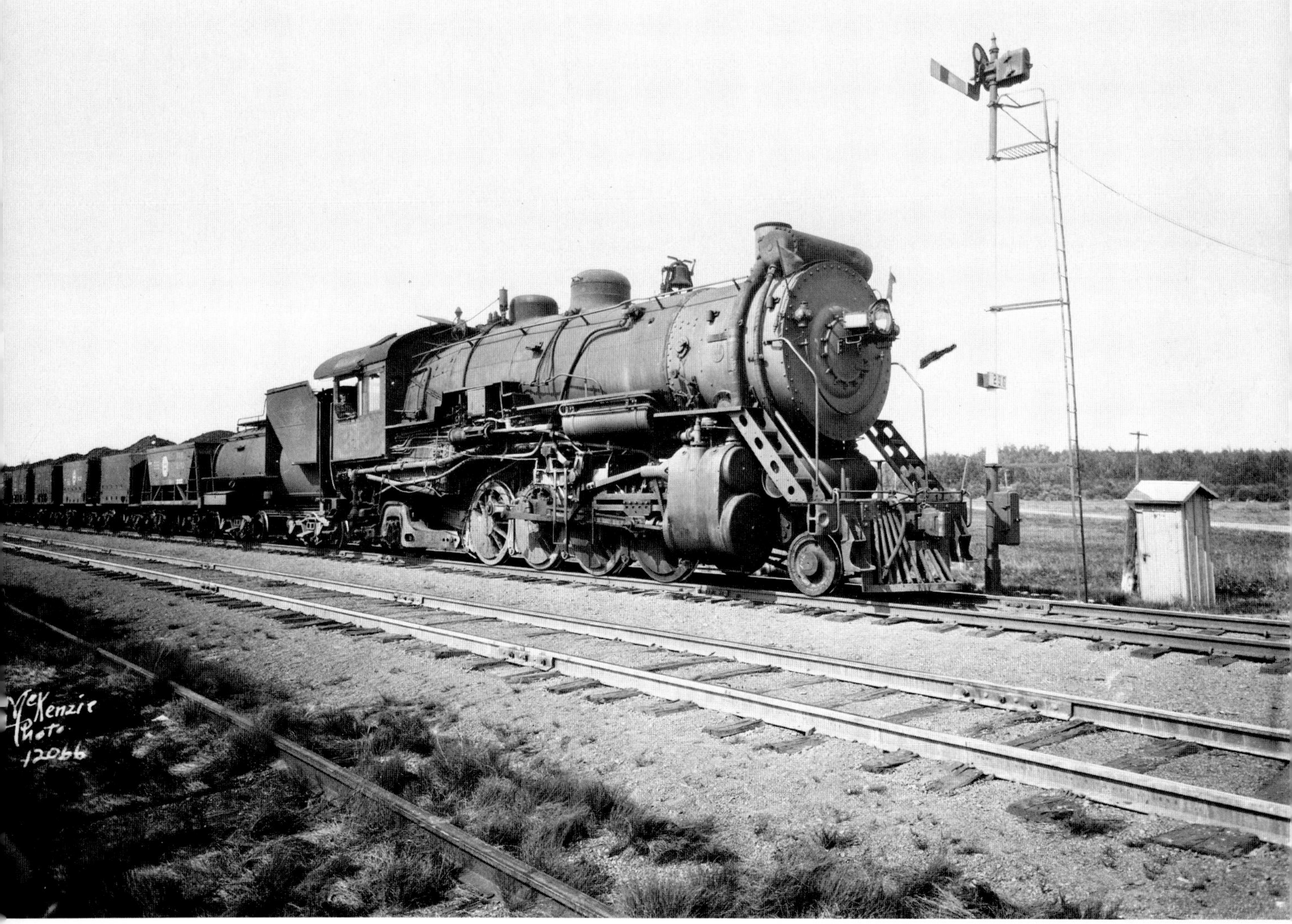
McKenzie
Photo.
12066

The last group of Mikados were class N-2, No.'s 309-311.
Left above, the 309 sits at Two Harbors soon after delivery, while
below, the second N-2, No. 310, poses with an ore train
some years later. The same engine is shown with another ore train
(above) at "Mud cut" near Two Harbors.
Below, a builders view of the 311.

All photos, author's collection

DM&IR collection

Frank A. King

Like many engines on the DM&IR, the N-2's went in for their share of modifications, even to the extent of losing their Elesco feedwater heaters in later years, and being reclassed N-3. Above, the 1310, formerly D&IR No. 310, is on work-train duty in August, 1950. Another view shows the years and results of various shoppings.

Frank A. King

Author's collection

Sister engine 1311 still sports her original feedwater heater in a photograph taken at Endion Roundhouse at Duluth. Later, she had much the same appearance as the 1310. The tenders on these locomotives are of interest . . . note the extended sides for added coal capacity.

Author's collection

Author's collection

Ore tonnage increased sharply during World War I. To handle the traffic, the DM&N ordered six big 2-10-2 types from Baldwin. These locomotives were delivered in 1916. Above, the first of the E class, No. 500, stands at the Baldwin plant soon after completion. The next two photographs taken at the Proctor coal dock show the 500 in different configurations . . . with and without its Coffin feedwater heater, after being absorbed by the DM&IR. At right, it was a cold day in 1958 when No. 503 climbed Proctor Hill with a train of empty ore cars. The locomotive has its familiar Elesco feedwater heater and top-mounted air tanks.

Frank A. King

94

No. 500 on the cinder pit at Proctor.

Both photos, Frank A. King

In 1916, brand new No. 505 weighs in on the Proctor ore scales with a 130-car train.

In 1936, DM&N E class Santa Fe No. 504 heads 135 loads of iron ore out of Rust Crusher yard in Hibbing, bound for Proctor. Note the left hand running on double track. The booster-equipped 2-10-2's were the workhorses of the Missabe division until receipt of the five rebuilt Mallets in 1941. The 2-10-2's were seldom used on road ore service after arrival of the additional ten "Yellowstones" in 1943.

Two photos, author's collection

DM&IR Santa Fe No. 507 is in ore-sorting service at the Two Harbors yard.

Frank A. King

Two views of 2-10-2 No. 506. The first of E-1 class USRA engines, while on a railfan special at Mitchell, near Hibbing, Minnesota, during the waning days of steam on the DM&IR.

Both photos, Frank A. King

Both photos, author's collection

Above, the second E-1 is seen at Proctor, while still on the DM&N. The close-up shows off the 507's various details such as the injector and stoker. Also note the booster truck steam connections.

Above, Engine 509 in her original USRA configuration. She still has the "US" stenciled on her tender. Below, the 508 depicts the many modifications to the E-1's in this photograph taken at Proctor in August, 1956. Right, a very interesting and rare aerial view of several DM&N ore trains, taken at Adolph, Minnesota in the 1920's. That's one of the E-1's on the train on the right.

All photos, author's collection

Frank A. King

Author's collection

The two interesting photographs of engine 510 show the changes made on the same locomotive over the years. There are differences in piping, bell mounting and tender.

Above right, in their later years, the E-1's were a far cry from their USRA origins. Both the 512 and 514 are loaded with piping and plumbing, especially between the steam dome and cab. Note, too, the sand box on the pilot deck.

Both photos, Frank A. King

103

Frank A. King

E-1 No. 514 was the last steam locomotive to operate on the DM&IR. Here she is on her last trip: At Virginia, Minnesota on a special train for the St. Louis County Historical Society on September 29, 1962.

Several views of No. 513. She was the only Missabe locomotive equipped with experimental number boards, mounted directly ahead of the Elesco feedwater heater. Like many other locomotives on the Missabe, the air pump filters were mounted high on the boiler top to avoid ore dust contamination.

Author's collection

Frank A. King

M-4 Yellowstone No. 230 working hard upgrade near Saginaw, Minnesota in 1959, with its usual train, a long string of loaded ore cars.

Frank A. King

# V. ARTICULATEDS: MALLETS TO YELLOWSTONES

The first decade of the 20th century found American railroads hard-pressed to meet the ever-increasing transportation demands of the nation's burgeoning industrial economy. That the Duluth, Missabe & Northern shared in this growth is an understatement, for ore shipments from the newly opened Mesabi Range in Minnesota mushroomed from 3,888,941 tons in 1900 to 13,470,641 tons by 1909 — a 350 percent increase!

It was painfully apparent that the 6.5 miles of 2.2 percent grade separating the giant ore-sorting yard at Proctor, Minn., and the ore docks at Duluth presented an intolerable operating bottleneck. Traffic density on "the Hill" had been a problem almost from the inception of the railroad — so much so that this stretch of railroad was double-tracked during the 1890s. By 1909, the Missabe's fleet of 51 sturdy Consolidation-type locomotives were handling all ore traffic over the road as well as on the Hill. The problem lay not so much in the capacity of the engines to move ore to the docks as in their limited ability to haul empties back up the steep ascent from Duluth. These engines could handle solid trains of 55 steel, 50-ton-capacity cars containing 2,750 or more tons of ore between the mines and Proctor, but their hauling capacity was reduced to a mere 28 empties while ascending the 2.2 percent back up from the docks.

During periods of peak ore shipments, trains were dispatched to the docks as frequently as every 15 minutes. This was bad enough in itself, but, when coupled with the extreme fog conditions often encountered at the western end of Lake Superior, it created an operating safety hazard of no little concern. Obviously the solution would have to be a bold one; *i.e.*, a locomotive capable of hauling no fewer than 55 empties upgrade from the docks. Electrification was studied first, for the area's Great Northern Power Company had recently completed a giant hydroelectric power generating complex on the St. Louis River, 20 miles upstream from Duluth, and was seeking customers. Also, the recent electrification of Grand Trunk's St. Clair Tunnel and Great Northern's Cascade Tunnel, under their namesake river and mountains, both looked to be successful applications of electricity by trunkline railroads to overcome severe operating bottlenecks. However, DM&N concluded that a Mallet type locomotive could be designed to do the job and earn a better return on investment.

The Mallet was not a novelty. Neighbor Great Northern had been accumulating experience with the type in the Cascades since 1906. Missabe's operating people watched with interest in 1909 as a homemade GN 2-6-8-0, No. 2000, trundled ore loads parallel to DM&N's main north of Alborn, Minn. A success, the ungainly 2000 was the prototype of 35 additional Mallets of this unusual wheel arrangement built by Baldwin during 1909-1910.

Its decision made, Missabe asked the Baldwin Locomotive Works to prepare specifications for eight monstrous 16-drivered Mallets; in power and size, they would exceed anything seen on North Country rails. The railroad wanted a locomotive which, because of its increased capacity, could cut traffic density on the Hill by 50 percent, compared with the Consolidation type. Baldwin conservatively promised that 2-8-8-2 compounds, practically identical with Virginian No. 600 which it was building for coal trains, would handle 55 steel empties weighing 32,300 pounds each, plus a four-wheel, 20,000-pound caboose, up the 2.2 percent at 12 mph. This requirement was easily met. Upon application of mechanical stokers, the Mallets handled as many as 85 empties per trip, although at a reduced speed, because of boiler limitations. They weighed 448,100 pounds, carrying 406,600 pounds of that on their 57-inch drivers. Their 200-pound-pressure steam was used first in the rear engine's 26 × 32″ high-pressure cylinders, then reused in the 40 × 32″ low-pressure cylinders on the front engine, producing 91,000 pounds tractive effort. Overall length of the engine and its stubby tank was just over 99 feet.

The M-class Mallets, Nos. 200-207, construction Nos. 35165-35172, began arriving in Proctor for service on the Hill for the opening of the 1910 ore season. Weighing in at over 320 tons for engine and tender, and stretching almost half a block long, they were more than twice the size of the biggest 2-8-0's DM&N owned. After one look, a number of "old head" engineers bid other jobs. Firemen were concerned about the Mallets' huge coal demands. Although two firemen were initially employed on the 200-series machines, difficulty was experienced at times in keeping up steam.

At the time the 200's were built, superheating was in its infancy. Instead, Baldwin was equipping Mallets with a recently developed feedwater heater. The boiler was constructed in two sections, united by a riveted separable joint; the front section, located just behind the smokebox, contained this heater. The firetube-equipped feedwater section was constantly filled with water, which was heated to about 250 degrees before being discharged through an outlet into the rear evaporating section or boiler proper. The Baldwin feedwater heaters did not prove to be a complete success and were removed in 1916. This reduced weight on drivers by 14,000 pounds, and heavy steel plates were placed in the forward section of the boiler to offset this adhesive weight loss. However, the plates retained so much heat that boilermakers could not enter the engines to make repairs until they had cooled down for several hours. For this reason, the plates were soon removed, and the locomotives thereafter operated with 12,000 pounds less weight. Little difficulty was experienced with slipping, though, for even with the weight loss the 200's had an ample adhesion factor of 4.31.

With the concept of superheating accepted, Schmidt superheaters were installed on the 200-series engines. All received Standard mechanical stokers in 1925, and in about 1930 most of the Mallets received conventional Elesco feedwater heaters. These were the only significant modifications made to these highly successful locomotives, some of which continued to render excellent service on the Hill for more than 40 years.

The year 1915 saw new tonnage records set at the Duluth docks, with a high of 211,616 tons of ore being loaded into vessels in a single day. Another new high was reached in 1916, with 21,838,056 tons, a figure not topped until 1942, when almost 24 million tons were shipped. Duluth has never again attained that figure. With the tempo of war in Europe increasing, the Missabe placed orders with Baldwin for two additional Mallet 2-8-8-2's for use on the Hill, and six Santa Fe types (2-10-2's) for road-haul work.

The 1916 Mallets, while of the same wheel arrangement and tractive power as their 1910 predecessors, were thoroughly revised in design, with improvements in their piping and machinery layout, and reinforcements of frames, braces, trucks, and other components. Engines Nos. 208 and 209 of M1 class, constructions nos. 43530-43531, came equipped with Standard stokers, Schmidt superheaters, and brick firebox arches. Total engine weight was modestly increased from the 448,100 pounds of the 1910 design to 470,000 pounds. Grate area remained the same at 84 square feet, but boiler diameter was increased from 84 to 86 inches. The new Mallets possessed a more compact appearance, inasmuch as their overall length was reduced by approximately five feet through moving the firebox forward that distance over drivers of the rear engine. They could easily have been designed as 2-8-8-0's had it not been for the need to operate them on the Hill in both directions without turning; for such service, the trailing truck of the 2-8-8-2 offered better back-up guidance. Two identical Mallets, M2 class nos. 210 and 211, construction nos. 45769 and 45793, respectively, were received from Baldwin in 1917.

By the late Twenties the railroad found that it did not require the services of 12 Mallets on Proctor Hill, where they averaged only 7,292 miles per locomotive (in 1927). Unfortunately, the plodding compounds were unsuited for road service. Meanwhile, neighbor Great Northern had been experiencing some startling operating results with N1 Mallet 2-8-8-0's, rebuilt in 1925 as single-expansion N2 2-8-8-0's, and employed in ore service on the Mesabi Division to replace lighter 2-6-8-0's. As Mallets, the N1's had boosted average tonnage per train from 6,827 to 9,687 and gross ton-miles per train-hour from 62,740 to 83,883 over their predecessors in 1924. In 1927, after being simpled, the GN N-2's pushed train tonnage to 11,412 and gross ton-miles per train-hour to 121,652! Ultimately, one of these engines handled a record train of 205 cars grossing an estimated 19,100 tons into GN's dockyard at Allouez, Wis. — a performance Missabe Road never equaled with steam because of its lack of GN's water-level grades.

Missabe officials observed all this with interest. Could not their four newest Mallets, Nos. 208-211, be simpled for road service with similar results? Approval was given to convert one engine to single expansion, No. 210 being selected.

Three photos, author's collection

A successful experiment . . . taking a tip from the Great Northern, who experienced startling results with rebuilt N-1 2-8-8-0's like the No. 2008 (at right). The Missabe decided to experiment with one of its older class M Mallets (such as the 201) by converting it to single expansion. The engine picked, (No. 210) was completely rebuilt. Working with Baldwin, the railroad incorporated such features as new steel frames, 23½ × 32″ cast-steel cylinders, a cast-steel ashpan, type E superheater, Coffin feedwater heater and a Franklin tender booster. The results (right and below) were quite impressive and plans were made by the DM&N's management to convert several of the older Mallets to simple machines (class M-1's and M-2's). Engines 207 and 209 were rebuilt in 1930 and 1931, respectively, followed by the 211, also in 1931, and the 209 in 1937.

Frank A. King

Working with Baldwin, the railroad incorporated such major features in the rebuilding as Hilastic steel frames, 23½ × 32" cast-steel cylinders, a new cast-steel ashpan, Type E superheater, Coffin feedwater heater, and a Franklin tender booster. Lesser improvements included an American multiple throttle, Nicholson thermic syphons, automatic cut-off control, and a Franklin radial buffer between engine and tender. The locomotive was fitted with two stacks, one for each engine. (These were later replaced by a single stack with a Norfolk & Western-design annular ported nozzle.) While weight on drivers was increased by only 1.4 percent to 421,100 pounds, tractive effort was boosted by 11 percent to 101,000 pounds. Total tractive effort, including that of the booster, totaled 114,000 pounds — a 25 percent increase over that of the compounds; use of the booster enabled the 210 to haul an additional 1,500 tons of ore per trip.

No question, No. 210, classed M-2S, came out of the Proctor backshop a modernized machine. The heaviest and most powerful engine on the DM&N, she became affectionately known among shopmen and engine crews as *Madame Queen*. Missabe people broadcast the fact that she could even outpull her rebuilt counterparts on the Great Northern.

During 1929 *Madame Queen*'s road performance and costs were closely watched and compared with those of the Missabe's Santa Fe types. That year she made 92 road trips, handling a total of 896,448 short (2,000-pound) tons of ore. She averaged 158 cars and 9,744 short tons of ore per trip. Compared with Missabe's standard 2-10-2 road power, No. 210 averaged 13 percent more cars and 35 percent more ore tonnage per train. (The discrepancy in the average number of cars per train, when compared with average tonnage, resulted from the fact that the Santa Fe type engines handled trains made up of 50-ton-capacity cars, whereas the No. 210 moved trains with a substantial number of new, 75-ton-capacity cars.)

This ability of the rebuilt No. 210 to eliminate one train out of three, as compared with the 2-10-2's, presented a potential for substantial savings. Management was sufficiently impressed to prepare plans to similarly simple Mallets Nos. 208-209 into Class M-1S and No. 211 into M-2S class. They were only 12 to 13 years old and had many years of service life in them. About this time, Mallet No. 207, one of the 1910 machines, was so seriously damaged in a wreck on Proctor Hill that consideration was given to not repairing her, since she was almost 20 years old. But after considerable study a decision was reached to rebuild her as a single-expansion engine, the work being performed in 1930. No. 207 received much the same treatment as *Madame Queen* had the year before, but emerged with a vastly different appearance than the No. 210 and subsequent rebuilds. First, there was no denial of her 1910 ancestry because of her longer boiler. Second, she received no tender booster. And third, air pumps were mounted on her smokebox front, anticipating a feature incorporated on Missabe's famed Yellowstones 11 years later. Mallets Nos. 208 and 211 were simpled in 1931. Because of the depression, No. 209 had to await her rebuilding until 1937. Rebuilding these locomotives with home shop forces kept people working in the road's shops and provided improved motive power at lowest cost.

Leasing of the Duluth & Iron Range by the DM&N in 1930 created today's Duluth, Missabe & Iron Range. It was apparent that operating economies could be realized by employing heavier power on ore trains over the sawtooth profile of the D&IR main line from the iron country down to Two Harbors, Minn. D&IR's biggest and most powerful road power were three 1923 Baldwin-built N2 class Mikados, and although ranked as among the most powerful 2-8-2's in the country at that time, these booster-fitted engines were limited to 3,600 long tons (4,000 short tons) of ore between Biwabik on the Mesabi Range and Two Harbors. On this run there were maximum ruling grades against loads of 0.62 percent at three locations, varying in length from 1.25 to 3 miles. The rebuilt Mallets increased train tonnage 60 percent by handling approximately 100 ore loads per trip. By then, the 210 — along with the other simple articulateds — had been equipped with larger 24 × 32" cylinders, upping tractive effort to 110,000 pounds, exclusive of tender boosters. During the remainder of the Thirties, and up until 1941 when the Yellowstone came, the five rebuilds could usually be found lugging ore trains over the Iron Range Division into Two Harbors.

In 1938, a recession year, ore tonnage dropped to slightly over 8 million. But the storm clouds of World War II were on the horizon, and soon the flow of war materiel from the United States to the Allies began to mount. More than 18 million tons of ore were moved in 1939. The following year that figure climbed to just short of 28 million.

Missabe Road was faced with the double dilemma of possessing an aging if well-maintained motive power fleet, not having purchased a new road locomotive in 20 years, and the imminent possibility of being required to cope with ore tonnage on a scale not seen since World War I. President Charles Edwin Carlson directed the road's mechanical department to proceed immediately with design specifications for new motive power. George W. Bohannon, the road's capable mechanical engineer (he later became Chicago & North Western's chief mechanical officer and ultimately president of the Pullman Company), was given the responsibility of working out design requirements, soliciting operating and maintenance personnel for their suggestions and thoughts. The new engines would go to the Iron Range Division, where operating requirements dictated a locomotive capable of handling 115-car, 8,750-ton trains over .62 percent grades without stalling — a 25 percent increase in train tonnage over that attainable with the "simplified Mallets." There was no question that the new engines would have to be big — far bigger than anything yet seen on the Missabe Road.

According to Bohannon, the design of the new engines was largely based upon the Western Pacific's very heavy, single-expansion 2-8-8-2's of Class M-137 built by Baldwin in 1931 and 1938. Certain changes, including lengthening of the back engine frame partially to accommodate a roomier cab, brought about an increase in weight, necessitating a four-wheel trailing truck. But in many important respects, the DM&IR and WP locomotives were alike. Both had 63" drivers and 26 × 32" cylinders. Steam pressure on the Missabe engines was set at 240 pounds, whereas on the WP engines it was pegged at 235 pounds; this produced a tractive force of 140,000 pounds for the 2-8-8-4's, compared with 137,000 pounds for the 2-8-8-2's. Boilers of the two locomotives were very close in size and steam-generating capability, the biggest difference being in firebox grate areas; the DM&IR engines had 125 square feet for burning high-quality, 13,500 BTU eastern soft coal, vs. 145 square feet for the oil-burning WP engines. Total engine weights were 695,000 pounds for the 2-8-8-4, and 663,100 pounds for the 2-8-8-2.

Robert A. Le Massena, author of *Articulated Steam Locomotives of North America* (Sundance Publications 1979), contributes this critique: "The big differences between the DM&IR and WP locomotives were inside the 'wrapping for the package.' Firebox width and length were alike, as were the boilers' first ring and maximum diameters. Yet, the DM&IR engine did not use all 145 square feet of grate area, that being cut to 125 feet. Flue/tube length was shortened from 23 to 21 feet, which makes good sense, for the last couple of feet contribute very little to a boiler's steam production. A substantial gain in horsepower was obtained by lengthening the combustion chamber from WP's 6 feet to 7 feet. The tube/flue arrangement differed remarkably: $27 \times 2\frac{1}{4}"$ and $75 \times 5\frac{1}{2}"$ (WP) vs. $82 \times 2\frac{1}{4}"$ and $245 \times 3\frac{3}{4}"$. The DM&IR boiler had about 25 percent more superheater area and about 6 percent more combined heating surface. In just about every other respect, the DM&IR engine had a superior boiler. The DM&IR locomotives had integrally cast frames and cylinders and roller bearings throughout. WP (like Rio Grande) did not feel that roller bearings were worthwhile on slow-moving engines. Of course, the DM&IR 2-8-8-4 had a longer wheelbase: $67'2"$ vs. $61'5"$."

Designing and building a large steam locomotive was always an intriguing business. To begin with, a railroad's motive-power department considered it sacrilege to accept another design, notwithstanding the precedent of the highly successful USRA designs of World War I, without making some changes, however trivial or arbitrary. (Electro-Motive would soon put an end to this provincial nonsense as well as the steam locomotive, unfortunately.) Next, the steam locomotive designer was confronted with the politics of whether to use an Elesco feedwater heater instead of a Worthington, say, or a Standard stoker instead of a Hanna. At times the choice was based on reciprocity in the marketplace and not necessarily from a mechanical standpoint. Finally, by 1940, builders had the additional problem of competing with defense factories for special steels and other scarce materials.

In designing the Yellowstones, every effort was made to produce the best possible locomotive for the money (the first batch cost $246,570 each) that would do the work demanded. Fortunately, roller bearings on all engine and tender axles were musts from the beginning. Heavy rolled slab frames were suggested by some as a means of holding down the cost of quarter-million-dollar locomotives, but Baldwin resisted including them on such large and powerful engines. The plan was to have used cast-steel frames on the forward engines and slab frames on the rear. Fortunately, cast-steel frames with integral cylinders won out for both engine units. The original tender specifications called for a conventional rectangular design, with a capacity of 26 tons of coal and 22,000 gallons of water, mounted on a pair of six-wheel Buckeye trucks. At the time, though, Union Pacific's 4-8-8-4 Big Boys were nearing completion. Their radically different 4-10-0, pedestal-type tenders, introduced in 1939 on UP 4-8-4's, appealed to both Baldwin and the DM&IR, and this design, which allowed a 3,000-gallon increase in water capacity, was selected.

Class M3 Yellowstones, Nos. 220-227, builder construction Nos. 62526-62533, were delivered in 1941. They were visually differentiated by their feedwater heaters, the Nos. 220-222 being equipped with Worthington SA's and the Nos. 223-227 with Elesco bundle types.

The first of the Yellowstones, No. 221 if memory serves me correctly, arrived in Duluth one balmy spring day in May 1941. Giant multicolored placards affixed to each side of her almost 10-foot-diameter boiler proudly acclaimed to all that she was a product of the great Baldwin Locomotive Works in far away Eddystone, Pa., just outside Philadelphia. Glistening in the afternoon sun, with her Russian-iron finish, gloss black appurtenances and running gear, she presented an elegant as well as awesome appearance even before steam-up. Her routing to Duluth had been circuitous, for the more direct lines from Chicago to the Head of the Lakes would not support her tremendous weight — listed on the freight waybill as being in excess of 400 tons even with no coal or water. I cut my last class in high school that afternoon to go to the downtown yards to get a close look at her. That night at the dinner table, I exclaimed to my father, who then headed the Missabe's plant protection department, that nothing would suffice but that we drive to Two Harbors and have a closer look at this most wondrous of all locomotives.

Upon arrival in Two Harbors the next evening, we found the 2-8-8-4 inside the new concrete, 8-track, rectangular enginehouse that had just been completed to house and service the eight new Yellowstones. The old 30-stall roundhouse and 100-foot turntable could not handle the new 128-foot giants.

A small army of mechanics and departmental brass was swarming over and about the great machines, looking like nothing so much as a colony of ants. There were four giant main rods to connect and a myriad of tests to be performed once the engine was connected to the enginehouse steam line. We walked around the half city-block-

| | NORTH COUNTRY COMPOUNDS | | | SIMPLED, A GN IDEA | | | |
|---|---|---|---|---|---|---|---|
| | DM&N | DM&N | DM&N | DM&N | DM&N | DM&N | DM&N |
| Type | 2-8-8-2 | 2-8-8-2 | 2-8-8-2 | 2-8-8-2 | 2-8-8-2 | 2-8-8-2 | 2-8-8-2 |
| Class | M | M-1 | M-2 | MS | M-1S | M-2S | M-2S |
| Series | 200-207 | 208-209 | 210-211 | 207 | 208-209 | 210 | 211 |
| Fuel | Bituminous | Bituminous | Bituminous | Bituminous | Bituminous | Bituminous | Bituminous |
| Cylinders, diameter/stroke, in. | 26×40×32 | 26×40×32 | 26×40×32 | 24×32 | 24×32 | 24×32 | 24×32 |
| Driver diameter, in. | 57 | 57 | 57 | 57 | 57 | 57 | 57 |
| Boiler pressure, p.s.i. | 200 | 200 | 200 | 200 | 200 | 200 | 200 |
| Grate area, sq. ft. | 84 | 77 | 84 | 84 | 84 | 84 | 84 |
| Evaporative heating surface, sq. ft. | 6883 | 5424 | 5424 | 5534 | 5592 | 5441 | 5621 |
| Superheater heating surface, sq. ft. | None | 1130 | 1130 | 2480 | 2480 | 2480 | 2480 |
| Weight on drivers, lbs. | 460,600 | 415,200 | 415,200 | 444,650 | 421,100 | 421,100 | 421,100 |
| Weight on lead truck, lbs. | | 28,300 | 28,300 | 17,225 | 26,750 | 26,750 | 26,750 |
| Weight on trailing truck, lbs. | | 26,700 | 26,700 | 32,265 | 46,600 | 46,600 | 46,600 |
| Total engine weight, lbs. | 448,100 | 470,200 | 470,200 | 494,500 | 494,450 | 494,450 | 494,450 |
| Tender weight, lbs. | 171,900 | 195,200 | 195,200 | 195,200 | 195,200 | 195,200 | 195,200 |
| Tender capacity, tons-gals./gals. | 16/9000 | 21/9000 | 21/9000 | 21/9000 | 21/9000 | 21/9000 | 21/9000 |
| Tractive force, engine | 91,000 | 91,000 | 91,000 | 110,000 | 110,000 | 110,000 | 110,000 |
| Tractive force, booster | None | None | None | None | None | None | None |
| Builder/date | Baldwin/1910 | Baldwin/1916 | Baldwin/1917 | Baldwin/1910 rebuilt 1930 | Baldwin/1916 rebuilt 1931 & 1937 | Baldwin/1917 rebuilt 1929 | Baldwin/1917 rebuilt 1931 |

long power plant on rails, eagerly absorbing every detail of her construction, giving especially close scrutiny to the huge pedestal tender. Almost 50 feet in length, this tender appeared to be supported by a continuous line of wheels. We had never seen one like it, what with a 25,000-gallon water capacity plus space for half a hopper car of coal.

My father, who had been a locomotive engineer 30 years before, suggested that we climb the vertical ladder leading to her second-story-level cab — and what a cab! Of vestibule design, almost 11 feet across and over 10 feet in length, it was the most commodious we had ever seen. It contained four cushioned seats, two for the engine crew, one for the brakeman, and an extra for a traveling dignitary or whoever. Father found the maze of controls and gauges intriguing, commenting that though he had not put his hand on a throttle for over three decades, he felt confident that, given minimal instruction, he could successfully operate the big beast. He told me that handling of the air with long trains would have been his greatest concern. I hinted to Dad that we must take a trip soon on one of these giants. That would follow a month later.

Prior to the arrival of the M3's, the railroad committed large capital expenditures for roadway and shop improvements to allow their use. New 115-pound rail was installed on the southbound main into Two Harbors. Water plugs (standpipes) were raised to accommodate the 14-foot height of the tender manholes. Adjacent tracks were respaced on certain curves to provide sufficient lateral swing clearance for the big boilers. New shop machinery and tools were necessary for their maintenance.

From all recollections, the first trip of an M-3, which turned at Biwabik near the eastern end of the Mesabi Range, went quite smoothly. Even though the big engine was not loaded down to her maximum tonnage, she had no trouble besting the biggest trains handled by the rebuilt 2-8-8-2's. DM&IR Superintendent of Motive Power & Cars P.M. Sullivan was quoted in the November 1941 issue of *Baldwin Locomotives*: "The locomotives broke in with practically full tonnage and were released for pool service after three supervised trips. No trouble was encountered during the break-in or subsequent trips. No alterations and very few adjustments were necessary. The locomotives steamed perfectly and exceeded the expected fuel performance." Along the route, crowds of spectators gathered to cheer her on. Within a short time, the M-3's were routinely handling trains 25 percent larger than those hauled by the older articulateds. As the Yellowstones took over the tonnage into Two Harbors, the replaced power began to slip away to Proctor, where it was badly needed to move the staggering tonnages moving through the port in Duluth. On the Missabe Division main, the rebuilt Mallets were expected to handle 180 loads of ore per trip into Proctor, a substantial increase over that possible with the popular booster-

| PERCURSOR | MISSABE'S FINEST | | OTHER MEMBERS OF THE YELLOWSTONE CLUB | | | BACKWARDS YELLOWSTONE |
|---|---|---|---|---|---|---|
| Western Pacific | DM&IR | DM&IR | Northern Pacific | Southern Pacific | Baltimore & Ohio | Southern Pacific |
| 2-8-8-2 | 2-8-8-4 | 2-8-8-4 | 2-8-8-4 | 2-8-8-4 | 2-8-8-4 | 4-8-8-2 |
| M-137-151 | M-3 | M-4 | Z-5 | AC-9 | EM-1 | AC-11 |
| 251-260 | 220-227 | 228-237 | 5000 | 3800-3811 | 7600-7619 | 4245-4274 |
| Oil | Bituminous | Bituminous | Sub-bituminous | Bituminous | Bituminous | Oil |
| 26 × 32 | 26 × 32 | 26 × 32 | 26 × 32 | 24 × 32 | 24 × 32 | 24 × 32 |
| 63 | 63 | 63 | 63 | 63½ | 64 | 63½ |
| 235 | 240 | 240 | 250 | 250 | 235 | 250 |
| 145 | 125 | 125 | 182 | 139.3 | 117.5 | 139 |
| 6811 | 6780 | 6758/6780 | 7673 | 6918 | 5298 | 6470 |
| 2152 | 2770 | 2770 | 3219 | 2831 | 2118 | 2616 |
| 549,600 | 560,257 | 564,974 | 554,000 | 531,200 | 485,000 | 531,700 |
| 48,134 | 41,219 | 41,362 | 45,500 | 48,300 | 50,700 | 76,400 |
| 65,310 | 93,564 | 93,364 | 115,500 | 110,400 | 93,000 | 49,800 |
| 663,100 | 695,040 | 699,700 | 715,000 | 689,900 | 628,700 | 657,900 |
| 403,350 | 436,635 | 438,335 | 401,000 | 400,700 | 382,000 | 393,300 |
| 60000/23,000 | 26/25,000 | 26/25,000 | 27/21,200 | 28/22,120 | 25/22,000 | 6100/22,000 |
| 137,000 | 140,000 | 140,000 | 139,900 | 124,300 | 115,000 | 124,300 |
| 13,900 | None | None | 13,400 | None | None | None |
| Baldwin/1938 | Baldwin/1941 | Baldwin/1943 | Alco/1928 | Lima/1939 | Baldwin/1944 | Baldwin/1942-43 |

equipped Santa Fe's, then the standard power on that district.

One bright early morning in June 1941, my father and I drove up to Two Harbors for my big day. Checking at the callboy's office, we found that there was a trip scheduled to Biwabik at about 10 a.m. Louis Amundsen, our engineer, was a kindly little man who had started his career on the old Duluth & Iron Range, hand-firing 4-8-0's. Introducing ourselves, we walked with Louis to our engine, 225 I believe. The engine crew was a bit apprehensive, knowing that my father was an official for the company, but upon learning that he had been a locomotive engineer, their reserve soon melted away.

After the customary inspection and air tests, our conductor waved the highball to leave Two Harbors. Being a small man, Louis had to rise up from his seatbox a bit to grasp the throttle. Gently, effortlessly, the giant engine moved ahead — with 140,000 pounds tractive effort there was no need to take slack. Slowly we moved around Pork City Hill while carmen inspected the train. Everything being OK, Louis gave a long blast on the whistle and pulled back on the throttle; we began in earnest to get our 120 empties in motion on the 1.5 percent grade. In the next 13 miles from the start of the run on Lake Superior, the engine would have to lift our train some 1,100 feet. With the engine in full throttle, there was little to do but sit back and look ahead, blowing the deep-throated steamboat whistle for grade crossings and occasionally applying the sanders on slippery rails. Passing through Highland, we found a southbound Yellowstone weighing her train. With the hill behind us, we glided as smoothly as a Pullman around the sweeping curve through Wales. We raced easily up and down the roller coaster line to Allen Junction, Amundsen having to reduce throttle much of the time to keep from exceeding the 35 mph speed limit. Coming back later that day with an 8,500-ton train would be a far different experience!

Picking up a message on the fly at Allen Junction instructing us to go on beyond Biwabik and turn back at Rainy Junction instead, we departed the main at Wyman and headed west along the Mesabi Range. The mining communities of Aurora, Biwabik, McKinley, Sparta, and Eveleth flashed by in succession. At most of these stations we found mine runs in the clear for our train. At

Largo Junction, we swung onto the Missabe Division's Virginia Branch and rolled at reduced speed to Rainy Junction Yard. After setting out our empties in the shadow of the giant Rouchleau ore-crushing plant, the engine was turned on the wye and then coaled and watered for the return trip to Two Harbors. Our orders read to pick up 60 loads at Rainy Junction, proceed to Fayal Yard, and fill out tonnage there. I wondered, why only 60 cars

to Fayal? The answer was soon obvious, for our big engine had all she could do to lug that many up the severe 0.75 percent grade at Leonidas Hill. At Fayal, another 40 loads were tacked onto our train and we prepared to move out with 100 cars to Two Harbors. Now, the conductor, wishing for some company, asked that we join him in the caboose, which we did. Up until then, all had gone well, too well it seemed. For as we pulled slowly

A panoramic view of the DM&N's ore docks at Duluth, taken in October, 1919. That's one of the big M class Mallets on the right taking off with a train of empties.

Author's Collection

Frank A. King

DM&IR Mallet No. 201 heads up Proctor Hill with a train of empties sometime during the late 1940's.

out of Fayal Yard, my father, who was standing on the rear platform with the conductor, facetiously asked if our return orders were in proper form. Turning white, the conductor quickly reexamined his orders and jerked open the angle cock at the rear of the caboose. (We never did learn what was wrong, nor did we feel we should ask.) As in all circumstances of this sort, the brakes on the rear end of the train reacted first, with the engine and cars on the head end continuing on for about 100 feet until the train dynamited and ground to an abrupt halt. Walking ahead, we found that the train had broken in two about 20 cars back of the engine, with a 100-foot-long gap separating the two sections. The weak link in the chain was an old 1906 U-3 class car on which the entire draft gear assembly on the front end was pulled out. Fortunately, a 1200-series 2-8-0 and switch crew were standing nearby and pulled the rear end of the train back and removed the damaged car from the consist. After an air test, we started out again for Two Harbors.

From then on, the return trip was uneventful, with Engineer Amundsen doing a masterful job of moving the heavy consist up and down the many hills to Two Harbors. Contrary to common opinion, the run is not all downhill, there being a number of adverse 0.62 percent grades. The worse stretch was, and still is, the 3-mile climb near Milepost 47 over which the 8,500-ton train was lifted some 100 feet in elevation! This is all the more remarkable considering that it was accomplished with a single unit. Dusk was overtaking us when we reached Highland, where the ore cars were weighed in motion at the rate of three cars per minute. This over, it was downhill to Two Harbors. Suddenly, a big Yellowstone, her headlight dimmed, thundered past with empties for the mines. We could hear her low, deep whistle blowing for grade crossings at Highland and beyond, finally fading away into the distance.

At Waldo, summit of the 3 percent grade down to Two Harbors, retainers were set up in a ritual performed there since air brakes were first applied to D&IR equipment in 1888. Dropping down Waldo Hill was, and still is, an awesome experience. Looking ahead from the caboose, we could see the red glow of hot brake shoes and smell their pungent, though not objectionable, odor. It was obvious that Louie had everything under control in the descent. In Two Harbors we bade our conductor and flagman goodbye and walked ahead to the panting engine to compliment Louie on a job well done. That day, almost 40 years ago now, remains for me a memorable experience. My last trip on a Yellowstone would come 17 years later.

On December 7, 1941, the United States became an active participant in World War II. Demands for iron ore off the Mesabi and Vermillion Ranges jumped sharply, with Missabe Road ore tonnage climbing from 37.5 million tons in 1941 to almost 45 million in 1942. Additional road power was needed, this time for the Missabe Division, and Baldwin received an order for 10 Yellowstones for 1943 delivery.

Classified M-4's, Nos. 228-237 (construction Nos. 64707-64716) left Eddystone in the winter of 1943. Though identical in design with the M-3's, the newcomers weighed more (699,700 vs. 695,000 pounds) because carbon steel had had to be substituted for certain alloy steels. Again, members of the class were visually differentiated by their feedwater heaters, Nos. 228-232 wearing Worthingtons and Nos. 233-237 Elescos.

The June 5, 1943, *Railway Age* contained a feature on the M-4's which included a statistical comparison of the new machines with other major articulateds, including Northern Pacific's prototype 2-8-8-4, Western Pacific's pattern 2-8-8-2, Union Pacific's Big Boy 4-8-8-4, Norfolk & Western's A-class 2-6-6-4, and Chesapeake & Ohio's 2-6-6-6. Interestingly, the DM&IR engine outranked all the others in weight on drivers and engine tractive effort.

Many of the new M-4's went directly to the hard-pressed Denver & Rio Grande Western, inasmuch as DM&IR had no employment for them until the following spring. That winter a total of 12 Yellowstones were leased to the Grande, as well as to the Great Northern and Northern Pacific, to assist them in moving wartime traffic. It was the second winter that D&RGW had borrowed DM&IR 2-8-8-4's for use as helpers over the 10,239-foot Tennessee Pass crossing of the Continental Divide. The Grande sent a telegram to the Missabe, stating that the Yellowstones were the finest steam engines ever to operate on its road. Vice President Paul H. Van Hoven, justly proud, read the wire to my father, who happened to be in his office when it arrived.

Receipt of the 10 M-4's greatly bolstered ore-hauling capability over the Missabe Division, over which they were rated at 18,100 tons — so much so that the five rebuilt Mallets, Nos. 207-211, were largely diverted to the cross-country ore haul between the Hibbing-Chisholm district and Biwabik, where the trains were turned over to Iron Range crews for movement to Two Harbors. Although tonnages peaked in 1942, they remained in excess of 40 million tons per year through 1945, a truly awesome amount of ore for one railroad to haul out of the limited area served by the Missabe.

Following the war, the old 1910 Mallets, which had given such an excellent account of themselves for nearly 40 years on Proctor Hill, began showing signs of fatigue. Mainframes were forever requiring welding to stay intact, and boiler and firebox repairs became increasingly troublesome and expensive. Missabe, not yet in a mood to dieselize, began looking for steam replacements. They came during 1949 from another U.S. Steel property, the Union Railroad, in the form of nine 0-10-2's rated at 90,900 pounds tractive effort. Employed on the Hill and in Proctor Yard, they compared favorably with the Mallets. But without the old plodding compounds and the soothing sound of their muffled exhaust, the operation was different, for the Hill now shook to the impatient snap of the 10-drivered Eastern invaders.

Additional power was needed, and it came from another U.S. Steel property in the spring of 1951. Missabe acquired 18 big Texas types from Bessemer & Lake Erie, engines rendered redundant by F7 diesels. They helped the DM&IR cope with a peak ore tonnage just shy of 50 million tons in 1953. Although the world's most powerful two-cylinder steam locomotives, the 2-10-4's exerted 30 percent less tractive effort than the Yellowstones and were assigned to mainline ore runs only as a last resort. Including the Texas types, DM&IR's steam roster attained an all-time high of 172 engines in 1951.

Diesel demonstrators then began appearing on the property. Among the first was a Baldwin 2000 h.p. C-C road-switcher. Then a four-unit, 6400 h.p. team of Alco FA2/FB2 cabs weighing approximately a million pounds, all on drivers, appeared. Dubbed the *Green Hornet* by Missabe crews, the demo experienced little difficulty in handling Iron Range Division trains grossing almost 13,000 tons into Two Harbors, this in territory where a Yellowstone's rating was 8,850 tons. The writing was on the wall.

During June 29-July 12, 1953, a pair of Fairbanks-Morse 2400 h.p. C-C Train Masters demonstrated, making five round trips out of Proctor to Mesabi Range yards at Mitchell and Fraser. On July 3, the 4800 h.p. team moved a train grossing 11,754 tons between Biwabik and Two Harbors, consuming only 1,162 gallons of fuel oil for the round trip from the latter point, a 39.5 percent reduction in fuel cost compared with steam. Even the staunchest steam supporter had to admit that steam would be dethroned.

Dieselization of the Missabe Road began in 1953 with receipt of fifteen 1200 h.p. SW9's from Electro-Motive Division. Dieselization of road operations commenced with the opening of the 1956 ore season with the delivery of EMD 1750 h.p. C-C SD9's. (The first 2400 h.p. EMD SD24 was tested on the DM&IR, but the railroad could not effectively utilize its high horsepower in low-speed drag service. The only exceptions to this were the six Alco RSD15's, 2400 h.p. high-nosed DL600B's Nos. 50-55, acquired in 1959 to handle the difficult sorting and dock-switching assignment at Two Harbors, subsequently leased to N&W, returned to DM&IR, transferred to B&LE, and eventually sold to U.S. Steel's Quebec Cartier, which also wound up with the 10 ex-UP Alco C630's Missabe had briefly in the early 1970s). Dieselization was completed three years later with delivery of SD18's. By then ore demand from the Mesabi Range had dropped to slightly over half of 1953's peak of almost 50 million tons, and a roster of 95 diesel units, together with a number of leased units, were adequate to replace all yard and road steam power.

Three Yellowstones were preserved: No. 225 at Proctor; No. 227 at the Lake Superior Museum of Transportation in Duluth; and No. 229 at Two Harbors.

My last trip aboard a Yellowstone was made during the summer of 1958 . . . and our big engine almost died on the main line for lack of steam! A beautiful morning found my invited guest, longtime friend and steam enthusiast Lowell Wood of Minneapolis, at the callboy's office in Proctor looking at the day's lineup. By then the Missabe was largely dieselized and we were taking our chances finding steam. Luck was with us, though, for the first ore extra out had Yellowstone No. 235 on the head end, called for a 9 a.m. departure. Walking over to the go-out track, we introduced ourselves to the engineer, amiable Walter "Mose" Bijold. Mose, fully expecting to get a diesel, was attired in sports clothes, and he made no effort to conceal his disappointment. Our destination was Taconite Junction at the far western end of the Mesabi Range.

Before leaving Proctor, Mose instructed his young fireman to hose down the cab deck and front of the coal pile to keep the dust down, since it promised to be a hot day. With 200 empties grossing 4,400 tons in tow, we left Proctor and started northward in earnest. About five miles out, Mose noted that our engine was losing speed and he instinctively glanced at the steam gauge. Pressure was nowhere near the normal 240 pounds. Mose beckoned the fireman over to the right-hand side of the cab, then walked over and opened the firebox door. He was aghast at what he saw, for immediately in front of the firing table was a huge pile of unburned "green" coal. The answer was obvious — the fireman had performed too good a job of dust control. Mose blurted out some oaths only to discover that the fireman had no previous Yellowstone experience. By now the speed of the engine was down to a crawl. Assisting Mose, we extricated the 20-foot fire rake from the tender. Meanwhile, Mose broke up the coal pile with the slash bar and turned up the blower. We pushed the green coal ahead and hand-shoveled some dry coal into the firebox. Slowly the steam pressure gauge began to climb and we started to pick up speed. Burning over the incident, Mose was determined to make up the lost time — after all, he intended to get in nine holes of golf that evening upon our return to Proctor!

Minutes later, our engine was moving along at a good 30 mph and soon afterward slammed downgrade across the Cloquet River bridge at about 40. At Coleraine Junction we veered left up the Alborn Branch. The track was straight as a taut string for miles and gave Mose a good opportunity to make up time. An automobile tried to beat us to a country crossing but the driver thought better of it upon seeing us bearing down on him. By the time we reached Taconite Junction, all time had been made up and Mose was happy.

After taking on coal and water at Taconite Junction, we backed to High Grade yard and coupled onto 180 loads of ore. After pumping up the train line and making the air test, we received the highball from the conductor. An SD9 coupled behind the caboose gave us a shove upgrade out of the yard onto the main, then cut off. At Holman Junction we swung onto the Great Northern, over which DM&IR had trackage rights. While blasting upgrade through Calumet, Mose called our attention to a bikinied young lovely sunbathing in her backyard near the track; everyone dashed to the righthand side of the cab for a look. Suddenly, our pretty sun-worshipper jumped up from her blanket, brushed herself off, and made a dash toward the house. At first we were perplexed. Then we realized the reason for her quick departure was because of the shower of hot cinders, which had rained down on her midriff from the hard-working stack of the 235.

Near Coleraine Junction we stopped, cut off from the train, and eased down light to the water plug. With our inexperienced fireman, Mose was taking no chances on running out of water before Proctor. The 0.3 percent grade between Cloquet River bridge and Saginaw brought our big engine and her 17,000-ton train down to 12 mph, but the rail was dry and we went over the summit in good form. (Today, a pair of SD18's or SD38's would attain only 8 to 10 mph on that grade with similar tonnage because of their lower horsepower.)

Drifting downgrade past Adolph, Mose smoothly slowed our heavy train, prepared to stop just short of the ore scales there. Another ore extra, this one headed by three leased Great Northern FT's, drifted in on an adjacent track as we awaited instructions to weigh. Cutting our train in half, we began weighing the head end at the rate of three cars per minute. A Proctor switch crew would be dispatched later to weigh the rear end. Upon completion of weighing, we set out the head end of the train in "A" yard, cut off the engine, and moved light to the tie-up track. The sun was still high in the sky, and Mose assured us he would still get his golf game in before calling it a day.

The next year there was little steam activity because of a marked tonnage drop. During 1960 ore rebounded to 28 million tons, making it necessary to bring out a number of Yellowstones for steam's final curtain call on the Missabe Road. The last steam ore run was made over the Missabe Division by engine No. 222 on July 5, 1960.

An even half century of steam articulateds on the DM&IR had ended.

Author's collection

Grimy and coated from ore dust, No. 200, the first of the compound Mallets delivered to the DM&N — and considered one of the largest locomotives of its time — blasts away from the ore docks at Duluth with a long string of empties.

At right, years later, the 200 shows the effects of "modernization" with her top-mounted tanks and Elesco feedwater heater. The old gal is still doing what she was intended for . . . hauling long trains of ore cars!

Frank A. King

Author's collection

121

Above, the second of the DM&N's M class Mallets, No. 201 is seen pulling loaded ore cars in 1925. Because it was standard practice to back down Proctor Hill, the Mallets, like most of the DM&N's early power, were equipped with rear-mounted pilots. Below, looking quite different, the 201 churns up the Hill near the end of her 43-year career.

Both photos, author's collection

H. Van Horn collection

Author's collection

The DM&N's M class Mallets were typical examples of the slow-drag freight articulateds used by many American railroads early in the 20th century. What they lacked in speed they more than made up with raw power. The M class enjoyed a long and fruitful life on both the DM&N and later on the DM&IR, hauling mile-long trains of iron ore. No. 203 and 204 are examples of the class in later years. No. 203 is shown parked near the coal tower at Proctor, while both the engineer's and fireman's side of the 204 are at the same location. The close-up of 204's cab illustrates the piping and other details of this massive engine.

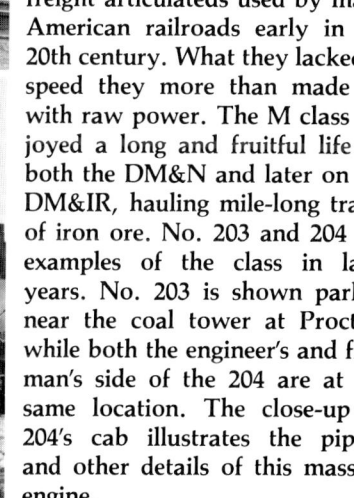

Frank A. King

Author's collection

Here are several interesting rear-end views showing the tender-mounted pilots. Above, in this rather blurred photograph, is one of the big mallets backing out of Proctor with a train bound for the Duluth ore docks. Below, this close-up of the rear of No. 204 gives an even better look at the high-mounted air hose that enabled coupling with the high-mounted hoses on the ore cars.

Two photos, author's collection

124

Before and after views of mallet No. 205. This engine retained its long lean look and was little changed, except for a few "modern" appliances, right up to the end. Below, the same engine rolls past the Proctor elevated locomotive coal dock with its customary train of empties from the Duluth ore docks. That's quite an interesting string of wood cabooses in the background.

Three photos, author's collection

Author's collection

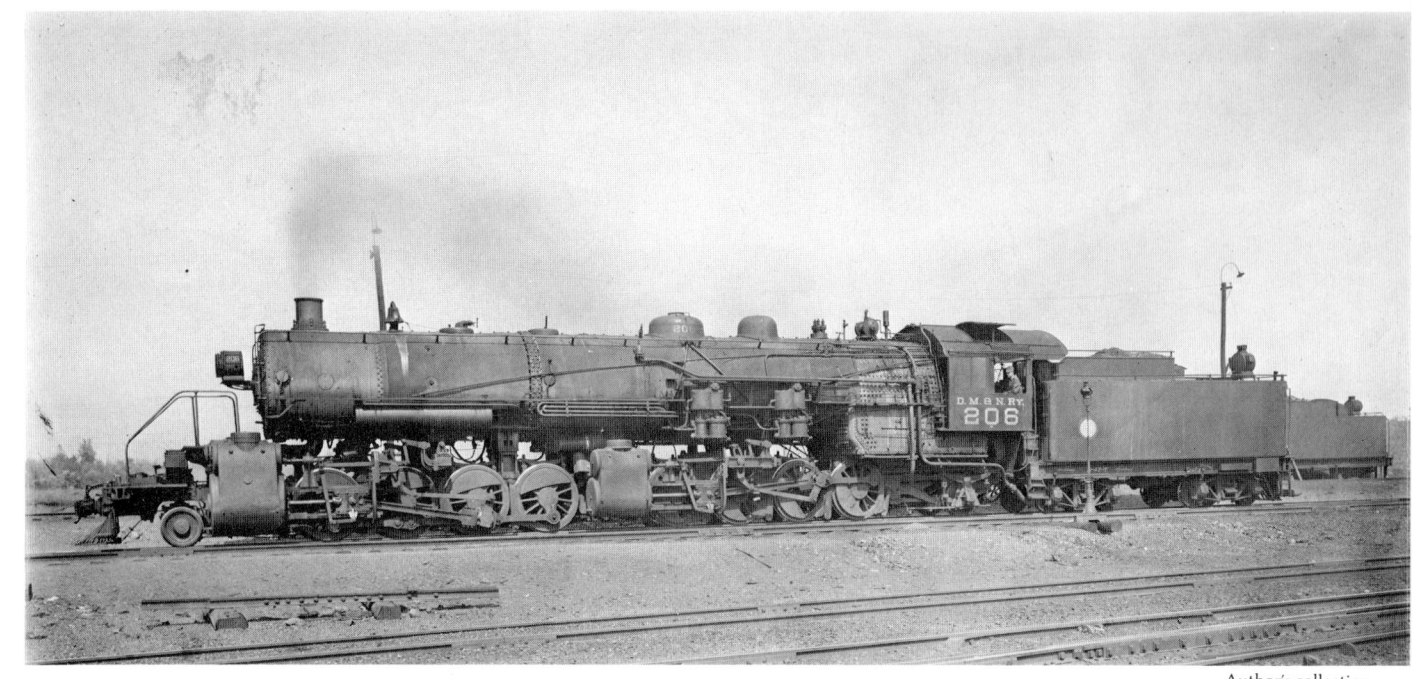

The M class 2-8-8-2's were equipped with shorty tenders that made the long locomotives appear even longer . . . of course, as in this photo of No. 206, the camera lens helps, too! In the lower photograph taken by Jim Scribbins on May 31st, 1947, a modernized 206 is seen ascending Proctor Hill with 57 empties.

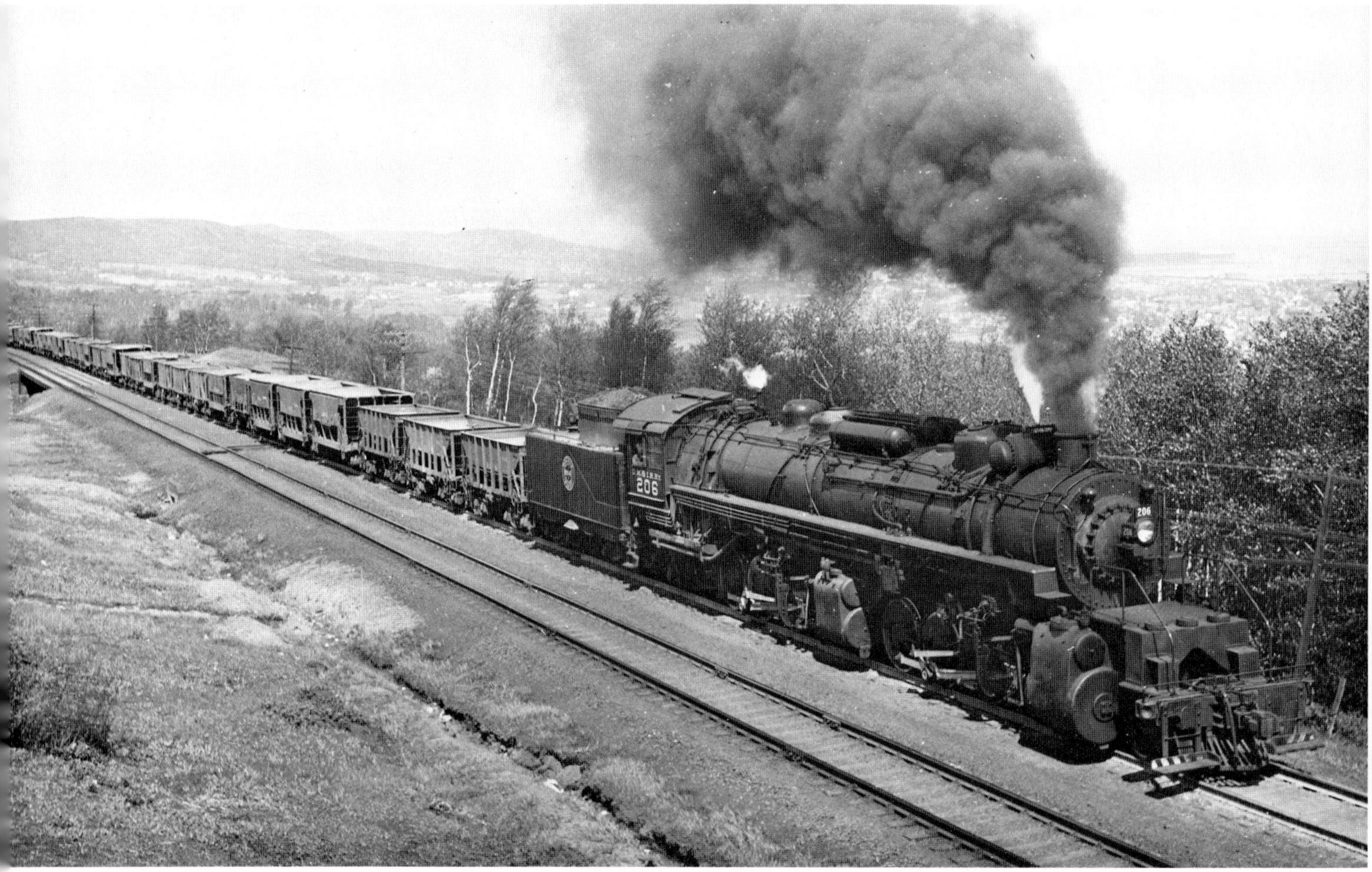

The mallets saw heavy service for over 40 years. In this picture, the 207 looks the worse for wear and in bad need of shopping. The road name and number are so faded on the cab side they're hard to read . . . even with a magnifier. In fact, the number on the front cylinder was made by the photographer for ease of identification!

The 207 was involved in a messy collision on Proctor Hill in late 1929. It looks like the tender and cab got the worst of it. By the time the photographer arrived the wrecking crew had begun to shore up the big hog with timbers. The locomotive was eventually rebuilt . . .

Three photos, author's collection

Author's collection

Frank A. King

. . . and here she is, better than ever! In the process the locomotive was converted to single expansion, following the lead of sister engine, No. 210. The Elesco feedwater heater, and front-mounted pumps give her a pleasing, modern appearance.

Like the 207, the 208 was also rebuilt to single expansion, making her quite different from the original Baldwin product of 1916. As built these massive locomotives had 57-inch drivers, and a total engine and tender weight of 647,000 pounds. Note tender booster.

Three photos, author's collection

Here's No. 208 again, and at that familiar and well-photographed location, you guessed it . . . Proctor Hill! The date was around 1952.

Frank A. King

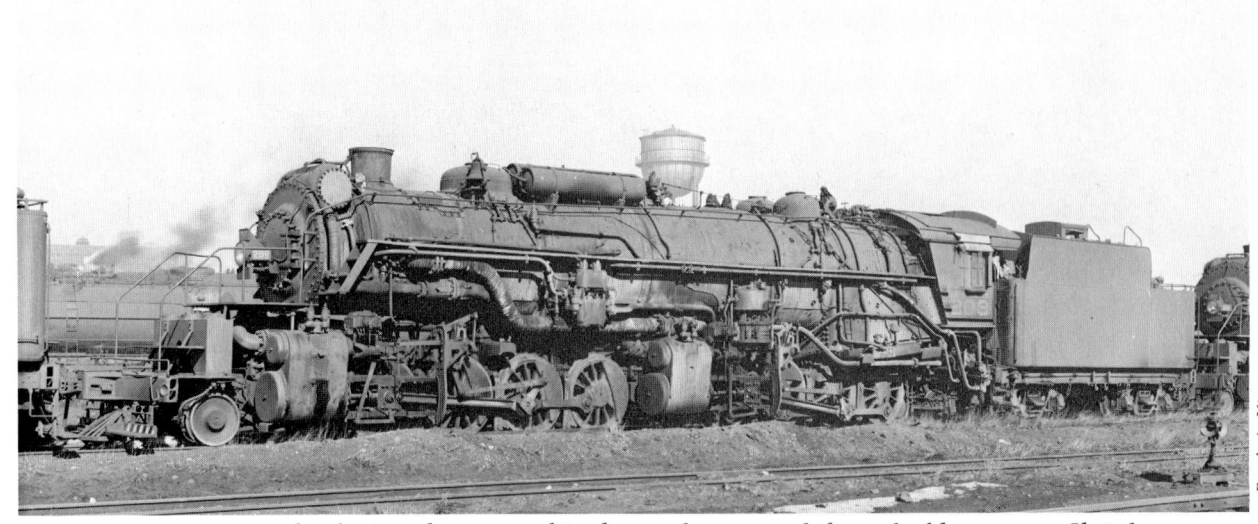

Engine 209 was a plumber's nightmare in this photo taken toward the end of her career. She's been simplified, rebuilt, modernized and sports a slant-front cab as well as a tender with increased coal capacity. That's sister engine No. 211 sitting right behind her.

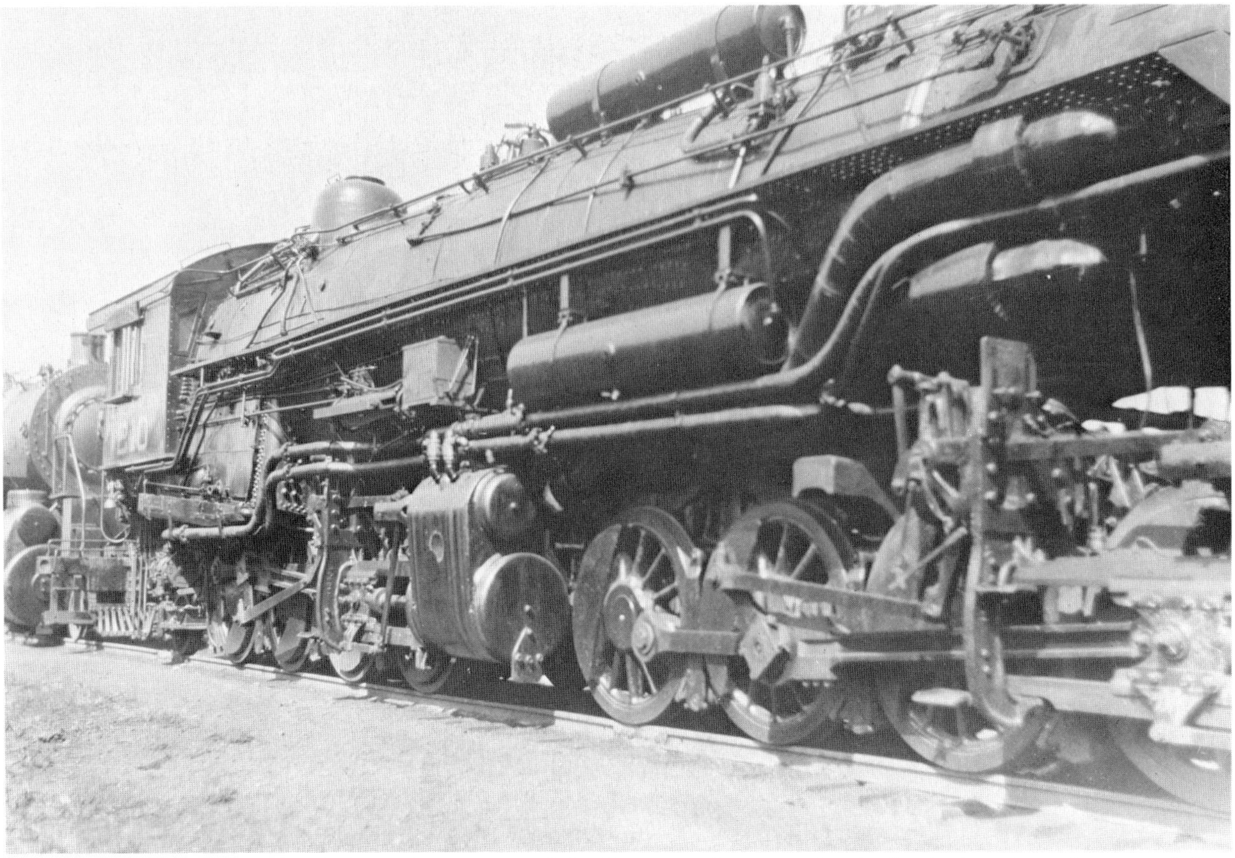

Author's collection

The problem with the early compound Mallets was they were basically designed as slow-speed drag freight engines, and as such, unsuited to the faster freight schedules inaugurated by the railroads in the 1920's. Many roads either bought new and faster power, or converted their older articulateds to more modern efficient machines. Taking a page from neighboring Great Northern, the Missabe rebuilt several engines in the M class to single expansion, starting in 1929. This close-up of the engineer's side of the 210 depicts the locomotive soon after conversion. No. 210, affectionately nicknamed the "Madam Queen" by Missabe crews, was the first in its class to be rebuilt.

Robert F. Collins  Here's a beautiful picture of the modern 210 passing a loaded train while climbing Proctor Hill with a string of empty ore cars that seem to stretch far around the curve.

Author's collection

Here's more fine action shots of the 210. Above, in familiar territory on Proctor Hill, while at right, on a Northbound "cross country" ore extra at Sparta, Minnesota in 1955. After being simplified the engines were reclassed. No. 207 became class MS ("S" meaning simple) and Nos. 208 and 209 went from class M1 to class M1S. The 210 and sister 211 were reclassed from M2's to M2S.

Frank A. King

Wayne Olsen

It's amazing to note the changes on the M class over the years. Looking at the before and after photos of the last of the Missabe's Mallets, No. 211, it's as if you were looking at two entirely different locomotives, and in a sense, they were. The 211 weighed 494,450 pounds after rebuilding and developed 110,000 pounds of tractive effort. The rebuilt engines of the M class regularly hauled trains of 180 cars of ore between the Mesabi Range and Proctor. The 211 was sold for scrap in 1957.

Two photos, author's collection

A few years away from retirement, the 211 rolls an ore train Northbound through Sparta, Minnesota.

In 1955 the author paced a "Cross-country" ore drag with 211 on the head end, taking these pictures along the way. Above, the train is near Iron Junction, while below the it's about the enter CTC-controlled track at Wolf, Minnesota. At right, the 211 easily rolls along with her long train through Sparta on its way to Biwabik.

All photos Frank A. King

*H. Van Horn collection*

The second in the series, No. 221, is seen enroute from the builder at Hudson, Wisconsin in 1941. Baldwin was proud of their product as evidenced by the sign on the side of the locomotive.

*H.L. Broadbelt collection*

*Author's collection*

Right and left builder's views of the 222, the third Yellowstone, resplendent in shiny black and gray, at the builder's plant in Eddystone, Pennsylvania. At right, the same locomotive is shown heading south with an ore train, at Allen Junction.

DM&IR collection

Frank A. King

Toward the end of steam operations on the Missabe, the Yellowstones were used on several fan trips. Above, M3 No. 222 is on such a trip at McComber, near Ely, Minnesota, on July 3rd 1960. This trackage was removed in 1983. At right, the same locomotive blasts away from Two Harbors on another fan trip. Yellowstone number four, the 223, is shown outside the Baldwin plant in this photograph from the Broadbelt collection. With its gray boiler and colorful Missabe emblem on the tender, 223 was a combination of beauty and sheer power.

Frank A. King

H.L. Broadbelt collection

Above, Yellowstone No. 224 hustles Northbound across the Eveleth branch with a train of empties. Note the crossing gate. At right, No. 225 thunders over a wood trestle while on a railfan special, near Calumet, on Great Northern trackage.

Yellowstone No. 225 makes ready to depart Saginaw for Proctor with an unlikely consist, a single coach from a railfan special

All photos Frank A. King

Howard Peddle

In this fine portrait, No. 226 poses for the camera before leaving Proctor with a string of empties, bound for the Mesabi Range.

Yellowstone No. 226 is about to start her train after dropping off an ore car that suffered from a "hot box." This scene is near Alborn, Minnesota, and you couldn't ask for a better combination of smoke and steam . . . photographically speaking that is, since the railroad frowned on excessive smoke!

Frank A. King

Frank A. King

On the next several pages is a series of outstanding action photos of the mighty Yellowstones in their natural element . . . hauling long trains of ore cars. Above No. 225 is on well-ballasted track near Wyeman, Minnesota. The 227 is shown with its customary long train. This engine is now on display at the Lake Superior Museum of Transportation in Duluth. Below, two massive Yellowstones stage a "meet" somewhere along the Missabe's main line North of Two Harbors.

Two photos, DM&IR collection

Frank A. King

No. 230's crew eyes the photographer as the big engine sprints Southbound through Alborn. Below, in a bird's eye view (actually from the nearby coal tower) 227 is also Southbound at Allen Junction.

Author's collection

Two photos, author's collection

No. 227 has been freshly painted and spruced up at Proctor before being placed on display at the railroad museum in Duluth.

Wayne Olsen collection

M4 No. 230 is shown heading through Fairbanks, Minnesota in the Fall of 1952. At right, in another view, No. 230 is seen working hard on the 0.3% grade southbound through Saginaw in 1959.

Frank A. King

Life on a locomotive.
Well known rail author and photographer, William Middleton had an opportunity to ride the cab of Yellowstone No. 228 and here are the results:
Bill caught the big engine getting ready at Proctor for a trip over the road in several views. The locomotive is seen at the Proctor coal tower before backing down to her train. The engineer awaits the highball, then she's off with her mile-long train of loaded ore cars. Meanwhile, the engineer and fireman go through their various chores, while the head brakeman takes it easy, with one foot up, watching the scenery roll by. The cabs of the Yellowstones were huge by anyone's standards . . . almost 11 feet across and 10 feet deep!
Last, 228 is about to pass sister engine 220 somewhere along the mainline.

Both photos, author's collection

Speaking of cabs . . . here's what the crew of a Yellowstone had to face . . . that's quite an array of gauges and valve handles.

Engine 231 gets ready to move off the Proctor turntable, while sister 234 waits her turn.

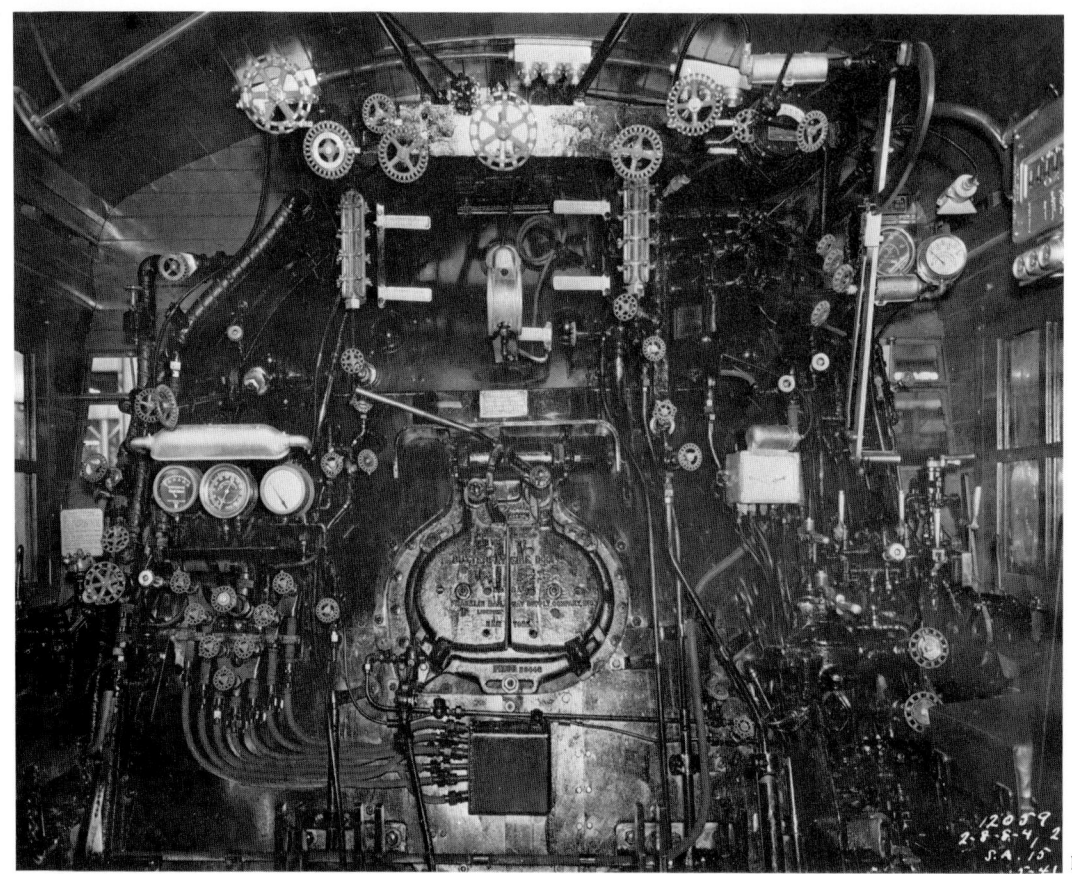

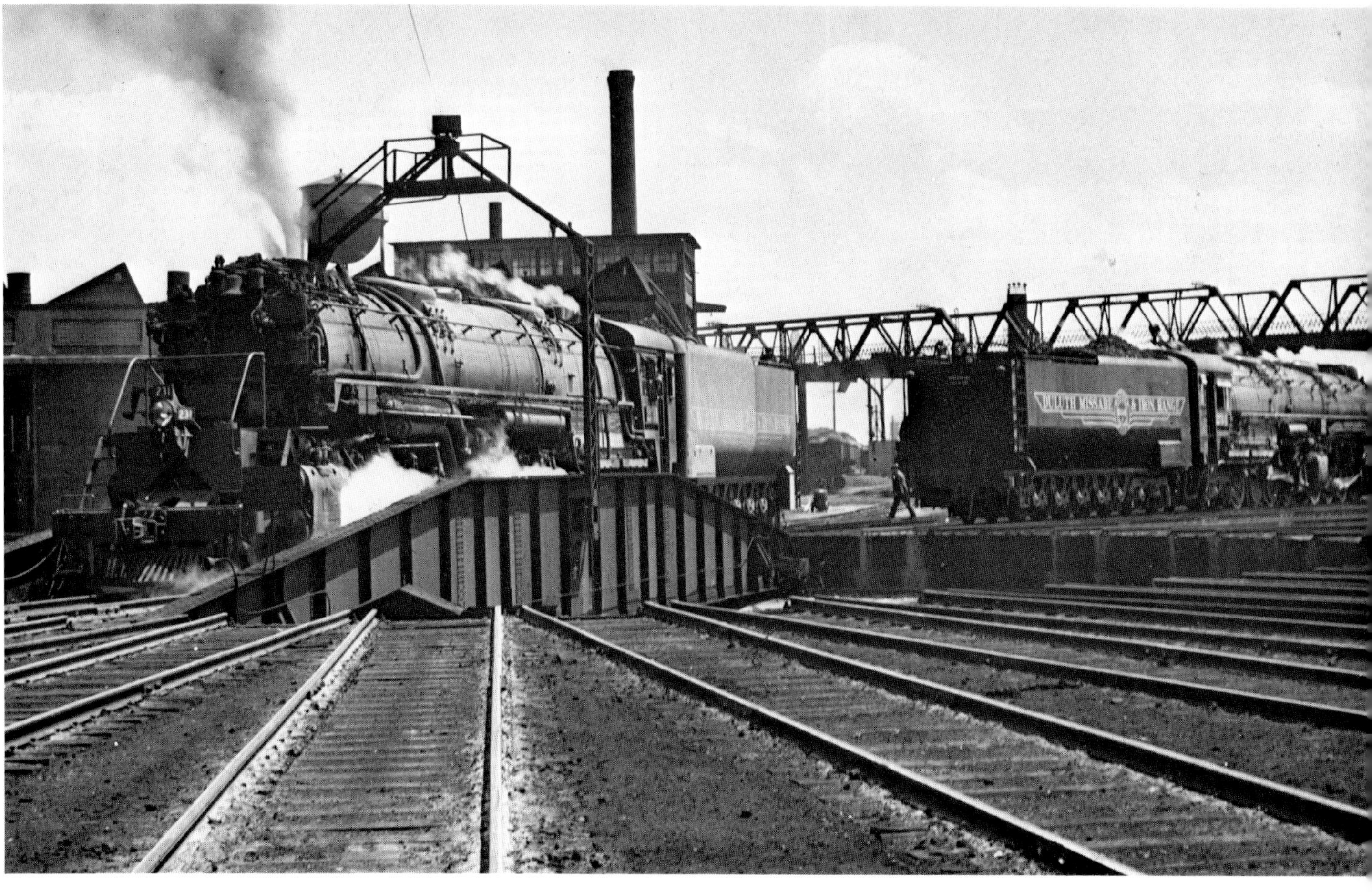

No. 232 weighs in on the ore scales at Highland, Minnesota, while the 231 thunders by with a train of empties.

This time it's No. 231 on the scales at Proctor. That's the Hibbing local along side on the left.

Both photos, Frank A. King

157

The delivery of 10 additional Yellowstones, class M4, during the war year 1943, created quite a stir in the railroad industry. An article on these locomotives was featured in the June 5th, 1943 issue of Railway Age, along with several pages of advertisements by Baldwin and other companies that supplied parts. A sample of these colorful ads are reproduced here. With their use of tints and different type faces, they were typical 1940's advertising.

Author's collection, courtesy of Railway Age

No. 232 is southbound through Saginaw . . . that steam in front of the tender, just below the cab, is from the unique tender-mounted rail washer.

Frank A. King

The 232 again . . . also going south ready to pass the tower at Coleraine Junction.

Author's collection

Several more views of the ore scales at Proctor. Above, an ore train with No. 233 on the head end, while below, No. 235 and leased Great Northern FT's wait to weigh in with their respective trains. The Proctor scales could handle three cars per minute.

No. 224 pounds across the Cloquet River bridge with a Northbound train of empties at a brisk 40 mph.

All photos Frank A. King

Frank A. King

The 235 was one of the last group of M4's built by Baldwin. They were the world's most powerful steam locomotives and the last to be used in ore service. Engine and tender weighed a whopping 568 tons and on the Iron Range division they were capable of pulling 100 loaded 70-ton capacity ore cars. On the Missabe division, the same engines were rated for 190 loaded cars!

No. 235, in a classic photo that must have been repeated wherever there was a steam locomotive, a small boy and a photographer.

164  DM&IR collection

In June, 1959, the author caught a Yellowstone on a southbound ore extra from the Bear Trap bridge.

*Frank A. King*

The 236 and her train are shown here working up the 1.5% grade out of Two Harbors.

Frank A. King

The 236 again, this time looking just a little weather-beaten, stands in front of one of the ex-B&LE 2-10-4's, near the Proctor coal dock.

A loaded ore train, stretching as far as the eye can see, gets ready to leave Hull Rust yard in Hibbing, Minnesota, bound for the ore docks at Duluth.

Ore traffic boomed during World War II on the DM&IR. Here in 1945, the ore-sorting yard at Proctor is crowded with row after row of loaded cars.

This photograph has been reproduced many times, yet no study of the Yellowstones would be complete without it, since more than any other picture, it depicts the great size and length of these magnificent locomotives. No. 236 is Northbound out of Two Harbors, and in the next 13 miles she will climb over 1000 feet above the elevation of Lake Superior.

Frank A. King

It looks pretty cold . . . and it was! This is an overall scene of
the annual Fall ore thawing at Two Harbors.

Toward the end of steam on the Missabe, the once-mighty Yellowstones
were reduced to ore-thawing service at Two Harbors yard.

Mishaps did happen to the big Yellowstones — not often, but when they did, a special wrecking crane with a 250-ton capacity was required to get the massive locomotives back on the rails.

All too often when Missabe steam is mentioned, especially later-day power, the first engines that come to mind are the Yellowstones. Yet there was more to the DM&IR than big power and long ore trains. The Missabe and its predecessors provided excellent passenger service with a fleet of 10-wheelers and Pacifics, like the 402, shown here hustling along with two cars on the Iron Range division.

Author's collection

# VI. PASSENGER POWER

The initial D&IR passenger service was powered by two Baldwin American, 4-4-0 locomotives, Nos. 1 and 2 (Class A), which were received in 1884. These petite diamond stacked engines weighed 83,900 pounds in working order. Two passenger cars and a combination caboose comprised the initial rolling stock.

Completion of trackage linking Two Harbors with Duluth during December, 1886 brought about increased passenger travel. During 1888 the road acquired from Baldwin three additional locomotives of the 4-4-0 type, Nos. 23, 24 and 25 (Class C). These passenger service engines weighed 96,600 pounds, which was 11,700 pounds more than the first two 4-4-0's.

By the turn of the century, passenger business between Duluth and the booming mining towns served by the D&IR reached such proportions that it was necessary to provide heavier passenger power to cope with the longer and heavier trains. The 1.5 percent grade leading north out of Two Harbors taxed the 4-4-0's to the extent that it was often necessary to double head passenger trains to the summit. New passenger power arrived from Schenectady during 1900 in the form of six, Ten-Wheeler (4-6-0) engines, which were numbered 101 through 106. These engines, designated Class M, weighed 150,000 pounds and represented a 55 percent increase in weight over the heaviest 4-4-0's. Developing 26,125 pounds of tractive effort, they were often used in local freight service, displacing the small Class G and H Consolidations. An unusual feature of the Ten-Wheelers was the application of a clerestory cab roof, similar to that used on passenger cars.

Acquisition of all-steel passenger equipment during 1913 increased train weights beyond the capability of the 4-6-0's. To cope with this situation, the D&IR received four Pacific (4-6-2) Class A locomotives from Baldwin in 1913. These engines, Nos. 107 through 110, were equipped with 22 × 28″ cylinders, 69″ drivers, and weighed 219,000 pounds. They developed 33,400 pounds of tractive effort. Vanderbilt-type tenders, carrying 6,300 gallons of water and 14 tons of coal, were included. These were the last passenger locomotives acquired by the D&IR. By this time the D&IR operated two first-class passenger trains between Duluth and Ely, both of which carried cafe-parlor cars. In addition, the overnight freight between these two points was listed as a mixed train and carried passengers. For many years this train was known locally as the "High Ball." Leaving Duluth Union Depot at 10:10 p.m. and arriving at Ely at the unholy hour of 4:55 a.m., it averaged only 16 miles per hour. Only the hardiest souls could endure the trip, and it was not surprising that the train's clientele was mainly lumberjacks. Upon receipt of the Pacifics, branch line service across the Mesabi Range (between Allen Junction and Virginia), was powered by the Class M Ten-Wheelers or the Class C 4-4-0's, depending on operating requirements and locomotive availability.

D&IR 4-4-0 No. 1 was the first passenger engine retired; it was sold to the Deer Park Railroad in 1911. As passenger service declined, all the engines assigned to this service were retired, the last to go being Pacific No. 1107 in 1955.

Passenger locomotive development on the DM&N closely paralleled that of the D&IR. The first passenger engines to arrive were two 4-4-0's, Nos. 1 and 2 (Class A), which were built by Pittsburgh Locomotive Works in 1893. Weighing 89,800 pounds, these little shotgun-stacked locomotives developed only 14,510 pounds of tractive effort. They soon proved inadequate to haul trains up the 2.2 percent grade between Duluth and Proctor and were replaced by Class F Ten-Wheelers developing 22,500 pounds of tractive effort. Although designed primarily for ore and freight service, the 56″ driver Ten-Wheelers proved to be adequate passenger power, thanks to the DM&N's relaxed passenger schedules.

By 1906 faster passenger schedules and heavier trains were taxing the capacity of the Class F Ten-Wheelers. Two heavier 4-6-0's, Nos. 100 and 101, were purchased from Baldwin to cope with the problem. Weighing 166,200 pounds and with 67″ drivers, these engines were designated Class F1 and carried a price tag of $14,108 each. With wide fireboxes placed over the rear drivers, it seemed certain that they would have adequate steaming capacity. This was not the case, however. In fact the steaming problem became so serious that, according to then Road Foreman of Engines Patrick M. Sullivan, Baldwin dispatched no less than Samuel Vauclain, their renowned general superintendent of the works and ace troubleshooter, to see what could be done. According to Sullivan, Vauclain suggested a number of modifications, the main one being to reduce the cylinder diameter by 1.25" to lessen steam demand. To test the idea, No. 100 was left unchanged, while the cylinders of No. 101 were bushed down from 20" to 18.75" in diameter. Still, engine No. 101 was not quite right, for the following year two additional Ten-Wheelers were ordered and Baldwin suggested reducing the driver diameter from 67" to 63" and leaving the cylinder diameter at 20". These engines, Nos. 102 and 103, apparently gave a good account of themselves. They were designated Class F2 and cost the company $15,254 each. A duplicate 4-6-0, No. 104, was received in 1910; cylinder and driver diameters were the same as on engines 102 and 103. Later the cylinder diameter of engine 104, which had been reduced to 18.75", was changed back to 20", and she was reclassified an F3.

In 1912, the DM&N acquired all-steel passenger equipment that pushed train weights beyond the capacity of the Baldwin Ten-Wheelers. The new steel cars weighed from 50 to 100 percent more than the wooden ones. In addition, due to heavier passenger business, the number of cars per train also increased. The company placed an order with Baldwin for three Pacific (4-6-2) locomotives, Nos. 400, 401, and 402, for 1913 delivery at a cost of $24,444 each. Weighing 245,700 pounds and developing 38,800 pounds of tractive effort, the Class P Pacifics proved an instant success. They were equipped with 25 × 28" cylinders and 69" drivers. Interestingly, they were at the time the heaviest road power on the DM&N exceeding the Class C3 freight Consolidations by 33 percent in weight, while developing approximately the same tractive effort. Compared to the D&IR Pacifics, Nos. 107 through 110, the DM&N's Pacifics were superior machines in virtually all respects. They were excellent steamers and had little difficulty in maintaining schedules even under the most adverse winter weather and temperature conditions. The D&IR Pacifics, on the other hand, were under-boilered and had to be "flogged" to maintain schedules when pulling five or more steel passenger cars.

The DM&N, justly proud of its new Pacifics and all-steel passenger cars, extolled the virtues of the improved service in a 1913 brochure:

"The passenger equipment is of the most modern type to provide for the safety and comfort of travelers. Large, heavy, all-steel coaches with high-backed seats, electric-lighted, automatic ventilators and comfortable seating capacity for 80 people and vestibuled, show the superiority of these over the ordinary wooden coach by easy riding, clean, fresh air, and absence of dust. The observation cafe cars are models of excellence, both in appointment and cuisine, a large observation platform for those who wish to enjoy their ride in open air, and inside is a large observation parlor provided with writing desks, large easy chairs and wide windows, with a porter in charge to look after the comfort of passengers. A neatly appointed dining compartment is located in the forward end where meals are furnished on the a la carte plan and this department has the credit of satisfying all guests. A large smoking room for gentlemen and a pleasant, roomy parlor for ladies makes this car ideal for those who wish to see the country from the 'Head of the Lakes' to the Missabe Range."

The zenith of the passenger business of the D&IR and DM&N, as well as other railroads generally, was attained shortly after World War I. The peak for these two roads was 1920, when passenger train revenues, including handling of mail and express, attained an all-time high of $1,067,373. At the time, the DM&N provided two round trips daily between Duluth and Hibbing and one round trip between Duluth and Virginia, all offering cafe-parlor car accommodations. The D&IR operated two trains daily in each direction between Duluth and the end of the line at Winton, both providing cafe-parlor accommodations.

For those able to read it, however, the handwriting was on the wall for the short-haul passenger train. In 1913, two enterprising men at Hibbing (On the Mesabi Iron Range) bought a Hupmobile touring car and started a motorized jitney service that is credited as the beginning of today's vast Greyhound system. Shortly after 1920, intercity bus service began between Hibbing and Duluth, undercutting railroad fares and offering faster and more convenient schedules. With help from Henry Ford's Model T, use of passenger trains plummeted, and during 1923 DM&N trains 5 and 6 between Duluth and Virginia were discontinued. Four years later, cafe-parlor accommodations vanished. Highways along the D&IR were not as well suited for bus operations; passenger train service there continued without significant change until 1926.

To reduce costs, rail-motor car service was tried out with little success on the D&IR's Western Mesaba Branch in 1926. Car MC-1 was an open-platform, wooden combine powered by two below-floor Red Seal Continental engines which malfunctioned with such annoying regularity that the road had a Ten-Wheeler always fired up at the Biwabik enginehouse to bring her in. The DM&N tried out internal combustion on the Alborn Branch, using motorized wooden combine car M-108. But as on the D&IR, the combine proved less than satisfactory. Within a couple of years steam was back on the job, and the gas engines on the two combines were removed.

Steam continued to power all Missabe Road passenger trains until 1953, when a Budd-built RDC-3 (rail diesel car) with seating for 48 persons was placed in service between Duluth and Ely. Later, steam was discontinued between Hibbing and Duluth, and the RDC-3 was used to cover this schedule as well as the Ely run. It was a tight schedule, calling for a run of about 400 miles each day. For protection against breakdowns, which were frequent, the company kept a 400 class Pacific ready at the Mitchell enginehouse near Hibbing. Trim, Vanderbilt-tanked No. 1107 Pacific was kept on call at the Duluth Endion roundhouse. In addition, SD9's Nos. 129 and 130 were equipped with steam boilers and were occasionally used to power passenger and special runs.

Faster and more convenient schedules notwithstanding, passenger service revenues for the Duluth/Hibbing run totaled less than $7,500 in 1957. Passenger service on the Missabe Division was discontinued after 63 years of operation. By then even Greyhound was having a difficult time in the land of its birth. Passenger train service between Duluth and Ely via the old D&IR ceased on July 15, 1961, bringing down the curtain on 77 years of continuous passenger operation over this route.

D&IR No. 23, one of the class C 4-4-0's, sits at Biwabik, Minnesota with the "Scoot," a little train that ran between Allen Junction and Virginia, Minnesota.

DM&IR collection

One of the early D&IR "M" class ten-wheelers, No. 101, in a builder's view at the Schenectady plant. Below, the same locomotive in action with a train in the "Mud Cut" near Two Harbors.

The ten-wheelers came in for their share of mishaps. Sometime in the early 1900's, the 103 overturned and wound up half submerged in a rather large puddle. No cause is given, but perhaps all that water is a result of heavy rains which might have weakened the roadbed. Below, the 101 and 102 were involved in a side-swiping accident at some unknown location.

All photos, author's collection

The 4-6-2's on the D&IR were represented by class "A" No. 107, shown here in her DM&IR number as 1107. These handsome Baldwin-built machines had much the same lines, including the short Vanderbilt tender, as the Erie's famous K-1 class Pacifics.

Both photos, Frank A. King

The 1107 on the "Passenger Loop" at Two Harbors. At the time this photo was taken, steam-powered passenger service on the Missabe was about to come to a close.

D&IR No. 1108, on the Coleraine passenger, was the third Pacific type acquired by the road in 1913.

Below, Before and after views of the 1109. Except for the electric light and some added piping, it looks pretty much as-built.

Three photos, author's collection

Frank A. King

Here are several views of DM&IR train No. 5, with the 1107 on the head end. The photo at right shows the private car "Northland" on the rear of the train.

Wayne Olsen

Author's collection

Several excellent photographs of D&IR No. 110, later DM&IR No. 1110. Above, taken at Two Harbors in 1913. Below, with its train at Duluth Union Station in May, 1930.

Author's collection

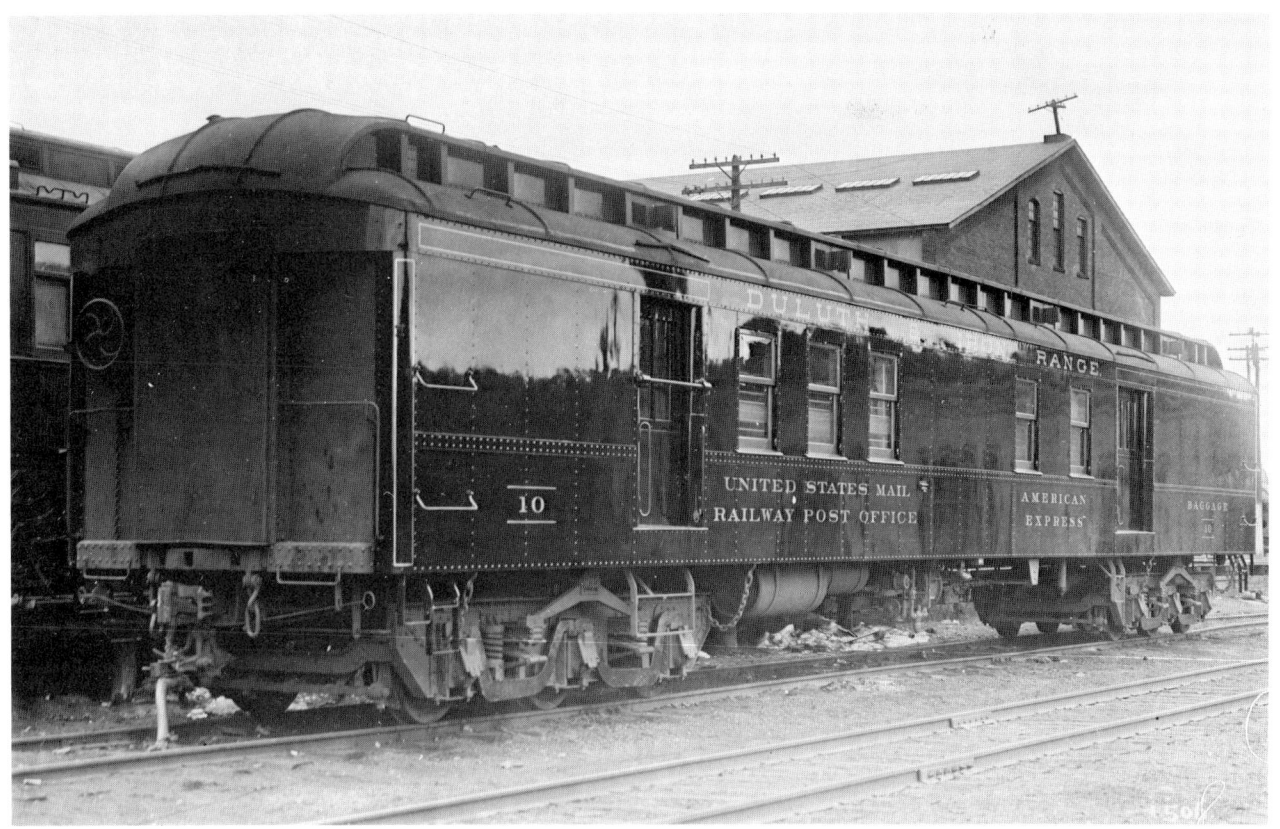

Exterior and interior views of the D&IR's all-steel mail car No. 10.

Two photos, author's collection

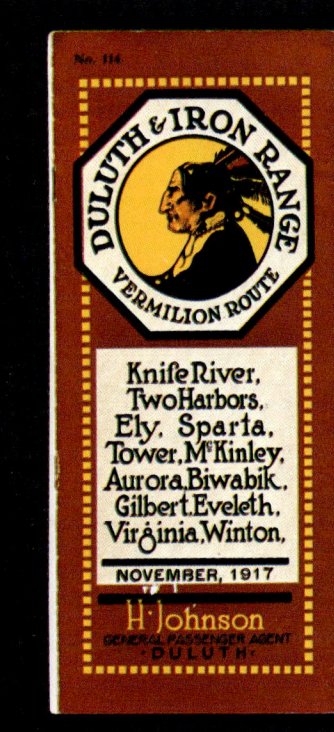

Author's collection

On this page are reproduced several examples of the colorful timetables and brochures issued by the DM&N and D&IR to promote tourism in the area they served. In that bygone era there was only one way to go . . . by train! Still in all, both roads provided the best in service.

DM&IR steel coach No.85 was a typical example of the cars used by the Missabe Road in passenger service.

Interior of DM&IR coach 29.

Two photos, author's collection

Two photos,
Wayne Olsen collection

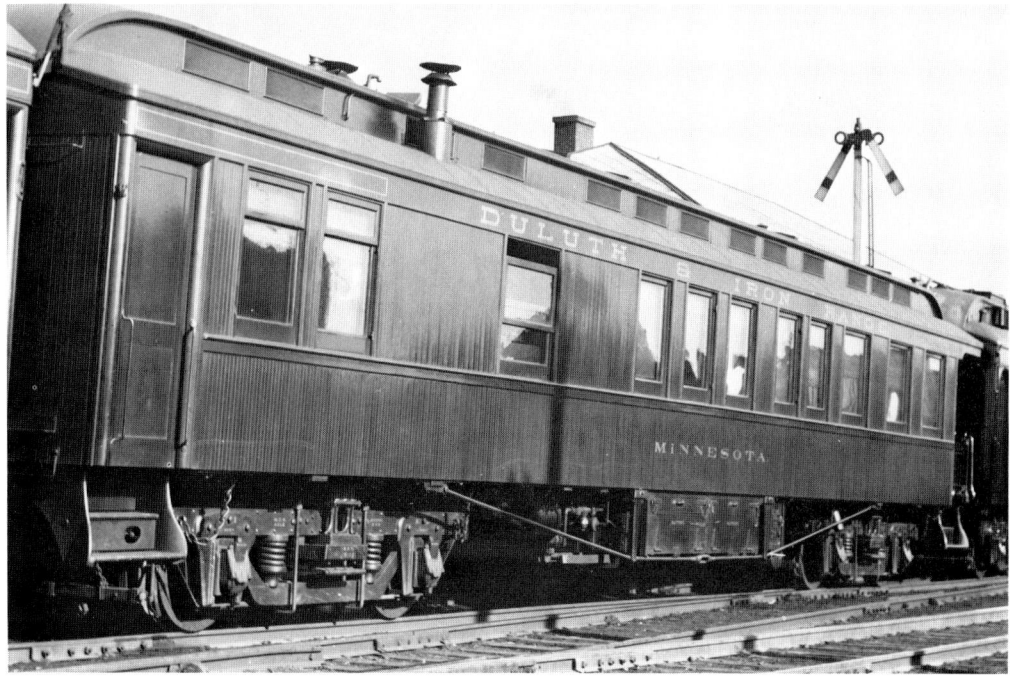

Author's collection

At one time, both the D&IR and DM&N provided passenger service, that in keeping with the era, was quite luxurious. The Northern lakes area in Minnesota was (and still is) a major tourist attraction and both roads outdid themselves with the best in trains and service. Left, above, several views of the DM&N's "shorty" business car "Olivette"... the D&IR's version, the "Minnesota," was a little longer! D&IR's parlor car No. 27, used on the road's best trains, was a classic example of the early car builders art.

Both photos, author's collection

The many depots along the DM&N and D&IR were interesting and colorful examples of depot architecture. Above the little depot at Hinsdale, with the agent and section crew striking a typical 1880's pose. The station at Brimson was also quite a simple structure. The DM&N's station at Mt. Iron, constructed in 1892, was austere compared to the depot at Biwabik, which was a study in Victorian elegance. The last picture is the original wooden structure at Two Harbors, which was later replaced with an imposing brick bulding.

Both photos, author's collection

Three photos, author's collection

DM&N No. 30, a 4-6-0 built by Pittsburgh in 1900, is on the headend of Train No. 2 at Iron Junction. Passenger business was brisk enough for the DM&N to borrow a baggage car from the Chicago & Northwestern. The 30 was finally retired in 1939. At left, two examples of the F-class Ten Wheelers on the DM&N in their later years. Both engines were built in 1893 for mainline ore service. No. 17 was scrapped in 1940, while the 19's boiler was used to provide steam at the Virginia, Minnesota engine house.

Three photos, author's collection

Engines 100-104 were built by Baldwin for the DM&N in 1906-1907. The 101 is shown in a builder's view; note how the striping on the driver spokes has been extended to the counterweights. This was a common touch in the days when labor and paint was cheap! The 101 is seen on a special train with her very capable-looking crew. No. 100 in her later years looking quite different with her centered headlight. The DM&N side-door caboose and NP round-roof boxcar on the right are also quite interesting.

Three photos, author's collection

Two early views taken at Alborn, Minnesota on the DM&N. Both pictures were obviously taken from the highest vantage point . . . the water tank! From the look of things, passenger traffic was quite heavy.

All photos, author's collection

Train No. 4 drops down Proctor Hill around 1910, heading for Duluth.

Another very early view of a DM&N passenger train, this time heading southbound at Proctor, circa 1905. The crowd in front of the station indicates that it might have been a special occasion.

DM&N 4-6-0, No. 102, heads a special train which includes the
business car "Missabe." The Lake Superior Transportation Museum
in Duluth is currently attempting to acquire this handsome car.

DM&N train No. 2, with one of the 400's up front, is about
ready to leave Hibbing for Duluth. The time is 12:15 and the year
is 1913. The Oliver Iron Mining Company shops can be
seen in the background.

Two photos, author's collection

Author's collection

Before and after views of DM&N Pacific type No. 400.
The top photo was taken in 1913, soon after delivery to the road.
Below, this graceful locomotive sits at Proctor later in her career.
It is easy to see a few changes have been made.

Frank A. King

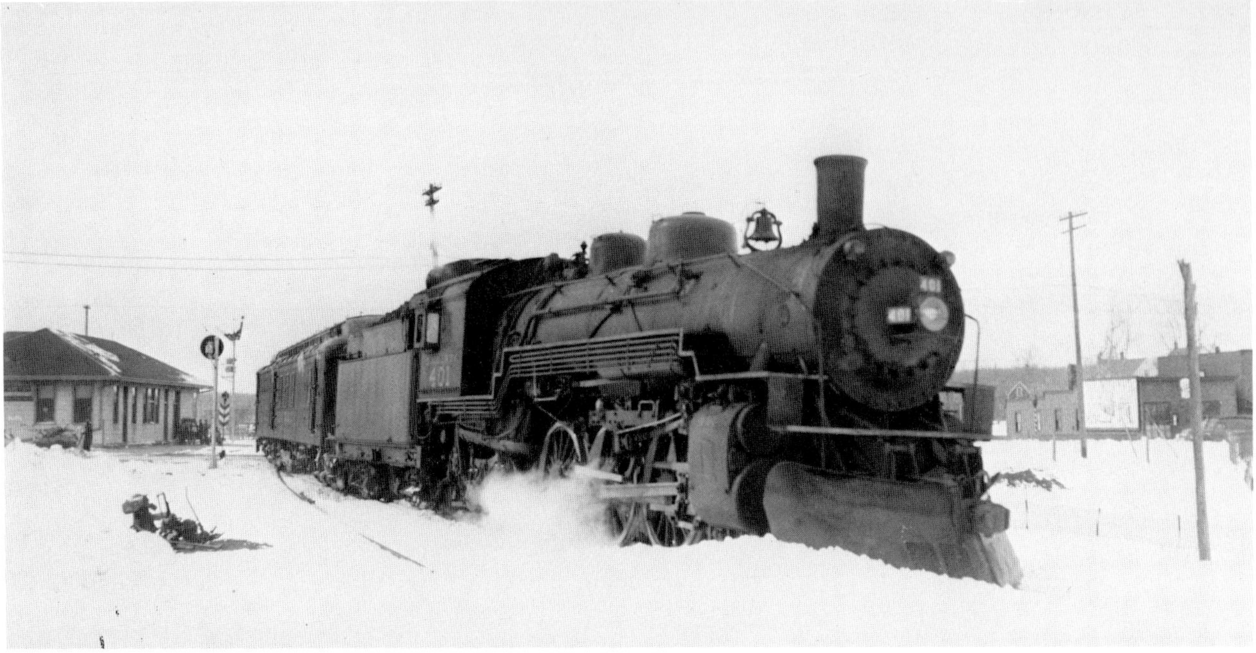
401

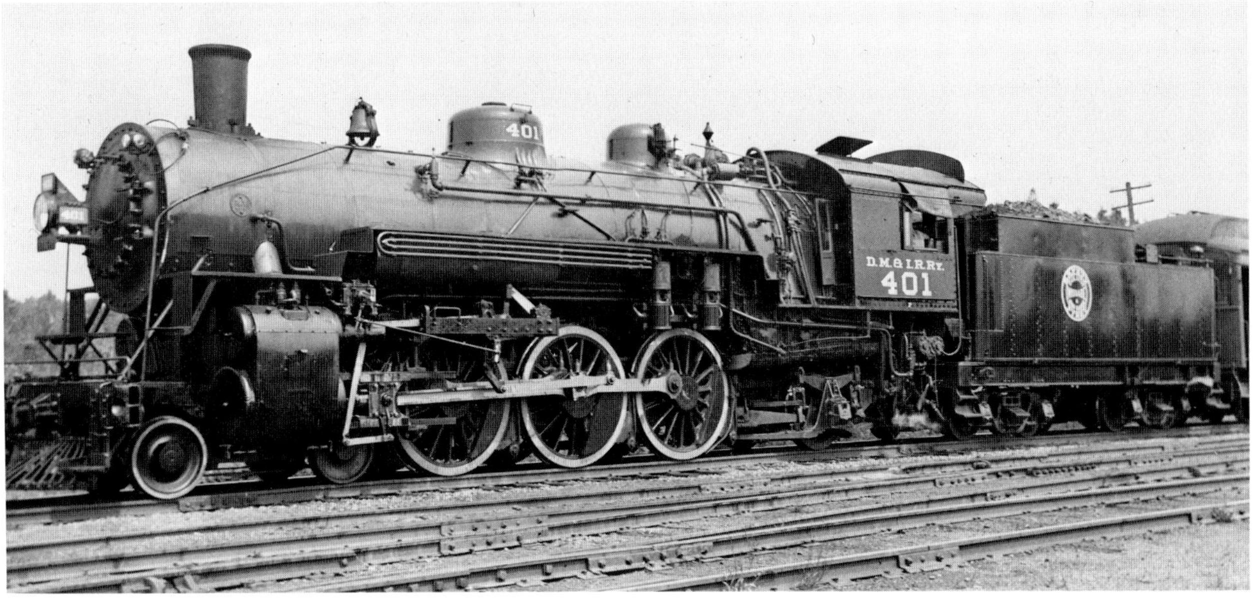
401
D.M.& I.R.RY.
401

401
D.M.& I.R.RY.
401

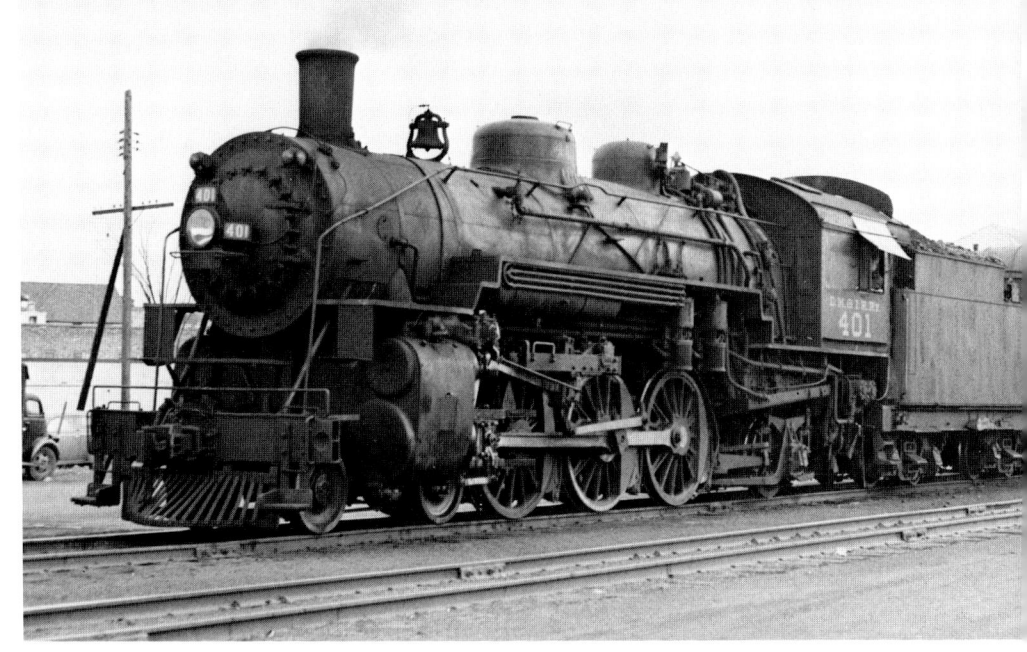

A rare aerial view of a 400 class on train No. 2 at Adolph, Minnesota sometime in the 1930's. Adolph, which looks like it's out in the middle of nowhere, is actually just north of Proctor.

Three photographs of the DM&N's second P class Pacific, No. 401. The lower photos show her on a train at Hibbing, Minnesota. The snow scene was taken at Proctor in April, 1950, and proves that winter takes its time leaving the North country.

All photos, author's collection

Author's collection

The last DM&N Pacific No. 402 is shown (above) in a builder portrait and below on train No. 6 passing through Lakewood, Minnesota on the Iron Range division. Though the engine has been shopped several times, it still retains its graceful lines. The fireman's side view was taken at Proctor in the late 1950's.

Frank A. King

Frank A. King

Author's collection

Like so many roads, the D&IR and DM&N experimented with self-propelled cars as a cost-saving measure in the 1920's. The top photos show gas-motor No. 55 pulling the business car "Missabe"; while below the car poses with officials soon after its conversion in 1927.

Three photos, author's collection

W-56 was a refugee from the Duluth Street Railway. It was converted to diesel electric power in 1939 by the DM&IR for use as a shop motor car at Proctor.

Frank A. King

A very rare view of M-108. This car was converted from an old wood-sheathed combine for use on the Alborn branch.

Author's collection

Frank A. King

Photos of the DM&IR Budd car No.1. Above, the car is seen on the turntable at Endion; while below, it makes its way along the shores of Lake Superior. The car was later sold to the Northern Pacific.

Author's collection

Frank A. King

Another photo of the No. 1 plodding through the snow near Lakeside in Duluth.

Author's collection

The predecessor to the famous Greyhound Bus Lines was supposedly the Northland Transportation Company. Here one of its buses, No. 40, poses on its run between Hibbing and Duluth.

Frank A. King

2-8-0 No. 1223 on the Proctor "Jitney" in January, 1959. The train was used between the southend shops and North roundhouse in Proctor when the W56 was out of service.

Ex-EJ&E Mike No. 1336 was sometimes used in later years on branchline trains 11 and 12 in these views taken near the end of passenger operations on the DM&IR in 1953. Above, engine and train are Northbound near Eveleth, Minnesota. The middle picture has the little train between Fayal and Virginia, Minnesota; while below the same train is shown at the Virginia depot.

All photos Frank A. King

The DM&IR used many different types of switchers in ore service . . . from tiny 0-4-0's to the mighty S-6 0-10-0's. In between was a group of 0-6-0's and 0-8-0's. Here, Baldwin-built 0-8-0 No.87 prepares to shove a long string of cars onto dock No.5 in Duluth in November, 1956.

Wayne Olsen

# VII. SWITCHERS

Few railroads had such a variety of switching power as the Missabe. Engines ranged from tiny 0-4-0's to giant 0-10-0's, the heaviest steam switchers ever built. The first switchers were two 0-4-0's received by the D&IR from Baldwin in 1884. These little diamond-stacked engines, Nos. 4 and 5, weighed only 69,000 pounds and developed 14,300 pounds tractive effort. At 34,500 pounds, however, their axle loading was considered very heavy. During 1886 another 0-4-0, No. 13, joined the D&IR's roster, and the following year two additional 0-4-0's, Nos. 14 and 15, were added. The sixth and last 0-4-0, No. 26, arrived from Baldwin in 1888.

Due to their small size, the 0-4-0's soon proved inadequate for most switching duties on the ore-carrying D&IR. The first to go were Nos. 15 and 26, which were sold to the Loraine Steel Company in Ohio during 1899. No. 14 shed her tender and was converted to a shop goat for use at Two Harbors about this time. The remaining three were sold to nearby mining companies during 1912 and 1914.

In 1889, the D&IR received a single 0-6-0 from Schenectady for use on the Two Harbors ore docks. Weighing 94,400 pounds on her 51" drivers, No. 27 exerted a tractive effort of 20,090 pounds. She was the only six-wheel switcher on the D&IR until 1906, when the road received four heavier engines of this type from Baldwin. No. 27 was converted for use as the Two Harbors shop switcher in 1914, replacing 0-4-0 No. 14, which was sold to a mining firm that year. She served as the shop switcher until scrapping in 1940, at that time bearing DM&IR No. 127.

The four 0-6-0's, Nos. 28 through 31, received by the D&IR during 1906, weighed 150,000 pounds and developed 33,000 pounds of tractive effort. These engines were assigned to ore sorting and ore switching at the Two Harbors docks. They served in this capacity until the late twenties, when they were sold. By then the D&IR had a surplus of the more powerful Class K 2-8-0's, which were assigned to ore sorting and dock switching, replacing the 0-6-0's.

The first switchers on the DM&N were six small 0-6-0's, Nos. 50 through 55, received from the Pittsburgh Locomotive Works in 1893 at a cost of $8,271 each. Weighing 84,000 pounds on their 50" drivers, they exerted 18,866 pounds of tractive effort. Initially these engines were assigned to the Proctor yard ore-sorting and the Duluth ore dock-switching service. They were later relegated to less demanding switching assignments as larger engines became available. By 1918, all six engines of this class (S) had been sold to other companies.

In 1900 the DM&N received two heavier 0-6-0 switchers, Nos. 56 and 57, at a cost of $11,900 each from Pittsburgh. They weighed 120,000 pounds and developed 28,721 pounds of tractive effort. These engines were used in Proctor yard ore sorting and served in this capacity until replaced by heavier engines of the 0-8-0 type during 1907. Engines Nos. 56 and 57 were sold to the Minnesota, Dakota and Western Railway in 1920, where they operated until the 1950s.

With the advent of steel ore cars during the early 1900s, Proctor and the Duluth ore docks needed more switching power. Four 0-8-0 switchers, Nos. 58 through 61, were ordered from Baldwin during 1907 at a cost of $13,756 each. These engines, weighing 164,000 pounds and developing 41,160 pounds tractive effort, were a marked improvement over the 0-6-0's which they replaced. During 1910, the road received three additional Baldwin 0-8-0's, Nos. 62 through 63, which were identical to the other 0-8-0's. Because of the 10' track centers on the early Duluth ore docks, these engines were restricted to an overall width of 8'6" (cab) and 9'4½" over the cylinders.

Mention should be made at this time of two mystery 0-8-0's, Nos. 70 and 71, which were supposedly ordered from Rogers in 1907. These engines were designated as Class S2 and weighed 200,000 pounds on their 50" drivers. There is no record that these engines were ever received by the DM&N. For some now obscure reason, these engines were acquired by the Oliver Iron Mining Company instead. However, during 1910 the DM&N did receive six heavy 0-8-0's from the Schenectady Works of the American Locomotive Company. These were practically identical to the

Oliver engines. The six Schenectady engines, Nos. 80 through 85, carried 207,500 pounds on their 51" drivers and developed 48,850 pounds of tractive effort. Their price tag was $16,830 each. These engines, designated as Class S2, were assigned to ore sorting at Proctor, where they replaced smaller engines of the same type.

When the Santa Fe type locomotives began road ore service in 1916, longer and heavier trains were brought into Proctor yard. This called for heavier locomotives for ore sorting, and four additional 0-8-0's, Nos. 86 through 89, were received from Baldwin during 1917 at a unit cost of $28,203. These engines, which weighed 216,000 pounds and developed 49,700 pounds of tractive effort, were described by Baldwin as representing the ultimate in eight-coupled switching power. In many respects they were very similar to the USRA 0-8-0 switchers which came out one year later. A comparison of the DM&N and USRA 0-8-0's is as follows:

|  | DM&N Class S5 | | USRA |
|---|---|---|---|
|  |  | (Later) |  |
| Tractive effort | 49,700 lbs. | 55,600 lbs. | 51,200 lbs. |
| Weight on drivers | 216,000 lbs. | 220,000 lbs. | 214,000 lbs. |
| Factor of adhesion | 4.35 |  | 4.18 |
| Engine wheelbase | 15'0" |  | 15'0" |
| Total wheelbase (engine & tender) | 50'9" |  | 52'10½" |
| Driver diameter | 51" |  | 51" |
| Cylinders | 24 x 28" |  | 25 x 28" |
| Steam pressure | 185 lbs. | 200 lbs. | 175 lbs. |
| Boiler diameter | 82" |  | 80" |

By 1928 the DM&N again needed heavier power for ore sorting in the Proctor yard. This time the road made a bold departure, bypassing the popular 0-8-0 type and ordering from Baldwin four giant 0-10-0 switchers, Nos. 90 through 93, weighing 352,250 pounds and developing 91,100 pounds of tractive effort, including the Franklin Tender Booster. These engines, which were the heaviest and most powerful ten-coupled switchers ever built, were also the most expensive locomotives acquired by the DM&N, costing $85,715.63 each. It is interesting to note that these engines, with their 70,400-pound axle loading, were about as heavy as the road's E and E1 Class Santa Fe road engines and at the time were exceeded in weight and power only by the 2-8-8-2 Mallets. On arrival, the big 0-10-0 switchers, 0-8-0's Nos. 86 through 89, were assigned to the Duluth ore docks, where they performed superbly until the end of steam, a quarter of a century later.

During the early 1930s, the limited steam cutoff on these engines was raised to 85 percent, thereby increasing engine tractive effort to 86,000 pounds. At that time, the tender boosters were removed to reduce maintenance costs. About 1935, two of the Class S6 0-10-0's were assigned to Two Harbors ore sorting and dock switching, replacing Mikados in this difficult service. These S6 engines, because of their heavy axle loading, were initially limited to switching in the Proctor and Two Harbors yards. Later, after bridge strengthening on Proctor Hill, the 0-10-0's were occasionally used in heavy transfer service between Missabe Junction (Duluth) and Proctor. During the 1940s, "Pneudyne" air throttles were applied, affording fingertip control, a feature which enabled smoother starting of these powerful engines when handling cuts of loaded ore cars often weighing over 10,000 tons.

Considering the great number of switching assignments on the Missabe, the number of true switching locomotives was low. Because of the heavy nature of the road's business, the practice of using Consolidation, Mikado, and even Santa Fe locomotives for switching was common. After World War II, the company received a large number of 0-10-2 and 2-10-4 locomotives from sister roads. These big engines were often used for Proctor ore sorting and Two Harbors sorting and dock switching during the 1950s. About 1950, the Missabe considered acquiring four very large 0-8-0 switchers from the Bessemer and Lake Erie. The plan was to assign these engines to switching on the Duluth ore docks, replacing lighter engines of the same type. Because of their limited service application, however, DM&IR management wisely dropped the idea.

Right, 0-4-0 No.14 was another example of the little switchers used by the D&IR in the early days. The 14, built in 1887, was later sold to the P. Meagher Mining Co.

One of the first 0-4-0's on the D&IR, class B No.4, is seen loading ore at the open pit Fayal mine in the Mesabi Range.

Both photos, author's collection

Lake County Historical Society

Author's collection

A group of workers pauses for the camera on the D&IR's ore dock No.1 at Two Harbors.
The long poles were separating the sticky iron ore from the dock pockets. 0-6-0 No. 27 can be seen in the background. No. 27 (top photo) was the only engine in its class.

Two photos, author's collection

Above, No. 31 was one of the F class switchers built by Baldwin for the D&IR in 1906. On the DM&N, early 0-6-0's like No. 56 were listed as class S1. Note the change of the engine number from the tender side to the more familiar location on the cab panel.

Wayne Olsen collection

211

Author's collection

H. Van Horn

No. 57 was a sister to 0-6-0 No. 56.
In 1920 both engines were sold to the Minnesota,
Dakota & Western Ry. The 56 was renumbered
to 8 by the MD&W.

Wayne Olsen collection

H.L. Broadbelt collection

It became obvious to the management of the DM&N that the 0-6-0's were too light for ore dock service so in 1907 the road placed an order with Baldwin for a group of larger 0-8-0 type switchers, classed as S3 and S4 respectively. No. 59 is shown on the job at dock No.1 at Duluth. The 61 poses in her builder stripes before delivery.
The S3's and S4's were later sold to the Oliver Iron Mining Co. Ex-DM&N No.64 is now on display (below) at Mountain Iron, Minnesota.

Frank A. King

Pile-driving operations for dock No. 5 in Duluth, with an S3 0-8-0 spotting cars in the background on dock No. 4.

Two interesting views of DM&N S-2 class 0-8-0 No. 81, built by Schenectady in 1910. Above, at Proctor, while below she is shown some years later with centered headlight and rebuilt tender. The engine was sold to the American Steel & Wire Co. in 1948 and later scrapped by them.

Three photos, author's collection

0-8-0's No. 82, 83 and 84 were further examples of the S-2 class. Like sister engine No. 81 they were sold in 1940 to the American Steel & Wire Co.

Three photos, author's collection

"PROCTOR SWITCHER" 16″ × 20½″ Watercolor
By Mike Pearsall

Author's collection

The heaviest 0-8-0's on the DM&N roster were the four engines in the S-5 class. All being built by Baldwin in the World War I era (1917), they were rated with over 53,000 pounds of tractive effort. These engines ultimately took over the heavy switching duties on the Duluth ore docks. They lasted until 1958.

Both photos, Frank A. King

The S-5 0-8-0's were well-proportioned chunky machines with neat lines. The 87 pauses in her duty as an ore dock switcher, while No. 88 appears freshly shopped with a coat of new paint.

Oliver Iron Mining Co. No. 401, shown at Coleraine, Minnesota, in 1936 was originally ordered by the DM&N as their No. 71, but never delivered.

Here's No. 86 in later years . . . about the only change seems to be her centered light. The laborers are applying hot water from the engine to loosen chunks of iron ore frozen in the cars. This picture was taken in 1942.

Two photos, author's collection

Both photos, author's collection

Both photos, Frank A. King

Wayne Olsen

On the next several pages are photographs of the ultimate switch engines used by the DM&N and later the DM&IR. The S-6 0-10-0's, Nos. 90 to 93, were awesome engines with 86,000 pounds of tractive effort, making them (at the time) the world's most powerful and heaviest switchers. As built, locomotives like No. 90 were equipped with tender boosters for added punch. Those proved to be a maintenance headache in later years and were removed. Used not only in heavy switching service and ore sorting, the big hogs were also used on Transfer runs, like No. 93, shown on such a run on Proctor Hill in August, 1956.

Author's collection

Author's collection

Frank A. King

The last of the S-6 class, No. 93 is depicted in several views: above left, at Proctor with high-mounted light and, left below, down in the center of the smokebox front. Above, the 93 is seen switching a cut of cars on dock No. 1 at Two Harbors. These good-looking switchers were cut up for scrap in 1958.

Author's collection

Frank A. King

Ex-Union Railway 0-10-2 No.301, now DM&IR No.601, shoves a cut of cars up to dock No.2 at Two Harbors. In the background, an ex-B&LE 2-10-4 is performing the same task at dock 1.

# VIII. POSTWAR POWER

By the postwar period, the DM&N C3 Consolidations were over 40 years of age and cost an incredible $1.94 per mile for repairs. The Missabe began shopping around for needed replacements. During 1948, the road leased five 1200 class Mikados and five Mountain (4-8-2) locomotives from the Rio Grande. The Mountain engines came to the Rio Grande from the Norfolk and Western during World War II and did a brief stint on the Missabe while on their way to new owners, Wheeling and Lake Erie. In addition, Mikado locomotives were leased from the Great Northern and the Omaha roads for short periods.

The first steam replacements were twenty-six 700 class Mikados received in 1948 from the Elgin, Joliet and Eastern Railway, a U.S. Steel sister road. Ten locomotives built by Alco in 1923 received DM&IR numbers 1312 through 1321 (Class N4), and four, built by Lima in the same year, were numbered 1322 through 1325 (Class N5). The remaining 12 locomotives, DM&IR Nos. 1326 through 1337 (Class N6), were built by Baldwin in 1929 and 1930. These engines were equipped with 28 × 30" cylinders, 63" drivers, and weighed 333,460 pounds in working order. Tractive effort was 63,467 pounds. Put to work with minimum modifications, these engines performed switching and mine run operations. While comparable in size to the ex-D&IR Mikados (Nos. 1300-1311), they were not as well liked by enginemen because their higher drivers (63" vs. 58") slipped when the engines pulled heavy cuts of ore.

About this time, the Missabe's 1910 Mallets, excellent performers on Proctor Hill for almost 40 years, were exhibiting signs of old age. Mainframes were cracking with alarming regularity and required continual welding to keep them intact. In addition, boiler and firebox repairs were becoming excessive. Replacements arrived during 1949 in the form of nine Baldwin-built 0-10-2 locomotives from U.S. Steel's Union Railroad at Pittsburgh. These Baldwins were placed in service on the Hill and in Proctor yard; later they were used in ore-sorting and dock-switching service at Two Harbors. With a tractive effort of 90,900 pounds, they compared favorably with the old Mallets. While the Baldwins came equipped with tender boosters, they were soon removed because of high maintenance. The 0-10-2's were also found to be somewhat "slippery," and to overcome this condition it was necessary to increase the weight on drivers from 343,000 to 364,600 pounds. This increase in weight was accomplished by shifting 10,000 pounds from the trailing truck, by relocating the fulcrum on the rear equalizers, and by adding 10,000 pounds of actual weight (steel plates) distributed between the front end and near the center of the engine. Total engine weight after this modificationn was upped to 422,000 pounds. Equipped with 28 × 32" cylinders and 61" drivers, these locomotives, Nos. 601 through 609, were classified as switching power on the Missabe and were designated as Class S7. Their former numbers on the Union Railroad were 301 through 309. It is interesting to note that these engines were originally to have been built to the 2-10-2 (Santa Fe) type. To keep the total engine and tender wheelbase within Union's 70-foot turntable length, Baldwin suggested omitting the front truck; this was possible because the top operating speed requirement was under 35 mph. The total wheelbase then was only 67'2¾", remarkable in a locomotive and tender almost 90 feet long!

The last steam engines acquired by the Missabe Road were 18 giant Texas (2-10-4) locomotives purchased from the U.S. Steel-owned Bessemer & Lake Erie Railroad. These engines, which arrived in 1951, ranged in weight from 520,000 pounds to 524,000 pounds. Total weight with tender was approximately 900,000 pounds, with 370,000 pounds on their 64" drivers. With huge 31 × 32" cylinders developing 96,700 pounds of tractive effort, they were considered the world's most powerful two-cylindered locomotives. The handsome Texas engines were numbered 700 through 717 and were designated Class E4 through E7. Although they assisted the Missabe to handle a peak tonnage of almost 50 million in 1953, they exerted 30 percent less drawbar pull than the big Yellowstones, and were assigned to handle main line ore runs only when a big articulated was not available. For the most part, they were employed in Proctor, Steelton Hill service, and in the "Cross-Country" ore movement between the Hibbing-Chisholm district and Biwabik. Occasionally they were used for ore sorting and switching in the Proctor and Two Harbors yards. Including the 18 Texas locomotives, the DM&IR's steam locomotive roster reached an all-time high of 172 units in 1951.

Author's collection

Both photos, Frank A. King

Two photos, author's collection

In 1948, the Missabe acquired a group of 2-8-2's from the Elgin, Joliet & Eastern. No sooner did these handsome engines arrive on the property when they were shopped, given a coat of fresh paint, renumbered and lettered, and put right to work by the DM&IR. Above, a builder's photo of EJ&E No. 756, which became No. 1322 on the Missabe. Class N4 No. 1313 (Ex-EJ&E No. 747) was Alco-built in 1923. Some roads refused to use the number "13" on their engines. Not being that superstitious the DM&IR used a double 13! No. 1321, shown here at Virginia, Minnesota was also classed N4. No. 1320, at Proctor, was ex-EJ&E No. 754. EJ&E No. 765, one of the engines built by Baldwin, went to the Missabe as their No. 1330. The engine is now on display at Gary, Indiana.

Frank A. King

Two photos, author's collection

Unquestionably the largest steam switchers ever built . . . the nine Ex-Union Railway 0-10-2's joined the Missabe's roster in 1949. No.606 and No.604 (Ex-URY. 306 and 304) pose alongside the shops at Two Harbors, while sister engine No.605 is seen smoking up the yards at Proctor. Left, the 607 hurls her exhaust skyward, pulling an endless string of loaded ore cars from Proctor yards enroute to Steelton. While these engines were fairly heavy, they were not heavy enough for the Missabe . . . note the stack of steel plates on the pilot deck for added weight.

Above, 0-10-2 No. 607 again . . . this time with a train of empties on Proctor Hill.

DM&IR No. 605 on the approach to Duluth ore dock No. 5 in August, 1950.

Both photos, author's collection

Also in 1948, the power-hungry DM&IR leased several engines from the D&RGW. (During WWII the Rio Grande had leased engines from the Missabe, like the big Yellowstones.) Above, D&RGW Mike No.1205 switches cars at Two Harbors; while below the much-traveled Rio Grande 4-8-2 No.1552 (Ex-N&W, Ex-D&RGW, soon to be W&LE) pushes a string of loaded ore cars, also at Two Harbors. At the time the engine was enroute to its new owners, the Wheeling & Lake Erie, but was "diverted" by the DM&IR.

Both photos, Frank A. King

In 1951, the Missabe purchased 18 2-10-4 Texas types from the Bessemer & Lake Erie. These engines had been bumped off the B&LE by a new fleet of F-7 diesels. While they were the world's most powerful two-cylinder steam engines they provided 30% less drawbar pull than the mighty Yellowstones, and consequently were used in mainline ore service only as a last resort. Above, in builder's livery, and below, one of the big engines steams away on a cold November day at Two Harbors yard.

Both photos, author's collection

The giant size of these engines is plainly obvious when compared to the man walking alongside the tender. The extra sandbox on the pilot deck was added by the DM&IR for greater capacity. The 707 was classed by the DM&IR as E4.

Frank A. King

Frank A. King

Frank A. King

A famous locomotive at a famous location . . . Texas No. 715 climbs the 2.2% grade on Proctor Hill.

Big Baldwin-built Texas No. 714 blasts her way up the 2.2% grade on Proctor Hill with a string of ore empties. Her sanders are wide open as attested by the cloud of dust below the drivers.

Frank A. King

Left, famed rail photographer Jim Shaughnessy found No. 709 on Proctor Hill in August, 1955 and this outstanding photograph was the result.

Another Shaughnessy photograph, taken at Saginaw, Minnesota. This time it's the 717 southbound with the Hibbing local. The track looks well kept, as do the two wood cars on the right.

Left, rail photographer and author William Middleton caught Texas type No. 711 reposing in the Proctor roundhouse. Below, in two photographs, also at Proctor, No. 700 (Ex-B&LE No. 621) looks a little grimey . . . she was built by Alco in 1937. On the other hand, No. 714 is fresh from the backshops after a complete overhaul. The 714 was built by Baldwin in 1943 as B&LE No. 641. Weight of the engine alone was a whopping 523,600 pounds! The DM&IR classed her as E-7.

Both photos, Frank A. King

William Middleton

Four EMD SD9's leave Biwabik yards with 170 loads bound for the docks at Two Harbors. By 1958 when this picture was taken, the roundhouse and coaling tower in the background were strangely quiet . . . steam was on its way out on the Missabe.

# IX. THE DIESELS

Even though neighboring Great Northern elected to dispose of its rebuilt 2-8-8-0's for F7's in ore service, the Missabe remained unimpressed. After all, the big Yellowstones represented a far more advanced steam power design. Also, the 18 Texas and nine Union (0-10-2) locomotives the Missabe had recently acquired were considered up-to-date steam. For this and other reasons, dieselization came hard. However, diesel demonstrators began making their appearance. The first was likely EJ&E No. 108, a 2,000 h.p. C-C center-cab Baldwin, during 1948. This writer recalls that this unit was used on the Wales Branch hauling out loads of pulpwood. She was also tested on the big hill out of Two Harbors, taking up trains of empty ore cars. On one trip she was loaded down too heavily and overheated her traction motors by the time she reached Highland. Tests were also conducted on Proctor Hill — moving loads down and empties up the 2.2 percent grade. Because she was unable to move as many empties up the grade as the plodding old 1910 Baldwin compounds, operating officials were unimpressed. A Baldwin AS-416, 1600 h.p. C-C road-switcher was probably second. Next, a four-unit 6400 h.p. lash-up of Alco FA2/FB2 cabs showed up. Weighing a million pounds, all on drivers, and dubbed the "Green Hornet" by Missabe crews, she had no trouble beating the big Yellowstones in the tonnage game. No doubt about it, her performance impressed Missabe operating people. For a period, one cab unit was removed from the four-unit consist and used in Iron Range Division passenger trains Nos. 5 and 6 in place of the customary Class A Pacific. Another Alco demonstrator, a 1600 h.p. C-C model RSD-4, was also on the property about this time. This writer well remembers watching her double head President Truman's special train up Proctor Hill to Hibbing in 1951.

Dieselization of the Missabe did not come first on the main line ore hauls but rather for switching with receipt of fifteen 1,200 h.p. SW9's from Electro-Motive. These locomotives, railroad class DS-1, Nos. 11 through 25, came equipped for multiple-unit operation, and two- and three-unit lash-ups became common practice. Electro-Motive suggested that the Missabe consider this type of unit for all their needs. Even though they were ballasted to 246,660 pounds weight, however, the road soon found that these were too small to handle most assignments without resorting to multiple-unit operation. For this reason, Missabe management wisely elected to buy six-motor C-C units and ultimately dispose of all of its SW9's.

During June and July of 1953, a duet of Fairbanks-Morse 2400 h.p. C-C Train Masters demonstrated on ore hauls into Proctor and Two Harbors. The results were impressive, with substantial fuel savings over steam. By then the handwriting was indeed on the wall, yet the Missabe did not feel the time was quite right to purchase units for main line ore movement. Instead, the company leased road units from other roads. First to arrive were four F7's from the Bessemer and Lake Erie, which showed up in 1954. These units were assigned Nos. 723 through 726 by the Missabe. They were used as two-unit locomotives hauling 180 loads of ore into Proctor. That same year a four-unit, 6,000 h.p., DR-4-4-15 Baldwin Sharknose consist arrived from the Elgin, Joliet and Eastern. They were in deplorable operating condition, and only two of the four units were used to any extent. These A and B units were assigned road numbers 727 and 728 by the Missabe. In all fairness to the Baldwins, it must be stated that they were good luggers on the Missabe Division ore haul, and when operating properly (which wasn't often) the two-unit consist could out-haul any pair of B&LE F7's. These units were used for one year on the Missabe and then returned to the EJ&E; ultimately they went to the Baltimore and Ohio. The Missabe found that repair cost for the Baldwins was $.56 per unit mile as compared to only $.13 for the B&LE F7's. The B&LE F7's continued to give a good account of themselves and remained on the property until 1958. By then repair costs for the B&LE F7's had climbed to $.43 per unit mile.

During 1954, the Missabe also leased five Alco RS-2, 1500 h.p. road-switchers from the Union Railroad in Pittsburgh. These units were used to perform switching and carried Union Nos. 611,

621 through 623, and 628. Numbers 621 through 623 were used for two years and then returned. Numbers 611 and 628 were returned in 1956, one year later. An Alco DL 600B 2400 h.p. demonstrator also appeared during 1954 and stayed on the property until 1955. Her performance ultimately resulted in five units of this type (Nos. 50 through 55) being acquired from Alco in 1959 for the difficult ore-sorting and dock-switching assignment at Two Harbors. They were designated road class RS-5.

The Missabe bought its first diesel road units in 1955, consisting of 10 EMD 1750 h.p. C-C SD9's. They were designated Class RS-1 and assigned Nos. 101 through 110. Ballasted to 387,000 pounds, they developed 96,750 pounds of starting tractive effort. In 1957, 20 additional SD9's arrived. These units, identical to the previous SD9's, were designated class RS-2 and numbered 111 through 130. During 1958 another 28 SD9 units arrived from EMD. These were assigned Class RS-3 and numbered 131 through 158. During a 1958 traffic upsurge, the Missabe leased seven EMD 1350 h.p. FT's and eight EMD 1500 h.p. F7's from the Great Northern. These units carried GN Nos. 311 through 317 and Nos. 636 through 643. To this writer's knowledge, they were used only one year on the Missabe. That year the road also leased four additional F7's from the B&LE. These were assigned Nos. 719 through 722 by the Missabe. By then a total of eight B&LE F7's were operating on the DM&IR.

During 1958 the road tested EMD's new 2400 h.p., C-C SD24 demonstrator unit. This locomotive was reputedly designed for sale to the last diesel holdouts: Norfolk & Western and DM&IR. The 650-horsepower increase over the SD9's did not seem necessary on the DM&IR, and during the following year the company — finally eager to dieselize — ordered 16 additional SD9's from EMD.

At this point, one might well ask why the Missabe was so late to dieselize? There were three basic reasons:

(1) The road had a fleet of modern steam power; the 18 Yellowstones and 18 Texas locomotives were sufficient for all main line assignments.

(2) The Missabe was largely a seasonal road with a 7½-month ore-shipping season. It was difficult to justify purchasing expensive diesel units which would be used for only two-thirds of the year.

(3) Steam locomotives were needed to supply steam for thawing frozen ore in cars and ore dock pockets during late fall and early spring. (The ore-thawing problem was ultimately solved by infra-red heating.)

During 1960 the Missabe acquired 19 EMD SD18, 1800 h.p. C-C units. Weight and tractive effort were identical to the SD9's. These units were classified RS-6 and were assigned numbers 175 through 193. For all practical purposes, this purchase resulted in complete dieselization of the Missabe.

To replace SD9 units leased or sold to B&LE and the EJ&E, and also to up-grade its diesel fleet, eight EMD 2000 h.p. SD-38's were acquired in 1971, and five SD-38-2's in 1975. These units are identical in weight and starting tractive effort to the earlier SD7's and SD18's. The SD-38's were classified RS-7's and given road numbers 201 through 208. The SD-38-2's were classified RS-8's and assigned road numbers 209 through 213.

In 1973, the Missabe purchased ten Alco 3000 h.p. C630 units from the Union Pacific. Built in 1966, they were classified RS-9's and given road numbers 900 through 909. They carried 394,000 pounds on drivers and developed 98,500 pounds of starting tractive effort. Because their maintenance requirements were not compatible with those of the EMD units, the DM&IR soon sought to dispose of the Alcos. During 1974, Nos. 905, 906, and 908 were leased to U.S. Steel's ore-hauling Cartier Railway in Quebec. Ultimately, all ten ex-UP units were leased to Cartier. The Missabe's five Alco DL 600 B's also went to Cartier after seeing service on the B&LE.

Diesel units 163 and 186 received chopped (low) noses for greater visibility during 1972 and 1971 respectively. (They were both involved in devastating wrecks and received this modification during their rebuilding.) During 1979 the road studied the economic feasibility of rebuilding the entire group of 52 diesel locomotives purchased between 1957 and 1960, as they were approaching the end of their anticipated 20-year life. The decision was made that year to completely dismantle and reconstruct a pilot model — No. 174 — to determine the feasibility of the concept. A low nose and the latest power assemblies were installed. Extensive electrical revisions included traction motors, main generators, and new power and control wiring. Also, solid-state, modular, electrical control equipment, identical to that included on the latest diesels, was specified. The rebuilt unit, now as efficient as the latest SD-38's, was given number 301 to set it apart from the others. The success of No. 301 led to rebuilding a second unit, No. 150, now No. 302. Due to poor economic conditions in northern Minnesota, however, the rebuild program has been suspended. Presently the Missabe has 86 RS units on its roster. Included in this figure are 21 units leased to the B&LE, EJ&E, and Cartier.

### DM&IR Diesel Locomotive update since 1972

| Orig. No. | Type & Class | Builder | Const. No. | Date Built | Dr. | Weight | HP | Tractive Effort | Final Disposition And Remarks |
|---|---|---|---|---|---|---|---|---|---|
| 209 | RS-8 | EMD | 74649-1 | 1975 | 40 | 387,000 | 2000 | 96,750 | |
| 210 | RS-8 | EMD | 74649-2 | 1975 | 40 | 387,000 | 2000 | 96,750 | |
| 211 | RS-8 | EMD | 74649-3 | 1975 | 40 | 387,000 | 2000 | 96,750 | |
| 212 | RS-8 | EMD | 74649-4 | 1975 | 40 | 387,000 | 2000 | 96,750 | |
| 213 | RS-8 | EMD | 74649-5 | 1975 | 40 | 387,000 | 2000 | 96,750 | |
| 301* | | EMD | 25260 | 1959 | 40 | 387,000 | 1750 | 96,750 | Orig. No. 174. Rebuilt by DM&IR 1979 |
| 302* | | EMD | 25274 | 1959 | 40 | 387,000 | 1750 | 96,750 | Orig. No. 160. Rebuilt by DM&IR 1980 |
| 900 | RS-9 | Alco | 3440-1 | 1966 | 40 | 394,000 | 3000 | 98,500 | Ex UP 2900** |
| 901 | RS-9 | Alco | 3440-2 | 1966 | 40 | 394,000 | 3000 | 98,500 | Ex UP 2901** |
| 902 | RS-9 | Alco | 3440-3 | 1966 | 40 | 394,000 | 3000 | 98,500 | Ex UP 2902** |
| 903 | RS-9 | Alco | 3440-4 | 1966 | 40 | 394,000 | 3000 | 98,500 | Ex UP 2903** |
| 904 | RS-9 | Alco | 3440-5 | 1966 | 40 | 394,000 | 3000 | 98,500 | Ex UP 2904** |
| 905 | RS-9 | Alco | 3440-6 | 1966 | 40 | 394,000 | 3000 | 98,500 | Ex UP 2905** |
| 906 | RS-9 | Alco | 3440-7 | 1966 | 40 | 394,000 | 3000 | 98,500 | Ex UP 2906** |
| 907 | RS-9 | Alco | 3440-8 | 1966 | 40 | 394,000 | 3000 | 98,500 | Ex UP 2907** |
| 908 | RS-9 | Alco | 3440-9 | 1966 | 40 | 394,000 | 3000 | 98,500 | Ex UP 2908** |
| 909 | RS-9 | Alco | 3440-10 | 1966 | 40 | 394,000 | 3000 | 98,500 | Ex UP 2909** |

*New number after rebuilding. No company classification assigned.
**Received from UP in 1977. Leased by DM&IR to Cartier Railway.

The Missabe not only leased steam for seasonable ore service, but diesels as well. Above, two leased Bessemer & Lake Erie F-7's wait on the ready track at Proctor; while below, Union Ry. Alco road-switcher is at Steelton yards in Duluth.
Neighboring Great Northern also provided power in the form of EMD F-7's. Two views of the GN units are shown on the Missabe near Saginaw, Minnesota, in the 1950's.

Both photos, Frank A. King

William Middleton

Two leased B&LE F-7's have all they can do to
lug 180 ore loads over Saginaw Hill.

Both photos, Frank A. King

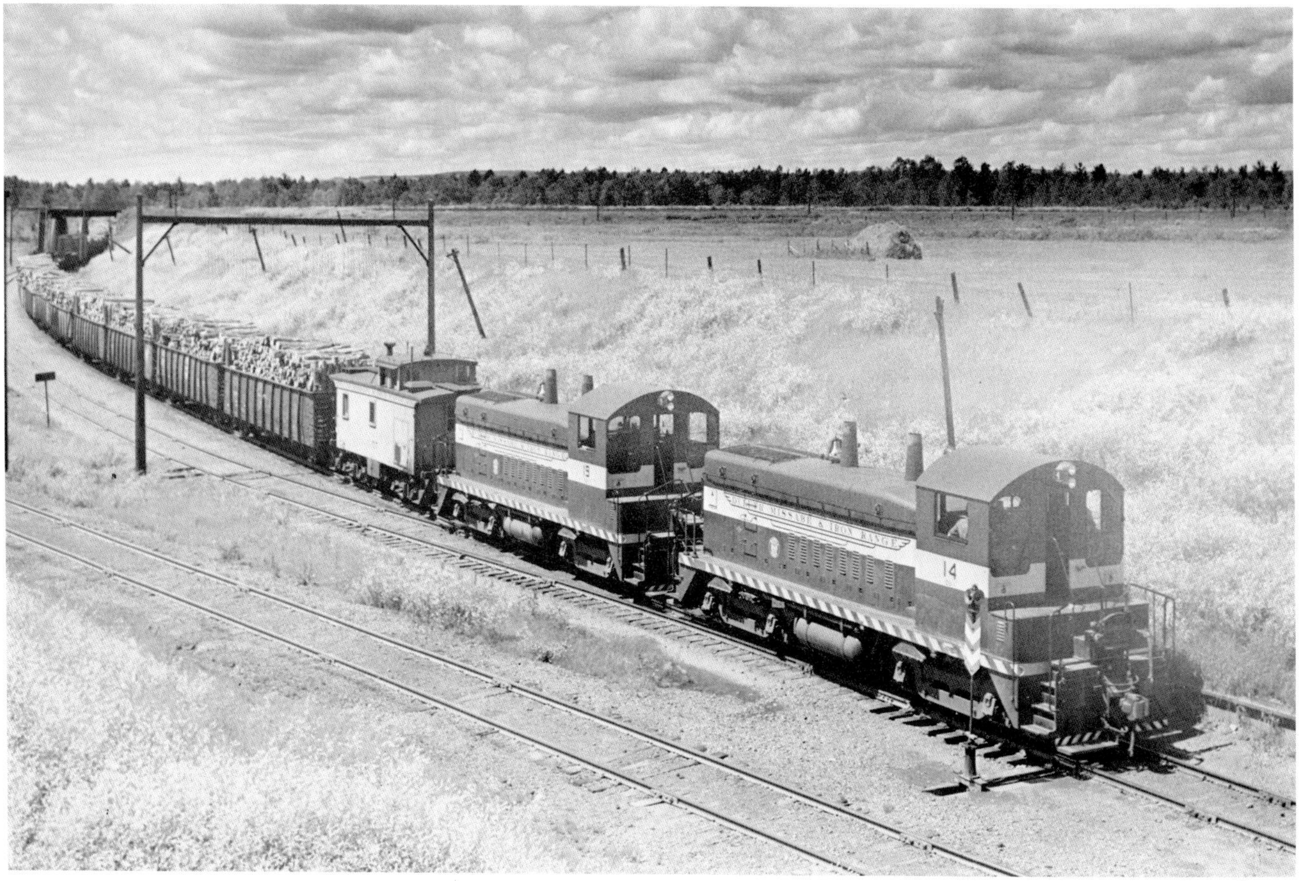


Author's collection

Frank A. King

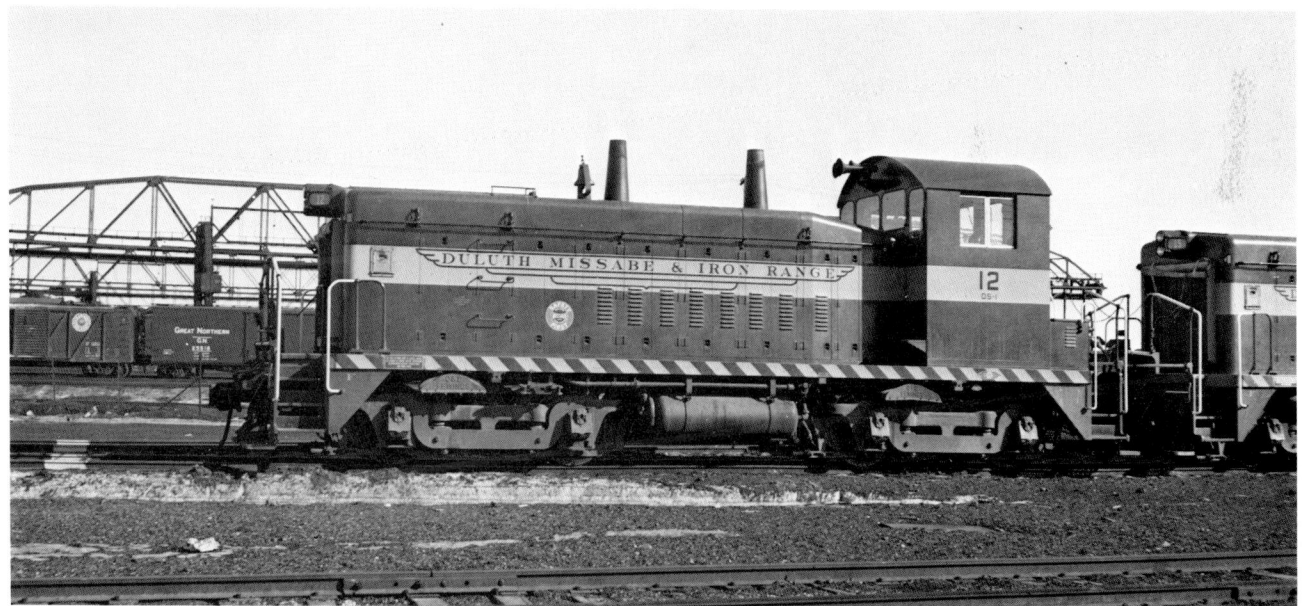

Because of its fleet of fairly modern steam locomotives, the DM&IR did not rush into dieselization like so many other railroads. Left, The road's first diesel facility was this small, corrugated metal structure located at Duluth. The Missabe's first diesel switchers were EMD SW-9's, delivered in 1953. Numbers 12 and practically obscured 15 are depicted in Duluth's Steelton yards; while above, units 14 and 15 work an Interstate Transfer run in Wisconsin soon after arriving on the DM&IR.

The old mixed with the new!
Two eras are depicted in Proctor yards with a trio of EMD SD9's on the ready track and several rows of stored steam power in the background.

A.P. Wallin

In a stunning night scene, SD9 158 waits on the dock 6 lead track.

Frank A. King

At right, several generations of diesels on the Missabe. Above, an interesting mix of leased GN units, brand new SD's, and remaining steam power at Proctor in 1958. This scene could be called a railfan's and modeler's dream since it features a little bit of everything! Also at Proctor in July 1974, SD 9 No. 171 shows off the DM&IR's original paint scheme. Right below, ex-UP Alco No. 909, in yellow and gray, helps SD9 No. 130 with an ore train on Proctor Hill on a rainy summer's day in 1974.

All photos Frank A. King

181
D.M.&I.R.Ry.
181
RS-6
155

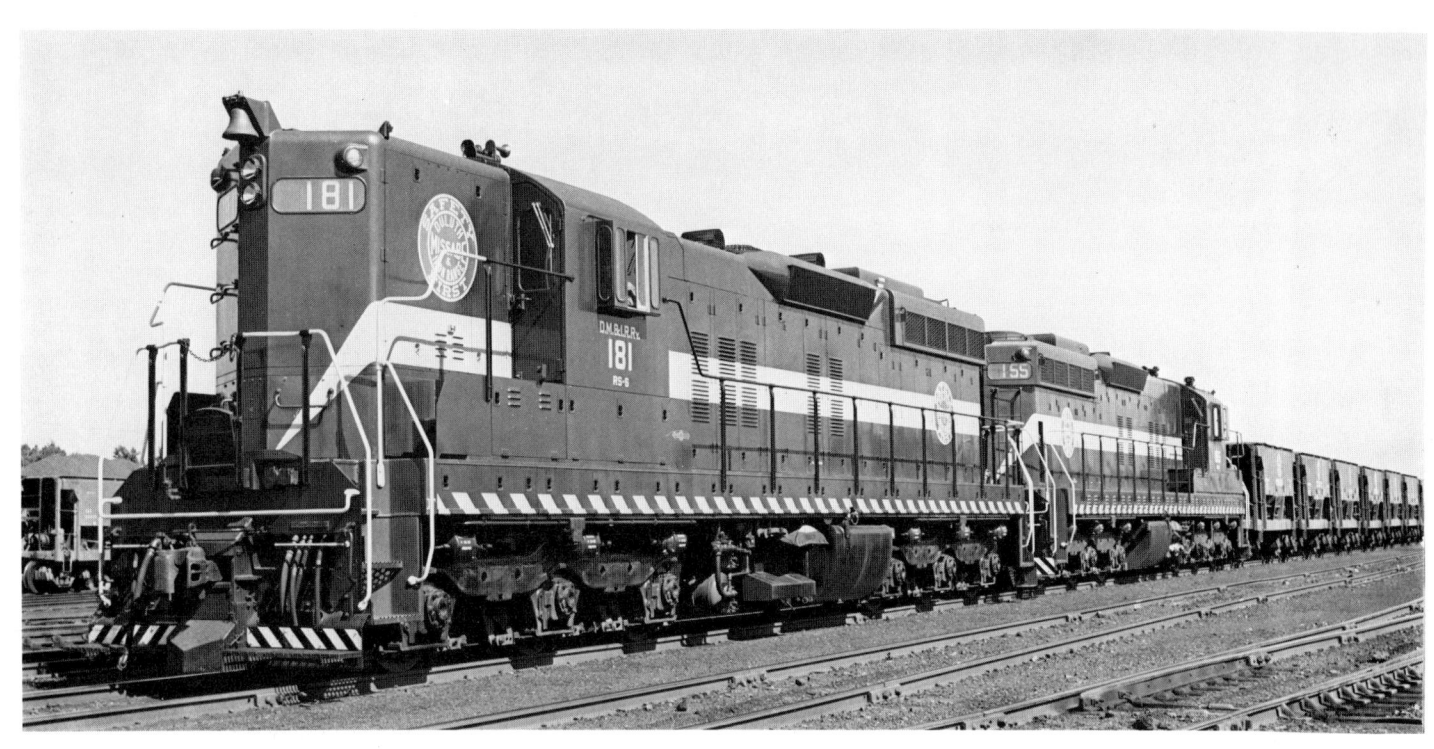

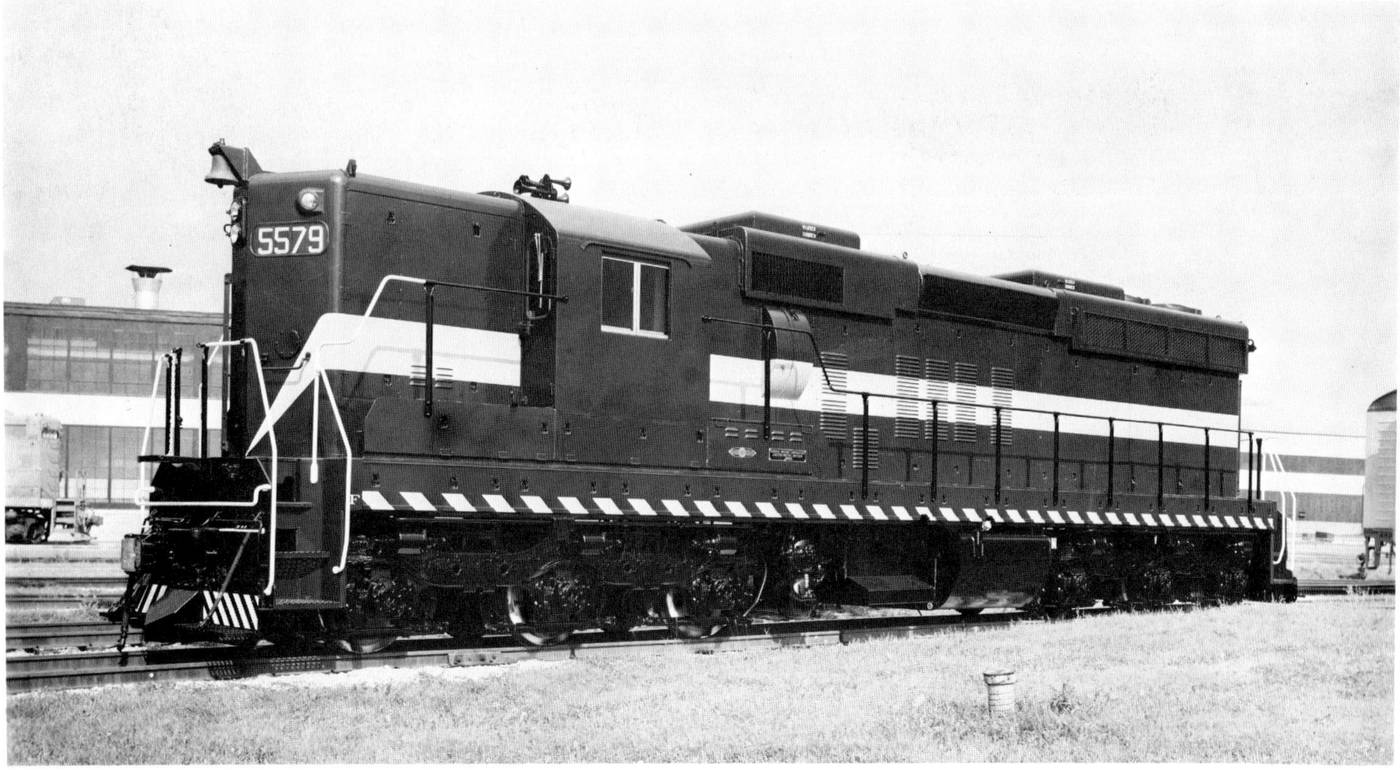
5579

The opening of the 1956 ore season saw the first use of the Missabe's new road diesels — EMD SD9's. At left above, Numbers 181 and 155 are getting ready to roll with a Missabe division ore run. Above, No. 177 and sister unit 178 cross highway 53 near Eveleth, Minnesota with an ore drag. (Below left) For a brief period an SD24 demonstrator in DM&IR colors was tested on the road. Management however, did not feel that the additional horsepower was necessary and consequently no orders were placed for SD24's.

All photos, author's collection

Frank A. King

The Missabe's management was impressed, however, with Alco's DL600. Above, one of the Alco demonstrators awaits testing at Proctor. Six units were purchased in 1959 . . . road numbers 50 to 55. Below, DL600 No.50 is in ore-sorting service at Two Harbors. At right, units 54 and 55 are on a log train on the DM&IR's Wales branch. The 2400-HP units went over to the B&LE in 1964, and later migrated to Canada's Cartier Mining Co. Railroad in the province of Quebec. Cartier is a subsidiary of US Steel and became a bastion for US-built Alco diesels. The units were in storage at Cartier's as of 1981.

Author's collection

DM&IR collection

Between June 29 and July 12, 1953 two 2400 HP Fairbanks-Morse "Trainmasters" were demonstrated on the DM&IR. The units went into service on the Iron Range division and completed eight round trips out of Two Harbors. After road tests were concluded, one unit was placed in service on the Proctor Hill ore run, while the second unit was placed in yard service at Biwabik. While the Missabe was impressed with their performance and fuel costs, they decided not to purchase the units since at that time the railroad still maintained a large fleet of relatively modern steam power. Nevertheless, the handwriting was on the wall, and the diesel would soon replace the mighty steam locomotives.

Three photos, author's collection

Four units on the point of an ore train near Allen Junction on its way to the docks at Two Harbors.

Both photos, Frank A. King

Blamey's Studio, Duluth

Leased DM&IR SD9's 129 and 130 on Amtrak's "Northstar" at Duluth. These two Missabe locomotives are equipped with steam boilers for passenger service.

Brand new SD9 No. 110 waits at Proctor yards for its train.

Author's collection

New power on the Missabe: A brace of EMD SD-38's leads an ore train down the 2% grade on Proctor Hill. Below, a beautiful pan shot of No. 208, the lead unit, on Fairlane unit train near Payne, Minnesota in April 1972. At right, the entire train is seen at Burnett, Minnesota on the same day.

All photos Howard S. Patrick

Snow comes early to the North Country. Above new SD-38's at Two Harbors on December 14, 1971. Right, two views of a DM&IR local freight with two SD9's up front, also near Two Harbors on a snowy day in February, 1972. These excellent photographs and those on the preceding pages were taken by photographer Howard Patrick who then resided at Two Harbors.

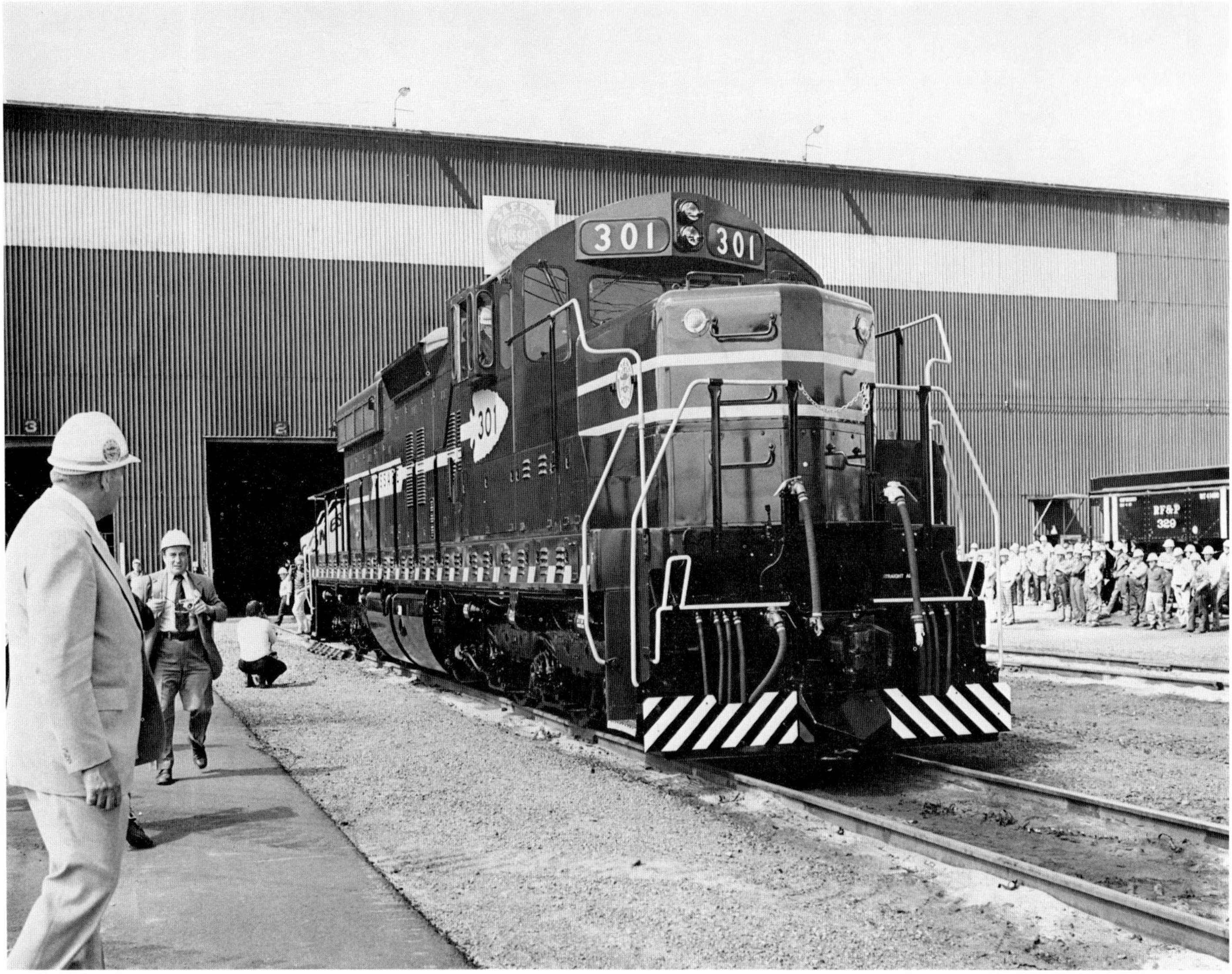
301
301
301
RF&P
329

301
301

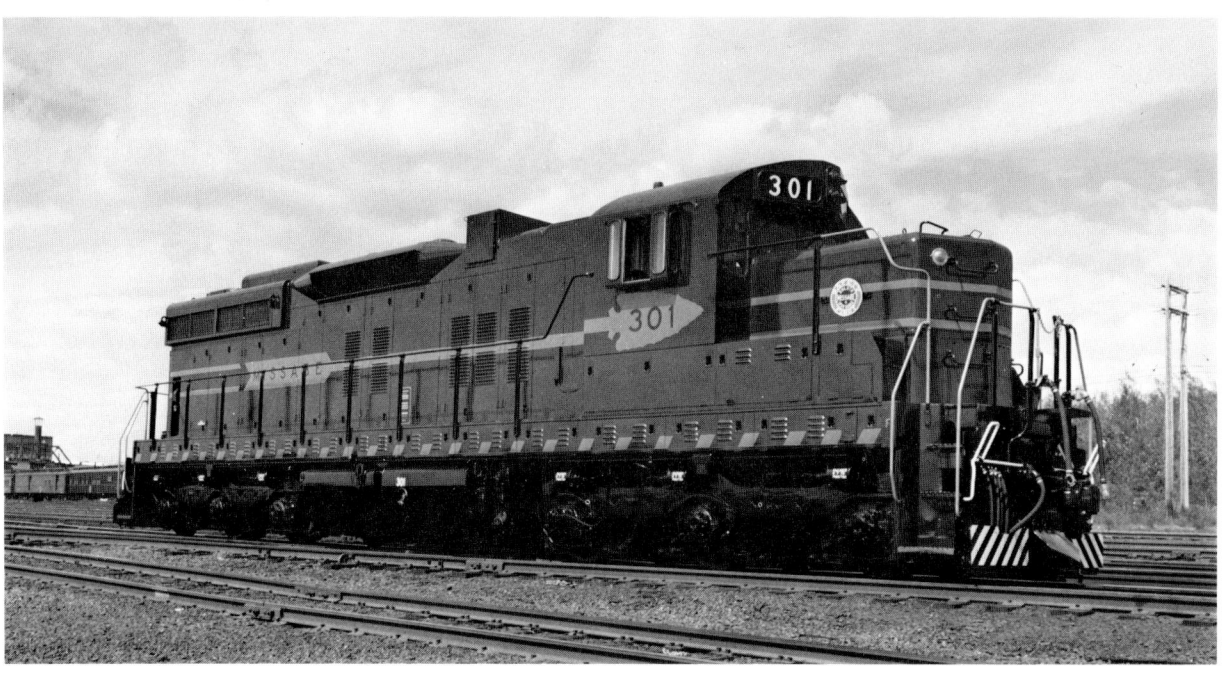

Interior view of the DM&IR diesel locomotive shop at Proctor, Minnesota. Built specifically to repair diesels, this facility is one of the finest of its kind in Minnesota.

Left, glistening in the late summer sun, born-again 301 makes her public debut. No.301, formerly SD9 No.174, was remanufactured at the Proctor diesel shop during 1979 at which time she received the latest power assemblies, electrical equipment wiring and solid-state units comparable to that contained in the latest diesels. She was the first unit to be rebuilt.

All photos, DM&IR collection

Several views of SD9 No. 129 on a DM&IR special train which included the business car "Northland" in the consist. As mentioned, No. 129 is one of the two SD9's equipped with steam boilers for passenger service. These photos were taken on the Spirit Lake Branch by Tom Hoff.

269

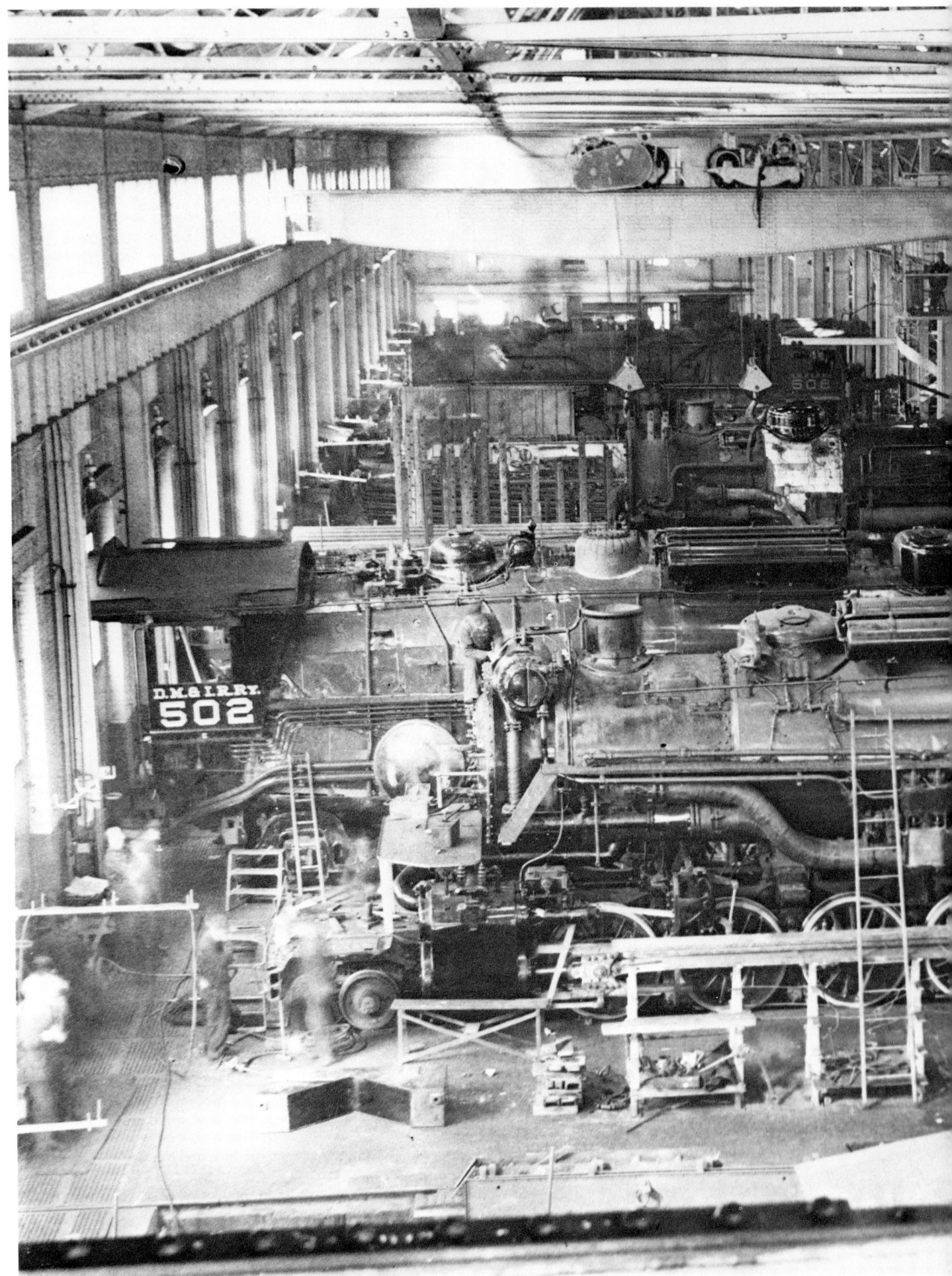

# Proctor Backshops

## The Proctor Backshops

During the heyday of steam many railroads employed vast shop complexes for servicing and maintaining their steam locomotives. The DM&IR's locomotive backshops were located at both Proctor and Two Harbors. With a large and skilled workforce, using all the most modern machine tools available, the DM&IR backshops could perform anything from light scheduled maintenance to rebuilding entire locomotives.

At left, inside the Proctor backshop during the late 1930's, work is being done on several locomotives at once, including big rebuilt No. 209 and a group of 2-10-2's. All major work on the Yellowstones, however, was performed at Two Harbors inasmuch as the transfer table at the Proctor backshop was not of sufficient length to handle the giant locomotives.

On the next several pages is a series of fascinating pictures depicting the history and development of the roundhouses, shops and locomotive servicing facilities down through the years.

Author's collection

DM&IR Coffin feedwater equipped Mikado No. 1301 on the cinder pit at Two Harbors. Acrylic on masonite by Jim Finnell.

(Above) The D&IR's first roundhouse at Two Harbors, circa 1884, was a 12-stall board-and-batten wood affair. (Below) 4-8-0 No. 71 gets a spin on the turntable near the D&IR's new brick roundhouse at Two Harbors in 1900. Notice the three men manning the lever . . . it really was an "Armstrong" turntable!

Two photos, author's collection

A panoramic view of the D&IR's backshop and roundhouse at Two Harbors in 1910. (Left) An interior view of the same shops taken a few years later in 1915.

All photos, author's collection

(Above) A very early photograph of the DM&N's roundhouse and backshops at Proctor, taken in 1905 as the facilities were nearing completion. (Below) A few years later, the same shops present a busy scene as seven locomotives can be counted on the ready track.

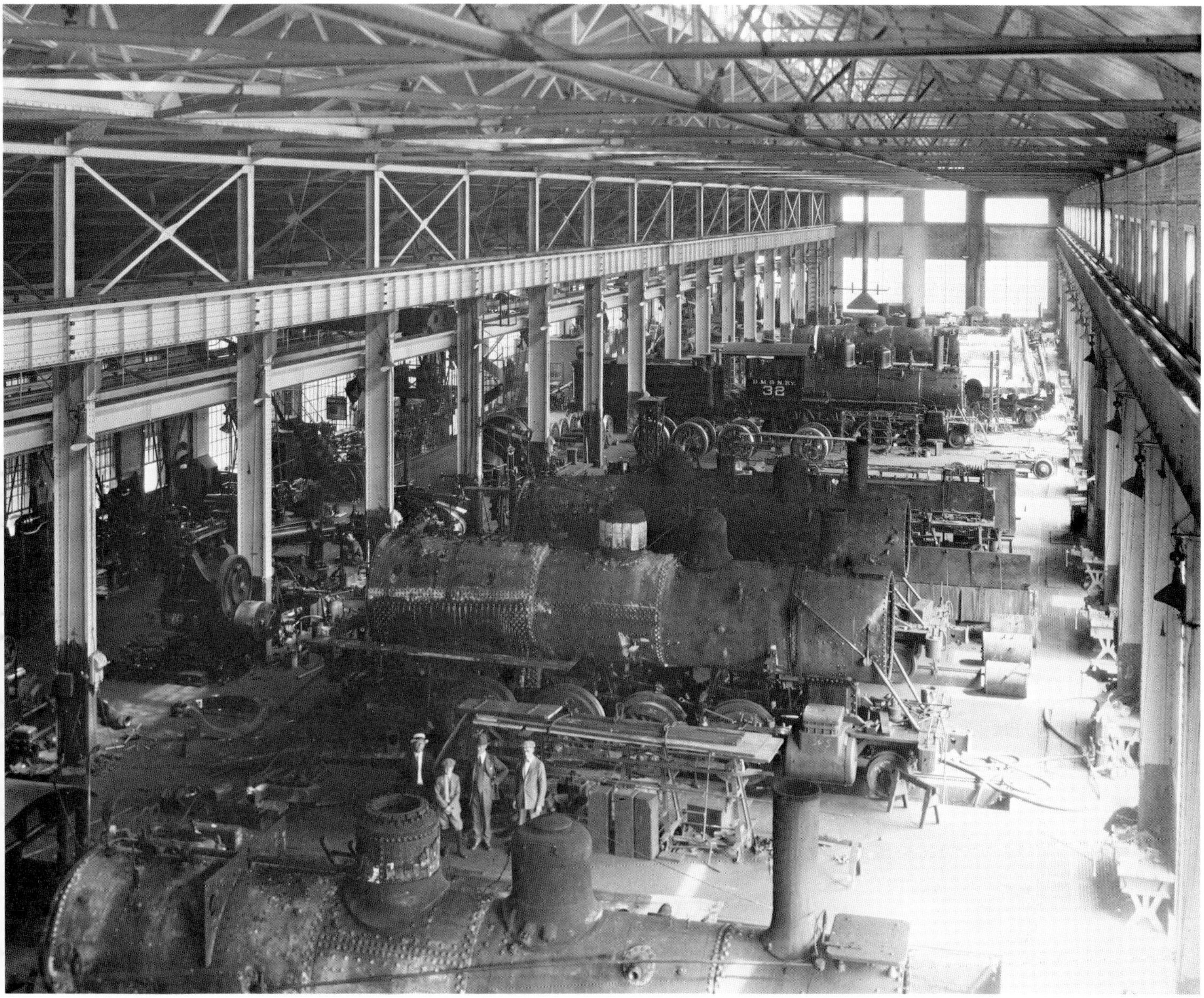

An interior view of the Proctor backshop taken some time in the "twenties." Three 2-8-0's, ten-wheeler No. 32, and a Santa Fe are in the process of being overhauled.

The DM&N's North Proctor roundhouse presents a tidy appearance in 1918.

Two photos, author's collection

An overall view of the original Proctor roundhouse and backshops in the 1920's. (Below) a close-up of the transfer table and control shack.

Two photos, author's collection

By the time this picture was taken during the late steam era, quite a few changes and improvements can be seen, especially when compared to the earlier photographs on the previous pages. (Below) Shop workers are busy relagging the boiler of a C-3 class 2-8-0.

Two photos, author's collection

Author's collection

An overhead view of the Endion roundhouse and yards along the shores of Lake Superior with the City of Duluth in the background. The interesting night scene of the same roundhouse shows a Budd RDC car and an unknown Mike sharing stalls. The engine servicing facilities and yards were compact enough to be a model layout designer's dream.

Frank A. King

The DM&IR's wood enginehouse at Virginia, Minnesota looked a little weatherbeaten when this photograph was taken in the 1930's. The structure dated from the 1890's and was eventually replaced with a large modern concrete building in 1940.

The DM&N's coaling tower located at the Proctor North engine terminal. Note the interesting spiral stairway.

Both photos, author's collection

Here's a small early wooden coal dock located on the D&IR. In the background is a brace of 25-ton wood ore cars. (Below) Several more of this early type car can be seen by the Spruce mine shaft No. 1 at Eveleth, Minnesota.

The town of Iron Junction still had a frontier look in 1910. The standpipe for the water tank is seen just to the left of the two cars in the background.

Three photos, author's collection

Lake County Historical Society

Large elevated coal docks were in vogue in the early days. The D&IR's coaling station at Biwabik is shown in the 1890's, while below, a close-up of the DM&N's original dock at Proctor in 1895.

Author's collection

In contrast, here are two photos of the DM&IR's more modern coaling facilities. (Above) The water tank and coal tower at Fraser were of modern design, using structural shapes . . . the Missabe used ore cars to deliver the coal.
(Below) The massive concrete coaling tower at Two Harbors in the 1950's. That's one of the ex-B&LE 2-10-4's moving past the tower.

Both photos, author's collection

The Missabe's first diesel facility was located at Steelton yards. (Below) The new and modern diesel shop at Proctor soon after construction.

Both photos, author's collection

# Ore Cars and others...

(Above left) An interesting "reefer" built for the DM&N in 1908 for handling on-line produce. In later years it was used in LCL service. (Mid-left) A rare car indeed on the Missabe Road was this stock car. The car, with its archbar trucks and truss rods lasted quite late . . . until the mid-50's.
(Below left) D&IR rack flat No. 6222 was a 36-foot car used in pulpwood service and had a capacity of 30 tons.

Three photos, author's collection

Here are several examples of the different types of ore cars used by the Missabe and its predecessors. (Above right) One of the first was this tiny 35-ton wooden car — one of the 800 built by Pullman in 1900. No. 7013 was one of the last wooden ore cars used by either the DM&N or D&IR. (Mid-right) U5 class car No. 12026 was built by Clark Steel Car Company for the DM&N in 1910. The car had a capacity of 50 tons and was one of the first steel cars used by the road. (Below right) Two workers apply a trapping wrench to dump the ore from car No. 19116. This car, also of 50 tons capacity, was one of 1000 received by the DM&N in 1914. Ultimately trapping machines were used for opening and closing the car doors, resulting in substantial savings in manpower.

Three photos, author's collection

During the peak ore hauling year of 1953, the DM&IR boasted the world's largest fleet of ore cars, owning 5420 50-ton cars and 7922 70-ton cars for a grand total of 13,342. Car No. 30167 was built by Pullman-Standard in 1949 as part of an order of 1000 cars. Later, approximately 1000 of this type were modified with extended sides for use in Taconite hauling service.

(Mid-left) DM&N hopper car No. 4700 was one of the 300 of this class of car used in coal and limestone hauling.

(Below) During 1971 a number of hoppers were rebuilt with extended sides for greater capacity.

Three photos, DM&IR collection

# Mining Locomotives

A group of mining officials and their wives are about to view the Adams mine near Eveleth, Minnesota, aboard a narrow gauge excursion car in 1903. The locomotive was one of several built by Porter in the 1890's for the Lake Superior Consolidated Iron Mines. Narrow gauge equipment was commonly used in mine stripping operations.

Here's another narrow gauge Porter locomotive (3') in surface stripping operation at the Fayal mine at Eveleth, Minnesota. The weight of the little saddle tanker was a mere 10 tons. Just below is a builder's photo of standard gauge 0-6-0T, built by Pittsburgh Locomotive Works for the Oliver Mining Company as their No. 4. (Below left) A brand new Baldwin 0-6-0 is being outfitted for the Mahoning Ore Co. at Hibbing, Minnesota in 1900.

Three photos, author's collection

Here's a busy scene at the Oliver Mine in Virginia, Minnesota depicting the loading of ore into 25-ton wooden ore cars in 1894. Note the steam shovel resting on a short length of temporary track and the brand new 0-6-0 spotting cars. That track in the foreground doesn't look too sturdy!

Baldwin-built Oliver Iron Mining Company No. 56 was typical of the many 0-6-0's used in the open pits during the early 1900's. The young, dapper, derby-wearing engineer on the right is the author's father, George R. King. (Below) A later view of the 50 series 0-6-0's taken around 1935. No. 50 has lost a little of its "gingerbread" but it's still a trim-looking machine.

Both photos, author's collection

Husky 0-6-0T No. 73 was built by Alco for the Mesabi Iron Company about 1920. The Mesabi Iron Co. shut down their Taconite processing operation during the mid-20's and No. 73, along with several other locomotives, was sold to the Chino Copper Co. in New Mexico.

Oliver Iron Mining Co. 0-6-0 No. 115 looks trim and well kept in this circa 1915 view. The revolving headlight made servicing easier and the full-length handrails along the running boards protected against falls.

Author's collection

Frank A. King  An 85-ton General Electric steeple cab spots the loading pocket at Cleveland Cliffs Mining Company's Gross-Marble mine in 1970. The offset pantograph facilitated shovel loading in the pit.

Author's collection

In 1923 a tug-of-war was staged between Hanna Ore Mining Co. electric locomotive No. 301 and 0-6-0 No. 205. The electric won the contest which took place at Buhl, Minnesota. A sister engine to the 301, No. 307, is on display at the Railroad Museum in Duluth.

Big Oliver Mining Company 0-8-0 No. 706 was built by Lima in 1927. Equipped with tender booster, she weighed 452,000 pounds with tender. This locomotive and her sisters represented the most powerful steamers used in the mines on the Mesabi Range.

This Alco 1000-hp diesel switcher, delivered in 1939, was the first diesel locomotive used on the Mesabi range. It's now on display at the Railroad Museum in Duluth.

Both photos, author's collection

The Balkan Mining Company operated the last steam locomotive on the Mesabi Range. This photo was taken by the author near the Danube Mine in August, 1964.

Frank A. King

# ROSTER OF LOCOMOTIVES

# STEAM LOCOMOTIVES: DULUTH & IRON RANGE RAILROAD

| Orig. No. | 2nd No. | 3rd No. | Type & Class | Builder and Construction No. | | Date Built | Dimensions Dr.—Cyls.—Wt. | Tractive Effort | Date Retired | Final Disposition and Remarks |
|---|---|---|---|---|---|---|---|---|---|---|
| 1 | | | 4-4-0  A | Baldwin | 7258 | 1884 | 63-17x24- 83,900 | 13,600 | 1911 | Deer Park RR 2 |
| 2 | | | 4-4-0  A | Baldwin | 7259 | 1884 | 63-17x24- 83,900 | 13,600 | 1911 | Sold for scrap |
| 3 | | | 2-6-0 | Baldwin | 6649 | 1883 | 52-16x24- 75,000 | 15,075 | 1899 | On exhibit at Two Harbors |
| 4 | | | 0-4-0  B | Baldwin | 7252 | 1884 | 51-16x24- 69,000 | 14,300 | 1912 | Section 30 Mining Co. |
| 5 | | | 0-4-0  B | Baldwin | 7358 | 1884 | 51-16x24- 69,000 | 14,300 | | |
| 6 | 36 | 136 | 2-8-0  G | Baldwin | 6874 | 1883 | 51-20x24-110,000 | 24,000 | 1933 | Sold for scrap |
| 7 | 37 | 137 | 2-8-0  G | Baldwin | 6937 | 1883 | 51-20x24-110,000 | 24,000 | 1933 | Sold for scrap |
| 8 | 38 | 138 | 2-8-0  G | Baldwin | 7347 | 1884 | 51-20x24-110,000 | 24,000 | 1933 | Sold for scrap |
| 9 | 39 | | 2-8-0  G | Baldwin | 7354 | 1884 | 51-20x24-110,000 | 24,000 | 1916 | Sold for scrap |
| 10 | 40 | | 2-8-0  G | Baldwin | 7374 | 1884 | 51-20x24-110,000 | 24,000 | 1916 | Sold for scrap |
| 11 | 41 | 141 | 2-8-0  G | Baldwin | 7381 | 1884 | 51-20x24-110,000 | 24,000 | 1939 | Sold for scrap |
| 12 | 42 | 142 | 2-8-0  G | Baldwin | 7921 | 1886 | 51-20x24-110,000 | 24,000 | 1933 | Sold for scrap |
| 13 | | | 0-4-0  B | Baldwin | 7964 | 1886 | 51-16x24- 69,000 | 14,300 | 1912 | P. Meagher |
| 14 | | | 0-4-0  B | Baldwin | 8646 | 1887 | 51-16x24- 69,000 | 14,300 | 1914 | P. Meagher |
| 15 | | | 0-4-0  B | Baldwin | 8647 | 1887 | 51-16x24- 69,000 | 14,300 | 1899 | Loraine Steel Co. |
| 16 | 43 | 143 | 2-8-0  G | Baldwin | 8633 | 1887 | 51-20x24-110,000 | 24,000 | 1933 | Sold for scrap |
| 17 | 44 | 144 | 2-8-0  G | Baldwin | 8634 | 1887 | 51-20x24-110,000 | 24,000 | 1933 | Sold for scrap |
| 18 | 45 | 145 | 2-8-0  G | Baldwin | 9261 | 1888 | 51-20x24-110,000 | 24,000 | 1933 | Sold for scrap |
| 19 | 46 | 146 | 2-8-0  G | Baldwin | 9257 | 1888 | 51-20x24-110,000 | 24,000 | 1933 | Sold for scrap |
| 20 | 47 | 147 | 2-8-0  G | Baldwin | 9265 | 1888 | 51-20x24-110,000 | 24,000 | 1933 | Sold for scrap |
| 21 | 48 | 148 | 2-8-0  G | Baldwin | 9266 | 1888 | 51-20x24-110,000 | 24,000 | 1933 | Sold for scrap |
| 22 | 49 | 149 | 2-8-0  G | Baldwin | 9273 | 1888 | 51-20x24-110,000 | 24,000 | 1933 | Sold for scrap |
| 23 | | | 4-4-0  C | Baldwin | 9272 | 1888 | 63-18x24- 96,600 | 15,700 | 1920 | Sold for scrap |
| 24 | | | 4-4-0  C | Baldwin | 9277 | 1888 | 63-18x24- 96,600 | 15,700 | 1916 | Sold for scrap |
| 25 | | | 4-4-0  C | Baldwin | 9278 | 1888 | 63-18x24- 96,600 | 15,700 | 1916 | J.H. Kaiser Lbr. Co. |
| | DM&IR No. | | | | | | | | | |
| 26 | | | 0-4-0  B | Baldwin | 9274 | 1888 | 51-16x24- 69,000 | 14,300 | 1899 | Loraine Steel Co. |
| 27 | 127 | | 0-6-0  D | Schenectady | 2838 | 1889 | 51-18x24- 94,400 | 20,090 | 1940 | Sold for scrap |
| 28 | | | 2-8-0 | Schenectady | 2832 | 1889 | 51-20x24-120,400 | 24,480 | 1892 | Chicago & Eastern Illinois 111-810 |
| 29 | | | 2-8-0 | Schenectady | 2833 | 1889 | 51-20x24-120,400 | 24,480 | 1892 | Chicago & Eastern Illinois 112-811 |
| 30 | | | 2-8-0 | Schenectady | 2834 | 1889 | 51-20x24-120,400 | 24,480 | 1892 | Chicago & Eastern Illinois 113-812 |
| 31 | | | 2-8-0 | Schenectady | 2835 | 1889 | 51-20x24-120,400 | 24,480 | 1892 | Chicago & Eastern Illinois 114-813 |
| 32 | | | 2-8-0 | Schenectady | 2836 | 1889 | 51-20x24-120,400 | 24,480 | 1892 | Chicago & Eastern Illinois 115-814 |
| 33 | | | 2-8-0 | Schenectady | 2837 | 1889 | 51-20x24-120,400 | 24,480 | 1892 | Chicago & Eastern Illinois 116-815 |
| 28 | | | 0-6-0  F | Baldwin | 27728 | 1906 | 51-20x26-150,000 | 33,000 | 1927 | Universal Portland Cement Co. |
| 29 | | | 0-6-0  F | Baldwin | 27729 | 1906 | 51-20x26-150,000 | 33,000 | 1927 | |
| 30 | | | 0-6-0  F | Baldwin | 27744 | 1906 | 51-20x26-150,000 | 33,000 | 1927 | |
| 31 | | | 0-6-0  F | Baldwin | 27761 | 1906 | 51-20x26-150,000 | 33,000 | 1927 | |

| Orig. No. | 2nd No. | Type & Class | | Builder and Construction No. | | Date Built | Dimensions Dr.—Cyls.—Wt. | Tractive Effort | Date Retired | Final Disposition and Remarks |
|---|---|---|---|---|---|---|---|---|---|---|
| 50 | 150 | 2-8-0 | H | Schenectady | 3738 | 1892 | 51-20x24-117,000 | 24,600 | 1933 | Sold for scrap |
| 51 | 151 | 2-8-0 | H | Schenectady | 3739 | 1892 | 51-20x24-117,000 | 24,600 | 1938 | Sold for scrap |
| 52 | 152 | 2-8-0 | H | Schenectady | 3740 | 1892 | 51-20x24-117,000 | 24,600 | 1936 | Sold for scrap |
| 53 | 153 | 2-8-0 | H | Schenectady | 3741 | 1892 | 51-20x24-117,000 | 24,600 | 1933 | Sold for scrap |
| 54 | 154 | 2-8-0 | H | Schenectady | 3742 | 1892 | 51-20x24-117,000 | 24,600 | 1934 | Sold for scrap |
| 55 | 155 | 2-8-0 | H | Schenectady | 3743 | 1892 | 51-20x24-117,000 | 24,600 | 1938 | Sold for scrap |
| 56 |  | 2-8-0 | H | Schenectady | 3744 | 1892 | 51-20x24-117,000 | 24,600 | 1899 | El Paso & Northeastern 51 |
| 57 | 157 | 2-8-0 | H | Schenectady | 3745 | 1892 | 51-20x24-117,000 | 24,600 | 1933 | Sold for scrap |
| 58 | 158 | 2-8-0 | H | Schenectady | 3805 | 1892 | 51-20x24-117,000 | 24,600 | 1933 | Sold for scrap |
| 59 | 159 | 2-8-0 | H | Schenectady | 3806 | 1892 | 51-20x24-117,000 | 24,600 | 1933 | Sold for scrap |
| 60 |  | 4-8-0 | J | Schenectady | 4041 | 1893 | 54-22x26-174,800 | 37,600 | 1928 | Sold for scrap |
| 61 |  | 4-8-0 | J | Schenectady | 4042 | 1893 | 54-22x26-174,800 | 37,600 | 1927 |  |
| 62 |  | 4-8-0 | J | Schenectady | 4043 | 1893 | 54-22x26-174,800 | 37,600 | 1928 | Sold for scrap |
| 63 |  | 4-8-0 | J | Schenectady | 4044 | 1893 | 54-22x26-174,800 | 37,600 | 1928 | Sold for scrap |
| 64 |  | 4-8-0 | J | Schenectady | 4045 | 1893 | 54-22x26-174,800 | 37,600 | 1928 | Sold for scrap |
| 65 |  | 4-8-0 | J | Schenectady | 4046 | 1893 | 54-22x26-174,800 | 37,600 | 1927 |  |
| 66 |  | 4-8-0 | J | Schenectady | 4047 | 1893 | 54-22x26-174,800 | 37,600 | 1927 |  |
| 67 |  | 4-8-0 | J | Schenectady | 4048 | 1893 | 54-22x26-174,800 | 37,600 | 1928 | Sold for scrap |
| 68 |  | 4-8-0 | J | Schenectady | 4049 | 1893 | 54-22x26-174,800 | 37,600 | 1927 |  |
| 69 |  | 4-8-0 | J | Schenectady | 4145 | 1893 | 54-22x26-174,800 | 37,600 | 1928 | Sold for scrap |
| 70 |  | 4-8-0 | J | Schenectady | 4327 | 1895 | 54-22x26-176,400 | 37,600 | 1929 | Sold for scrap |

| 71 | 171 | 4-8-0 | J | Schenectady | 4328 | 1895 | 54-22x26-176,400 | 37,600 | 1933 | Sold for scrap |
| 72 |  | 4-8-0 | J | Schenectady | 4329 | 1895 | 54-22x26-176,400 | 37,600 | 1929 | Sold for scrap |
| 73 |  | 4-8-0 | J | Schenectady | 4330 | 1895 | 54-22x26-176,400 | 37,600 | 1927 |  |
| 74 |  | 4-8-0 | J | Baldwin | 14717 | 1896 | 54-22x26-176,200 | 37,600 | 1923 | Illinois Steel Co. |
| 75 |  | 4-8-0 | J | Baldwin | 14718 | 1896 | 54-22x26-176,200 | 37,600 | 1929 | Sold for scrap |
| 76 | 176 | 4-8-0 | J | Baldwin | 14719 | 1896 | 54-22x26-176,200 | 37,600 | 1933 | Sold for scrap |
| 77 |  | 4-8-0 | J | Baldwin | 14720 | 1896 | 54-22x26-176,200 | 37,600 | 1929 | Sold for scrap |
| 78 |  | 4-8-0 | J | Baldwin | 14721 | 1896 | 54-22x26-176,200 | 37,600 | 1929 | Sold for scrap |
| 79 |  | 4-8-0 | J | Baldwin | 14722 | 1896 | 54-22x26-176,200 | 37,600 | 1923 | Illinois Steel Co. |
| 80 | 180 | 4-8-0 | J | Baldwin | 16747 | 1899 | 54-22x26-180,000 | 37,600 | 1933 | Sold for scrap |
| 81 | 181 | 4-8-0 | J | Baldwin | 16748 | 1899 | 54-22x26-180,000 | 37,600 | 1933 | Sold for scrap |
| 82 |  | 4-8-0 | J | Baldwin | 16749 | 1899 | 54-22x26-180,000 | 37,600 | 1933 | Sold for scrap |
| 83 |  | 4-8-0 | J | Baldwin | 16750 | 1899 | 54-22x26-180,000 | 37,600 | 1926 | Sold for scrap |
| 84 |  | 4-8-0 | J | Schenectady | 5412 | 1900 | 54-22x26-182,600 | 37,600 | 1933 | Sold for scrap |
| 85 |  | 4-8-0 | J | Schenectady | 5413 | 1900 | 54-22x26-182,600 | 37,600 | 1933 | Sold for scrap |
| 86 |  | 4-8-0 | J | Schenectady | 5414 | 1900 | 54-22x26-182,600 | 37,600 | 1933 | Sold for scrap |
| 87 |  | 4-8-0 | J | Schenectady | 5415 | 1900 | 54-22x26-182,600 | 37,600 | 1933 | Sold for scrap |

| Orig. No. | DM&IR No. | Type & Class | | Builder and Construction No. | | Date Built | Dimensions Dr.—Cyls.—Wt. | Tractive Effort | Date Retired | Final Disposition and Remarks |
|---|---|---|---|---|---|---|---|---|---|---|
| 88 | | 4-8-0 | J | Schenectady | 5416 | 1900 | 54-22x26-182,600 | 37,600 | 1933 | Sold for scrap |
| 89 | DM&IR No. | 4-8-0 | J | Schenectady | 5417 | 1900 | 54-22x26-182,600 | 37,600 | 1933 | Sold for scrap |
| 90 | | 4-8-0 | K | Baldwin | 25465 | 1905 | 54-22x26-193,400 | 37,600 | 1961 | Renumbered 199—Sold for scrap |
| 91 | 191 | 2-8-0 | K | Baldwin | 25466 | 1905 | 54-22x28-193,400 | 37,600 | 1957 | Sold for scrap |
| 92 | 192 | 2-8-0 | K | Baldwin | 25467 | 1905 | 54-22x28-193,400 | 37,600 | 1958 | Sold for scrap |
| 93 | 193 | 2-8-0 | K | Baldwin | 25509 | 1905 | 54-22x28-193,400 | 37,600 | 1958 | Sold for scrap |
| 94 | 194 | 2-8-0 | K | Baldwin | 25783 | 1905 | 54-22x28-193,400 | 37,600 | 1956 | Sold for scrap |
| 95 | 195 | 2-8-0 | K | Baldwin | 25805 | 1905 | 54-22x28-193,400 | 37,600 | 1958 | Sold for scrap |
| 96 | 196 | 2-8-0 | K | Baldwin | 25873 | 1905 | 54-22x28-193,400 | 42,553 | 1957 | Sold for scrap |
| 97 | 197 | 2-8-0 | K | Baldwin | 25874 | 1905 | 54-22x28-193,400 | 42,553 | 1958 | Sold for scrap |
| 98 | 198 | 2-8-0 | K | Baldwin | 25885 | 1905 | 54-22x28-193,400 | 42,553 | 1961 | Sold for scrap |
| 99 | | 4-4-0 | | Hinkley | | 1871 | 54-16x24- | | | Ex-Chicago & Eastern Illinois 12 (Rec'd D&IR 1887) (SC. C. 1910) |

| | DM&IR No. | | | | | | | | | |
|---|---|---|---|---|---|---|---|---|---|---|
| 101 | 1 1 0 1 | 4-6-0 | M | Schenectady | 5408 | 1900 | 58-19x26-150,800 | 26,125 | 1933 | Sold for scrap |
| 102 | | 4-6-0 | M | Schenectady | 5409 | 1900 | 58-19x26-150,800 | 26,125 | 1929 | Sold for scrap |
| 103 | 1 1 0 3 | 4-6-0 | M | Schenectady | 5410 | 1900 | 58-19x26-150,800 | 26,125 | 1933 | Sold for scrap |
| 104 | | 4-6-0 | M | Schenectady | 5411 | 1900 | 58-19x26-150,800 | 26,125 | 1929 | Sold for scrap |
| 105 | 1 1 0 5 | 4-6-0 | M | Schenectady | 5433 | 1900 | 58-19x26-150,800 | 26,125 | 1933 | Sold for scrap |
| 106 | DM&IR No. | 4-6-0 | M | Schenectady | 5434 | 1900 | 58-19x26-150,800 | 26,125 | 1929 | Sold for scrap |
| 107 | 1 1 0 7 | 4-6-2 | A | Baldwin | 39861 | 1900 | 69-22x28-219,000 | 33,400 | 1955 | Sold for scrap |
| 108 | 1 1 0 8 | 4-6-2 | A | Baldwin | 39862 | 1913 | 69-22x28-219,000 | 33,400 | 1953 | Sold for scrap |
| 109 | 1 1 0 9 | 4-6-2 | A | Baldwin | 39863 | 1913 | 69-22x28-219,000 | 33,400 | 1953 | Sold for scrap |
| 110 | 1 1 1 0 | 4-6-2 | A | Baldwin | 39864 | 1913 | 69-22x28-219,000 | 33,400 | 1954 | Sold for scrap |
| 200 | 1 2 0 0 | 2-8-0 | K | Baldwin | 27722 | 1906 | 54-22x28-196,050 | 42,553 | 1956 | Sold for scrap |
| 201 | 1 2 0 1 | 2-8-0 | K | Baldwin | 27738 | 1906 | 54-22x28-196,050 | 42,553 | 1958 | Sold for scrap |
| 202 | 1 2 0 2 | 2-8-0 | K | Baldwin | 27739 | 1906 | 54-22x28-196,050 | 42,553 | 1958 | Sold for scrap |
| 203 | 1 2 0 3 | 2-8-0 | K | Baldwin | 27740 | 1906 | 54-22x28-196,050 | 42,553 | 1955 | Sold for scrap |
| 204 | 1 2 0 4 | 2-8-0 | K | Baldwin | 27755 | 1906 | 54-22x28-196,050 | 42,553 | 1959 | Sold for scrap |
| 205 | 1 2 0 5 | 2-8-0 | K | Baldwin | 27773 | 1906 | 54-22x28-196,050 | 42,553 | 1956 | Sold for scrap |
| 206 | 1 2 0 6 | 2-8-0 | K | Baldwin | 30311 | 1906 | 54-22x28-198,850 | 42,553 | 1954 | Sold for scrap |
| 207 | 1 2 0 7 | 2-8-0 | K | Baldwin | 30322 | 1906 | 54-22x28-198,850 | 42,553 | 1956 | Sold for scrap |
| 208 | 1 2 0 8 | 2-8-0 | K | Baldwin | 30323 | 1906 | 54-22x28-198,850 | 42,553 | 1958 | Sold for scrap |
| 209 | 1 2 0 9 | 2-8-0 | K | Baldwin | 33308 | 1909 | 54-22x28-198,850 | 42,553 | 1956 | Sold for scrap |
| 210 | 1 2 1 0 | 2-8-0 | K | Baldwin | 33309 | 1909 | 54-22x28-198,850 | 42,553 | 1950 | Sold for scrap |
| 211 | 1 2 1 1 | 2-8-0 | K | Baldwin | 33310 | 1909 | 54-22x28-198,850 | 42,553 | 1954 | Sold for scrap |
| 212 | 1 2 1 2 | 2-8-0 | K | Baldwin | 33311 | 1909 | 54-22x28-198,850 | 42,553 | 1959 | Sold for scrap |
| 213 | 1 2 1 3 | 2-8-0 | K | Baldwin | 34740 | 1910 | 54-22x28-198,850 | 42,553 | 1958 | Sold for scrap |
| 214 | 1 2 1 4 | 2-8-0 | K | Baldwin | 34741 | 1910 | 54-22x28-198,850 | 42,553 | 1958 | Sold for scrap |
| 215 | 1 2 1 5 | 2-8-0 | K | Baldwin | 34742 | 1910 | 54-22x28-198,850 | 42,553 | 1959 | Sold for scrap |
| 216 | 1 2 1 6 | 2-8-0 | K | Baldwin | 34743 | 1910 | 54-22x28-198,850 | 42,553 | 1957 | Sold for scrap |
| 217 | 1 2 1 7 | 2-8-0 | K | Baldwin | 34744 | 1910 | 54-22x28-198,850 | 42,553 | 1958 | Sold for scrap |
| 218 | 1 2 1 8 | 2-8-0 | K | Baldwin | 34745 | 1910 | 54-22x28-198,850 | 42,553 | 1962 | Donated to Tower, Minnesota |
| 219 | 1 2 1 9 | 2-8-0 | K | Baldwin | 34813 | 1910 | 54-22x28-198,850 | 42,553 | 1958 | Sold for scrap |
| 220 | 1 2 2 0 | 2-8-0 | K | Baldwin | 34814 | 1910 | 54-22x28-198,850 | 42,553 | 1957 | Sold for scrap |

| Orig. No. | DM&IR No. | Type & Class | | Builder and Construction No. | | Date Built | Dimensions Dr.—Cyls.—Wt. | Tractive Effort | Date Retired | Final Disposition and Remarks |
|---|---|---|---|---|---|---|---|---|---|---|
| 221 | 1221 | 2-8-0 | K | Baldwin | 34841 | 1910 | 54-22x28-198,850 | 42,553 | 1959 | Sold for scrap |
| 222 | 1222 | 2-8-0 | K | Baldwin | 34842 | 1910 | 54-22x28-198,850 | 42,553 | 1956 | Sold for scrap |
| 223 | 1223 | 2-8-0 | K | Baldwin | 34843 | 1910 | 54-22x28-198,850 | 42,553 | 1959 | Sold for scrap |
| 224 | 1224 | 2-8-0 | K | Baldwin | 34844 | 1910 | 54-22x28-198,850 | 42,553 | 1959 | Sold for scrap |
| 300 | 1300 | 2-8-2 | N | Baldwin | 39671 | 1913 | 54-27x30-287,600 | 59,250 | 1958 | Sold for scrap |
| 301 | 1301 | 2-8-2 | N | Baldwin | 39672 | 1913 | 54-27x30-287,600 | 59,250 | 1962 | Sold for scrap |
| 302 | 1302 | 2-8-2 | N | Baldwin | 39916 | 1913 | 54-27x30-287,600 | 59,250 | 1962 | Sold for scrap |
| 303 | 1303 | 2-8-2 | N | Baldwin | 39917 | 1913 | 54-27x30-287,600 | 59,250 | 1959 | Sold for scrap |
| 304 | 1304 | 2-8-2 | N | Lima | 1311 | 1913 | 54-27x30-287,600 | 59,250 | 1961 | Sold for scrap |
| 305 | 1305 | 2-8-2 | N | Lima | 1312 | 1913 | 54-27x30-287,600 | 59,250 | 1959 | Sold for scrap |
| 306 | 1306 | 2-8-2 | N1 | Baldwin | 43303 | 1916 | 58-27x30-294,000 | 59,250 | 1958 | Sold for scrap |
| 307 | 1307 | 2-8-2 | N1 | Baldwin | 43304 | 1916 | 58-27x30-294,000 | 59,250 | 1959 | Sold for scrap |
| 308 | 1308 | 2-8-2 | N1 | Baldwin | 43305 | 1916 | 58-27x30-294,000 | 59,250 | 1958 | Sold for scrap |
| 309 | 1309 | 2-8-2 | N2 | Baldwin | 56507 | 1923 | 58-27x30-321,400 | 59,250 | 1959 | Sold for scrap |
| 310 | 1310 | 2-8-2 | N2 | Baldwin | 56508 | 1923 | 58-27x30-321,400 | 59,250 | 1959 | Sold for scrap |
| 311 | 1311 | 2-8-2 | N2 | Baldwin | 56509 | 1923 | 58-27x30-321,400 | 59,250 | 1958 | Sold for scrap |

## STEAM LOCOMOTIVES: DULUTH, MISSABE & NORTHERN RAILWAY

| Orig. No. | DM&IR No. | Type & Class | | Builder and Construction No. | | Date Built | Dimensions Dr.—Cyls.—Wt. | Tractive Effort | Date Retired | Final Disposition and Remarks |
|---|---|---|---|---|---|---|---|---|---|---|
| 1 | | 4-4-0 | A | Pittsburgh | 1409 | 1893 | 62-17x22- 89,000 | 15,214 | 1928 | Sold for scrap |
| 2 | | 4-4-0 | A | Pittsburgh | 1410 | 1893 | 62-17x22- 89,000 | 15,214 | 1925 | Cazenovia Southern Ry. |
| 5 | 5 | 4-6-0 | F | Pittsburgh | 1427 | 1893 | 56-19x26-123,000 | 23,000 | 1940 | Detroit, Caro & Sandusky Rw. |
| 6 | | 4-6-0 | F | Pittsburgh | 1428 | 1893 | 56-19x26-123,000 | 23,000 | 1935 | Sold for scrap |
| 7 | | 4-6-0 | F | Pittsburgh | 1387 | 1893 | 56-19x26-123,000 | 23,000 | 1901 | Indiana, Illinois & Iowa Ry.  41 |
| 8 | | 4-6-0 | F | Pittsburgh | 1388 | 1893 | 56-19x26-123,000 | 23,000 | 1901 | Indiana, Illinois & Iowa Ry.  40 |
| 9 | | 4-6-0 | F | Pittsburgh | 1389 | 1893 | 56-19x26-123,000 | 23,000 | 1901 | Indiana, Illinois & Iowa Ry.  42 |
| 10 | | 4-6-0 | F | Pittsburgh | 1429 | 1893 | 56-19x26-123,000 | 23,000 | 1901 | Indiana, Illinois & Iowa Ry.  44 |
| 11 | | 4-6-0 | F | Pittsburgh | 1430 | 1893 | 56-19x26-23,000 | 23,000 | 1933 | Sold for scrap |
| 12 | 12 | 4-6-0 | F | Pittsburgh | 1431 | 1893 | 56-19x26-23,000 | 23,000 | 1939 | Sold for scrap |
| 13 | | 4-6-0 | F | Pittsburgh | 1432 | 1893 | 56-19x26-23,000 | 23,000 | 1938 | American Steel & Wire Co. |
| 14 | | 4-6-0 | F | Pittsburgh | 1433 | 1893 | 56-19x26-23,000 | 23,000 | 1901 | Indiana, Illinois & Iowa Ry.  45 |
| 15 | | 4-6-0 | F | Pittsburgh | 1462 | 1893 | 56-19x26-23,000 | 23,000 | 1933 | American Steel & Wire Co. |
| 16 | | 4-6-0 | F | Pittsburgh | 1463 | 1893 | 56-19x26-123,000 | 23,000 | 1937 | American Steel & Wire Co. |
| 17 | 17 | 4-6-0 | F | Pittsburgh | 1464 | 1893 | 56-19x26-123,000 | 23,000 | 1940 | Sold for scrap |
| 18 | | 4-6-0 | F | Pittsburgh | 1465 | 1893 | 56-19x26-123,000 | 23,000 | 1901 | Indiana, Illinois & Iowa Ry.  43 |
| 19 | 19 | 4-6-0 | F | Pittsburgh | 1466 | 1893 | 56-19x26-123,000 | 23,000 | 1940 | Boiler at Virginia Enginehouse |
| 20 | | 4-6-0 | F | Pittsburgh | 1467 | 1893 | 56-19x26-123,000 | 23,000 | 1933 | American Steel & Wire Co. |

| Orig. No. | DM&IR No. | Type & Class | Builder and Construction No. | | Date Built | Dimensions Dr.—Cyls.—Wt. | Tractive Effort | Date Retired | Final Disposition and Remarks |
|---|---|---|---|---|---|---|---|---|---|
| 21 | 21 | 4-6-0 F | Pittsburgh | 1840 | 1898 | 56-19x26-123,000 | 23,000 | 1948 | American Steel & Wire Co. |
| 22 | | 4-6-0 F | Pittsburgh | 1841 | 1898 | 56-19x26-123,000 | 23,000 | 1923 | Northern Lumber Co. 22 |
| 23 | | 4-6-0 F | Pittsburgh | 1957 | 1899 | 56-19x26-123,000 | 23,000 | 1933 | Sold for scrap |
| 24 | | 4-6-0 F | Pittsburgh | 1958 | 1899 | 56-19x26-123,000 | 23,000 | 1923 | Northern Lumber Co. 24 |
| 25 | | 4-6-0 F | Pittsburgh | 1959 | 1899 | 56-19x26-123,000 | 23,000 | 1933 | Sold for scrap |
| 26 | | 4-6-0 F | Pittsburgh | 1960 | 1899 | 56-19x26-123,000 | 23,000 | 1933 | Sold for scrap |
| 27 | | 4-6-0 F | Pittsburgh | 2092 | 1900 | 56-19x26-123,000 | 23,000 | 1937 | American Steel & Wire Co. |
| 28 | | 4-6-0 F | Pittsburgh | 2093 | 1900 | 56-19x26-123,000 | 23,000 | 1933 | Sold for scrap |
| 29 | | 4-6-0 F | Pittsburgh | 2094 | 1900 | 56-19x26-123,000 | 23,000 | 1923 | Northern Lumber Co. 29 |
| 30 | 30 | 4-6-0 F | Pittsburgh | 2095 | 1900 | 56-19x26-123,000 | 23,000 | 1939 | |
| 31 | 31 | 4-6-0 F | Pittsburgh | 2096 | 1900 | 56-19x26-123,000 | 23,000 | 1940 | Detroit, Caro & Sandusky Ry. |
| 32 | | 4-6-0 F | Pittsburgh | 2097 | 1900 | 56-19x26-123,000 | 23,000 | 1928 | Sold for scrap |
| 33 | | 4-6-0 F | Pittsburgh | 2098 | 1900 | 56-19x26-123,000 | 23,000 | 1923 | Northern Lumber Co. 33 |
| 50 | | 0-6-0 S | Pittsburgh | 1455 | 1893 | 50-17x24- 84,000 | 18,866 | 1918 | Chickasaw Shipbuilding Co. |
| 51 | | 0-6-0 S | Pittsburgh | 1456 | 1893 | 50-17x24- 84,000 | 18,866 | 1916 | Minnesota Steel Co. |
| 52 | | 0-6-0 S | Pittsburgh | 1457 | 1893 | 50-17x24- 84,000 | 18,866 | 1916 | Pittsburg Iron Mining Co. |
| 53 | | 0-6-0 S | Pittsburgh | 1458 | 1893 | 50-17x24- 84,000 | 18,866 | 1916 | Universal Atlas Cement |
| 54 | | 0-6-0 S | Pittsburgh | 1459 | 1893 | 50-17x26- 84,000 | 18,866 | 1916 | Minnesota Steel Co. |
| 55 | | 0-6-0 S | Pittsburgh | 1460 | 1893 | 50-17x26- 84,000 | 18,866 | 1917 | Pittsburg Iron Mining Co. |
| 56 | 1 | 0-6-0 S1 | Pittsburgh | 2122 | 1900 | 50-19x26-120,450 | 28,721 | 1920 | Minnesota Dakota & Western Ry. 8 |
| 57 | 1 | 0-6-0 S1 | Pittsburgh | 2123 | 1900 | 50-19x26-120,450 | 28,721 | 1920 | Minnesota Dakota & Western Ry. 9 |
| 58 | | 0-8-0 S3 | Baldwin | 30487 | 1907 | 51-21x28-164,000 | 41,160 | 1927 | Oliver Iron Mining 800 |
| 59 | | 0-8-0 S3 | Baldwin | 30488 | 1907 | 51-21x28-164,000 | 41,160 | 1927 | Oliver Iron Mining 801 |
| 60 | | 0-8-0 S3 | Baldwin | 30501 | 1907 | 51-21x28-164,000 | 41,160 | 1927 | Oliver Iron Mining 802 |
| 61 | | 0-8-0 S3 | Baldwin | 30586 | 1907 | 51-21x28-164,000 | 41,160 | 1927 | Oliver Iron Mining 803 |
| 62 | | 0-8-0 S4 | Baldwin | 34754 | 1910 | 51-21x28-164,000 | 41,160 | 1927 | Oliver Iron Mining 804 |
| 63 | | 0-8-0 S4 | Baldwin | 34755 | 1910 | 51-21x28-164,000 | 41,160 | 1927 | Oliver Iron Mining 805 |
| 64 | | 0-8-0 S4 | Baldwin | 34756 | 1910 | 51-21x28-164,000 | 41,160 | 1927 | Oliver Iron Mining 806 |
| 80 | 80 | 0-8-0 S2 | Schenectady | 47925 | 1910 | 51-21x28-207,500 | 48,850 | 1948 | American Steel & Wire Co. |
| 81 | 81 | 0-8-0 S2 | Schenectady | 47926 | 1910 | 51-21x28-207,500 | 48,850 | 1948 | American Steel & Wire Co. |
| 82 | 82 | 0-8-0 S2 | Schenectady | 47927 | 1910 | 51-21x28-207,500 | 48,850 | 1948 | American Steel & Wire Co. |
| 83 | 83 | 0-8-0 S2 | Schenectady | 47928 | 1910 | 51-21x28-207,500 | 48,850 | 1948 | American Steel & Wire Co. |
| 84 | 84 | 0-8-0 S2 | Schenectady | 47929 | 1910 | 51-21x28-207,500 | 48,850 | 1948 | American Steel & Wire Co. |
| 85 | 85 | 0-8-0 S2 | Schenectady | 47930 | 1910 | 51-21x28-207,500 | 48,850 | 1948 | American Steel & Wire Co. |
| 86 | 86 | 0-8-0 S3 | Baldwin | 45704 | 1917 | 51-24x28-216,000 | 53,575 | 1954 | Sold for scrap |
| 87 | 87 | 0-8-0 S3 | Baldwin | 45705 | 1917 | 51-24x28-216,000 | 53,575 | 1958 | Sold for scrap |
| 88 | 88 | 0-8-0 S3 | Baldwin | 45706 | 1917 | 51-24x28-216,000 | 53,575 | 1958 | Sold for scrap |
| 89 | 89 | 0-8-0 S3 | Baldwin | 45707 | 1917 | 51-24x28-216,000 | 53,575 | 1958 | Sold for scrap |
| 90 | 90 | 0-10-0 S6 | Baldwin | 60213 | 1928 | 57-28x30-352,250 | 41,160 | 1955 | Sold for scrap |
| 91 | 91 | 0-10-0 S6 | Baldwin | 60263 | 1928 | 57-28x30-352,250 | 41,160 | 1958 | Sold for scrap |
| 92 | 92 | 0-10-0 S6 | Baldwin | 60293 | 1928 | 57-28x30-352,250 | 41,160 | 1958 | Sold for scrap |
| 93 | 93 | 0-10-0 S6 | Baldwin | 60294 | 1928 | 57-28x30-352,250 | 41,160 | 1958 | Sold for scrap |
| 100 | | 4-6-0 F1 | Baldwin | 27719 | 1906 | 67-20 x26-166,200 | 26,400 | 1933 | American Steel & Wire Co. |
| 101 | | 4-6-0 F1 | Baldwin | 27727 | 1906 | 67-18¾x26-166,200 | 23,200 | 1933 | American Steel & Wire Co. |
| 102 | | 4-6-0 F2 | Baldwin | 30436 | 1907 | 63-18¾x26-164,000 | 24,675 | 1932 | Boiler at Biwabik Enginehouse |
| 103 | | 4-6-0 F2 | Baldwin | 30437 | 1907 | 63-18¾x26-164,000 | 24,675 | 1933 | American Steel & Wire Co. |
| 104 | | 4-6-0 F3 | Baldwin | 34723 | 1907 | 63-20 x26-164,000 | 28,100 | 1933 | American Steel & Wire Co. |
| 200 | 200 | 2-8-8-2 M | Baldwin | 35165 | 1910 | 57-26x40x32-448,100 | 91,000 | 1953 | Sold for scrap |
| 201 | 201 | 2-8-8-2 M | Baldwin | 35166 | 1910 | 57-26x40x32-448,100 | 91,000 | 1953 | Sold for scrap |
| 202 | 202 | 2-8-8-2 M | Baldwin | 35167 | 1910 | 57-26x40x32-448,100 | 91,000 | 1953 | Sold for scrap |
| 203 | 203 | 2-8-8-2 M | Baldwin | 35168 | 1910 | 57-26x40x32-448,100 | 91,000 | 1950 | Sold for scrap |
| 204 | 204 | 2-8-8-2 M | Baldwin | 35169 | 1910 | 57-26x40x32-448,100 | 91,000 | 1950 | Sold for scrap |
| 205 | 205 | 2-8-8-2 M | Baldwin | 35170 | 1910 | 57-26x40x32-448,100 | 91,000 | 1950 | Sold for scrap |
| 206 | 206 | 2-8-8-2 M | Baldwin | 35171 | 1910 | 57-26x40x32-448,100 | 91,000 | 1950 | Sold for scrap |
| 207 | 207 | 2-8-8-2 M | Baldwin | 35172 | 1910 | 57-26x40x32-448,100 | 91,000 | | Rebuilt to Single-Expansion 1930 |
| 207* | 207 | 2-8-8-2 MS | Baldwin | 35172 | 1910 | 57-24x32 -494,500 | 110,000 | 1953 | Sold for scrap |
| 208 | 208 | 2-8-8-2 M1 | Baldwin | 43530 | 1916 | 57-26x40x32-448,100 | 91,000 | | Rebuilt to Single-Expansion 1931 |
| 208* | 208 | 2-8-8-2 M1S | Baldwin | 43530 | 1916 | 57-26x40x32-448,100 | 91,000 | 1954 | Sold for scrap |

DM&N No. 305 blasts up Proctor Hill with a string of empties in 1904. Notice the interesting mix of steel and wooden ore cars in the train.

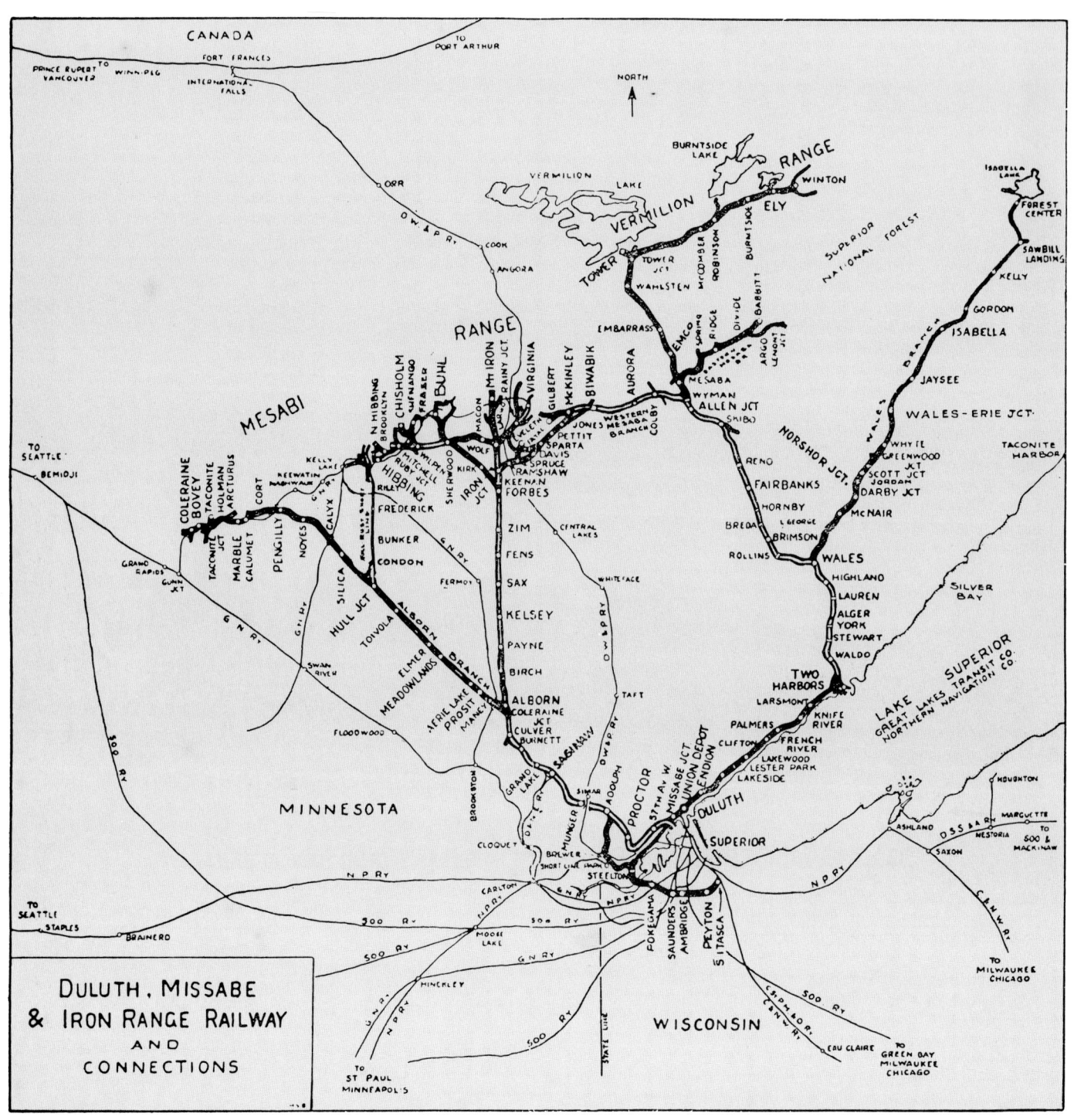

DM&N No. 305 blasts up Proctor Hill with a string of empties in 1904. Notice the interesting mix of steel and wooden ore cars in the train.

Author's collection

| Orig. No. | DM&IR No. | Type & Class | Builder and Construction No. | | Date Built | Dimensions Dr.—Cyls.—Wt. | Tractive Effort | Date Retired | Final Disposition and Remarks |
|---|---|---|---|---|---|---|---|---|---|
| 209 | 209 | 2-8-8-2 M1 | Baldwin | 43531 | | 57-26x40x32-470,000 | 91,000 | | Rebuilt to Single-Expansion 1937 |
| 209* | 209 | 2-8-8-2 M1S | Baldwin | 43531 | 1953 | 57-24x32  -494,450 | 110,000 | 1958 | Sold for scrap |
| 210 | 210 | 2-8-8-2 M2 | Baldwin | 45769 | 1917 | 57-26x40x32-470,000 | 91,000 | | Rebuilt to Single-Expansion 1929 |
| 210* | 210 | 2-8-8-2 M2S | Baldwin | 45769 | 1917 | 57-24x32  -494,450 | 110,000 | 1957 | Sold for scrap |
| 211 | 211 | 2-8-8-2 M2 | Baldwin | 45793 | 1917 | 57-26x40x32-470,000 | 91,000 | | Rebuilt to Single-Expansion 1931 |
| 211* | 211 | 2-8-8-2 M2S | Baldwin | 45793 | 1917 | 57-24x32  -494,450 | 110,000 | 1957 | Sold for scrap |
| 300 | | 2-8-0 C | Pittsburgh | 1525 | 1894 | 50-22x28-160,000 | 36,800 | 1927 | Duluth & Northwestern R.R. 23 |
| 301 | | 2-8-0 C | Pittsburgh | 1563 | 1895 | 50-22x28-160,000 | 36,800 | 1927 | Duluth & Northwestern R.R. 23 |
| 302 | | 2-8-0 C1 | Pittsburgh | 1966 | 1899 | 56-22x28-180,000 | 36,900 | 1933 | American Steel & Wire Co. |
| 303 | | 2-8-0 C1 | Pittsburgh | 2099 | 1900 | 56-22x28-180,000 | 36,900 | 1934 | American Steel & Wire Co. |
| 304 | | 2-8-0 C1 | Dickson | 26342 | 1902 | 56-22x28-180,000 | 36,900 | 1933 | American Steel & Wire Co. |
| 305 | | 2-8-0 C1 | Dickson | 26343 | 1902 | 56-22x28-180,000 | 36,900 | 1933 | American Steel & Wire Co. |
| 306 | 306 | 2-8-0 C1 | Dickson | 26344 | 1902 | 56-22x28-180,000 | 36,900 | 1948 | American Steel & Wire Co. |
| 307 | 307 | 2-8-0 C1 | Cooke | 27063 | 1903 | 56-22x28-180,000 | 36,900 | 1948 | American Steel & Wire Co. |
| 308 | 308 | 2-8-0 C1 | Cooke | 27064 | 1903 | 56-22x28-180,000 | 36,900 | 1948 | American Steel & Wire Co. |
| 309 | | 2-8-0 C1 | Cooke | 27065 | 1903 | 56-22x28-180,000 | 36,900 | 1933 | American Steel & Wire Co. |
| 310 | | 2-8-0 C1 | Cooke | 27066 | 1903 | 56-22x28-180,000 | 36,900 | 1933 | American Steel & Wire Co. |
| 311 | | 2-8-0 C1 | Cooke | 27067 | 1903 | 56-22x28-180,000 | 36,900 | 1933 | American Steel & Wire Co. |
| 312 | | 2-8-0 C1 | Cooke | 27068 | 1903 | 56-22x28-180,000 | 36,900 | 1933 | American Steel & Wire Co. |
| 313 | | 2-8-0 C2 | Pittsburgh | 28897 | 1904 | 56-22x28-180,000 | 37,026 | 1919 | Oliver Iron Mining Co. 513+ |
| 314 | | 2-8-0 C2 | Pittsburgh | 28898 | 1904 | 56-22x28-180,000 | 37,026 | 1919 | Oliver Iron Mining Co. 514+ |
| 315 | | 2-8-0 C2 | Pittsburgh | 28899 | 1904 | 56-22x28-180,000 | 37,026 | 1919 | Oliver Iron Mining Co. 515+ |
| 316 | | 2-8-0 C2 | Pittsburgh | 28900 | 1904 | 56-22x28-180,000 | 37,026 | 1919 | Oliver Iron Mining Co. 516+ |
| 317 | | 2-8-0 C2 | Pittsburgh | 28901 | 1904 | 56-22x28-180,000 | 37,026 | 1919 | Oliver Iron Mining Co. 517+ |
| 318 | | 2-8-0 C2 | Pittsburgh | 28902 | 1904 | 56-22x28-180,000 | 37,026 | 1919 | Oliver Iron Mining Co. 518+ |
| 319 | 319 | 2-8-0 C3 | Pittsburgh | 30730 | 1905 | 56-22x28-180,000 | 39,080 | 1955 | Sold for scrap |
| 320 | | 2-8-0 C3 | Pittsburgh | 30731 | 1905 | 56-22x28-180,000 | 39,080 | 1919 | Oliver Iron Mining Co. 520+ |
| 321 | | 2-8-0 C3 | Pittsburgh | 30732 | 1905 | 56-22x28-185,500 | 39,080 | 1928 | Mpls. Northfield & SO. Ry. 402 |
| 322 | | 2-8-0 C3 | Pittsburgh | 30733 | 1905 | 56-22x28-185,500 | 39,080 | 1919 | Oliver Iron Mining Co. 522+ |
| 323 | | 2-8-0 C3 | Pittsburgh | 30734 | 1905 | 56-22x28-185,500 | 39,080 | 1919 | Oliver Iron Mining Co. 523+ |
| 324 | 324 | 2-8-0 C3 | Pittsburgh | 30735 | 1905 | 56-22x28-185,500 | 39,080 | 1954 | Sold for scrap |
| 325 | 325 | 2-8-0 C3 | Pittsburgh | 31232 | 1905 | 56-22x28-185,500 | 39,080 | 1948 | Sold for scrap |
| 326 | | 2-8-0 C3 | Pittsburgh | 31233 | 1905 | 56-22x28-185,500 | 39,080 | 1928 | Mpls. Northfield & So. Ry. 403 |
| 327 | 327 | 2-8-0 C3 | Pittsburgh | 31334 | 1905 | 56-22x28-185,500 | 39,080 | 1955 | Sold for scrap |
| 328 | | 2-8-0 C3 | Pittsburgh | 31335 | 1905 | 56-22x28-185,500 | 39,080 | 1919 | Oliver Iron Mining Co. 522+ |
| 329 | | 2-8-0 C3 | Pittsburgh | 31236 | 1905 | 56-22x28-185,500 | 39,080 | 1928 | Mpls. Northfield & So. Ry. 404 |
| 330 | 330 | 2-8-0 C3 | Pittsburgh | 31237 | 1905 | 56-22x28-185,500 | 39,080 | 1953 | Sold for scrap |
| 331 | 331 | 2-8-0 C3 | Pittsburgh | 39586 | 1906 | 56-22x28-185,500 | 39,080 | 1955 | Sold for scrap |
| 332 | 332 | 2-8-0 C3 | Pittsburgh | 39587 | 1906 | 56-22x28-185,500 | 39,080 | 1955 | Duluth & Northeastern R.R. 28 On display at RR Museum, Duluth, Minn. |
| 333 | 333 | 2-8-0 C3 | Pittsburgh | 39588 | 1906 | 56-22x28-185,500 | 39,080 | 1950 | Sold for scrap |
| 334 | 334 | 2-8-0 C3 | Pittsburgh | 39589 | 1906 | 56-22x28-185,500 | 39,080 | 1955 | Sold for scrap |
| 335 | 335 | 2-8-0 C3 | Pittsburgh | 39590 | 1906 | 56-22x28-185,500 | 39,080 | 1955 | Sold for scrap |
| 336 | 336 | 2-8-0 C3 | Pittsburgh | 39591 | 1906 | 56-22x28-185,500 | 39,080 | 1954 | Sold for scrap |
| 337 | | 2-8-0 C3 | Pittsburgh | 42275 | 1907 | 56-22x28-185,500 | 39,080 | 1929 | Mpls. Northfield & So. Ry. 405 |
| 338 | 338 | 2-8-0 C3 | Pittsburgh | 42276 | 1907 | 56-22x28-185,500 | 39,080 | 1953 | Sold for scrap |
| 338 | 339 | 2-8-0 C3 | Pittsburgh | 42277 | 1907 | 56-22x28-185,500 | 39,080 | 1955 | Sold for scrap |
| 340 | 340 | 2-8-0 C3 | Pittsburgh | 42278 | 1907 | 56-22x28-185,500 | 39,080 | 1950 | Sold for scrap |
| 341 | 341 | 2-8-0 C3 | Pittsburgh | 42279 | 1907 | 56-22x28-185,500 | 39,080 | 1953 | Sold for scrap |
| 342 | 342 | 2-8-0 C3 | Pittsburgh | 42280 | 1907 | 56-22x28-185,500 | 39,080 | 1955 | Sold for scrap |
| 343 | 343 | 2-8-0 C3 | Pittsburgh | 42281 | 1907 | 56-22x28-185,500 | 39,080 | 1950 | Sold for scrap |
| 344 | | 2-8-0 C3 | Pittsburgh | 42282 | 1907 | 56-22x28-185,500 | 39,080 | 1927 | Mpls. Northfield & So. Ry. 400 |
| 345 | | 2-8-0 C3 | Pittsburgh | 42283 | 1907 | 56-22x28-185,500 | 39,080 | 1927 | Mpls. Northfield & So. Ry. 401 |
| 346 | 346 | 2-8-0 C3 | Pittsburgh | 42284 | 1907 | 56-22x28-185,500 | 39,080 | 1949 | Sold for scrap |
| 347 | 347 | 2-8-0 C3 | Pittsburgh | 42285 | 1907 | 56-22x28-185,500 | 39,080 | 1953 | Presented to Museum of Mining |
| 348 | 348 | 2-8-0 C3 | Pittsburgh | 42286 | 1907 | 56-22x28-185,500 | 39,080 | 1955 | Duluth & Northeastern R.R. 27 On display at Barnum, Minn. |

| Orig. No. | DM&IR No. | Type & Class | Builder and Construction No. | | Date Built | Dimensions Dr.—Cyls.—Wt. | Tractive Effort | Date Retired | Final Disposition and Remarks |
|---|---|---|---|---|---|---|---|---|---|
| 349 | 349 | 2-8-0 C3 | Pittsburgh | 42287 | 1907 | 56-22x28-185,500 | 39,080 | 1953 | Sold for scrap |
| 350 | 350 | 2-8-0 C3 | Pittsburgh | 42288 | 1907 | 56-22x28-185,500 | 39,080 | 1955 | Sold for scrap |
| 400 | 400 | 4-6-2 P | Baldwin | 39877 | 1913 | 69-25x28-245,700 | 38,800 | 1959 | Sold for scrap |
| 401 | 401 | 4-6-2 P | Baldwin | 39878 | 1913 | 69-25x28-245,700 | 38,800 | 1955 | Sold for scrap |
| 402 | 402 | 4-6-2 P | Baldwin | 39879 | 1913 | 69-25x28-245,700 | 38,800 | 1958 | Sold for scrap |
| 500 | 500 | 2-10-2 E | Baldwin | 43409 | 1916 | 60-28x32-346,600 | 71,200 | 1962 | Sold for scrap |
| 501 | 501 | 2-10-2 E | Baldwin | 43410 | 1916 | 60-28x32-346,600 | 71,200 | 1959 | Sold for scrap |
| 502 | 502 | 2-10-2 E | Baldwin | 43411 | 1916 | 60-28x32-346,600 | 71,200 | 1962 | Donated to Mus. of Transportation, St. Louis |
| 503 | 503 | 2-10-2 E | Baldwin | 43412 | 1916 | 60-28x32-346,600 | 71,200 | 1962 | Sold for scrap |
| 504 | 504 | 2-10-2 E | Baldwin | 43501 | 1916 | 60-28x32-346,600 | 71,200 | 1962 | Sold for scrap |
| 505 | 505 | 2-10-2 E | Baldwin | 43502 | 1916 | 60-28x32-346,600 | 71,200 | 1962 | Sold for scrap |
| 506 | 506 | 2-10-2 E1 | Brooks | 60075 | 1919 | 57-27x32-352,000 | 69,600 | 1962 | Donated to National Ry. Mus., Green Bay |
| 507 | 507 | 2-10-2 E1 | Brooks | 60076 | 1919 | 57-27x32-352,000 | 69,600 | 1962 | Sold for scrap |
| 508 | 508 | 2-10-2 E1 | Brooks | 60077 | 1919 | 57-27x32-352,000 | 69,600 | 1959 | Sold for scrap |
| 509 | 509 | 2-10-2 E1 | Brooks | 60078 | 1919 | 57-27x32-352,000 | 69,600 | 1962 | Sold for scrap |
| 510 | 510 | 2-10-2 E1 | Brooks | 60079 | 1919 | 57-27x32-352,000 | 69,600 | 1963 | Sold for scrap |
| 511 | 511 | 2-10-2 E1 | Brooks | 60080 | 1919 | 57-27x32-352,000 | 69,600 | 1959 | Sold for scrap |
| 512 | 512 | 2-10-2 E1 | Brooks | 60081 | 1919 | 57-27x32-352,000 | 69,600 | 1962 | Sold for scrap |
| 513 | 513 | 2-10-2 E1 | Brooks | 60082 | 1919 | 57-27x32-352,000 | 69,600 | 1962 | Sold for scrap |
| 514 | 514 | 2-10-2 E1 | Brooks | 60083 | 1919 | 57-27x32-352,000 | 69,600 | 1962 | Sold for scrap |
| 515 | 515 | 2-10-2 E1 | Brooks | 60084 | 1919 | 57-27x32-352,000 | 69,600 | 1959 | Sold for scrap |

\* —As Rebuilt  
‡ —92,100 lbs. Tractive Effort with Tender Booster  
+ —Converted to 0-8-0 type by Oliver Iron Mining Co.

## STEAM LOCOMOTIVES: DULUTH, MISSABE & IRON RANGE RAILWAY

| Orig. No. | Type & Class | Builder and Construction No. | | Date Built | Date Acq. | Dimensions Dr.—Cyls.—Wt. | Tractive Effort | Date Retired | Final Disposition and Remarks |
|---|---|---|---|---|---|---|---|---|---|
| 220 | 2-8-8-4 M3 | Baldwin | 62526 | 1941 | | 63-26x32-695,040 | 140,000 | 1962 | Sold for scrap |
| 221 | 2-8-8-4 M3 | Baldwin | 62527 | 1941 | | 63-26x32-695,040 | 140,000 | 1963 | Sold for scrap |
| 222 | 2-8-8-4 M3 | Baldwin | 62528 | 1941 | | 63-26x32-695,040 | 140,000 | 1962 | Sold for scrap |
| 223 | 2-8-8-4 M3 | Baldwin | 62529 | 1941 | | 63-26x32-695,040 | 140,000 | 1962 | Sold for scrap |
| 224 | 2-8-8-4 M3 | Baldwin | 62530 | 1941 | | 63-26x32-695,040 | 140,000 | 1962 | Sold for scrap |
| 225 | 2-8-8-4 M3 | Baldwin | 62531 | 1941 | | 63-26x32-695,040 | 140,000 | 1963 | Donated to Proctor Dev. Council |
| 226 | 2-8-8-4 M3 | Baldwin | 62532 | 1941 | | 63-26x32-695,040 | 140,000 | 1962 | Sold for scrap |
| 227 | 2-8-8-4 M3 | Baldwin | 62533 | 1941 | | 63-26x32-695,040 | 140,000 | | On display at RR Museum, Duluth, Minn. |
| 228 | 2-8-8-4 M4 | Baldwin | 64707 | 1943 | | 63-26x32-699,700 | 140,000 | 1962 | Sold for scrap |
| 229 | 2-8-8-4 M4 | Baldwin | 64708 | 1943 | | 63-26x32-699,700 | 140,000 | 1967 | Lake Co. Hist. Soc., Two Harbors |
| 230 | 2-8-8-4 M4 | Baldwin | 64709 | 1943 | | 63-26x32-699,700 | 140,000 | 1962 | Sold for scrap |
| 231 | 2-8-8-4 M4 | Baldwin | 64710 | 1943 | | 63-26x32-699,700 | 140,000 | 1962 | Sold for scrap |

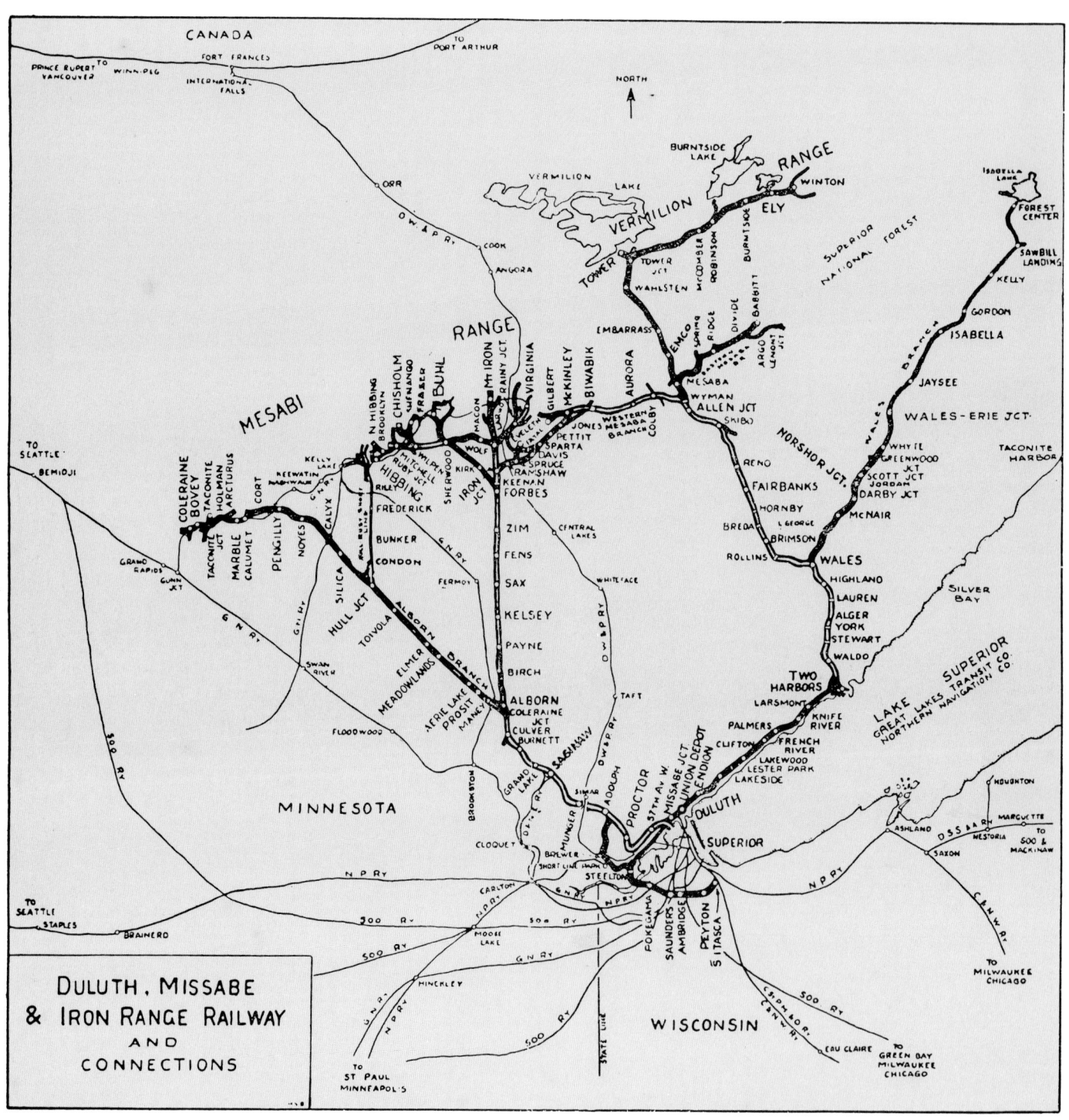

| Orig. No. | Type & Class | | Builder and Type | | Constr. No. | Date Built | Dimensions Dr.—Wt.—H.P. | Tractive Effort | Date Retired | Final Disposition and Remarks |
|---|---|---|---|---|---|---|---|---|---|---|
| 232 | 2-8-8-4 | M4 | Baldwin | 64711 | 1943 | | 63-26x32-699,700 | 140,000 | 1962 | Sold for scrap |
| 233 | 2-8-8-4 | M4 | Baldwin | 64712 | 1943 | | 63-26x32-699,700 | 140,000 | 1962 | Sold for scrap |
| 234 | 2-8-8-4 | M4 | Baldwin | 64713 | 1943 | | 63-26x32-699,700 | 140,000 | 1962 | Sold for scrap |
| 235 | 2-8-8-4 | M4 | Baldwin | 64714 | 1943 | | 63-26x32-699,700 | 140,000 | 1962 | Sold for scrap |
| 236 | 2-8-8-4 | M4 | Baldwin | 64715 | 1943 | | 63-26x32-699,700 | 140,000 | 1962 | Sold for scrap |
| 237 | 2-8-8-4 | M4 | Baldwin | 64716 | 1943 | | 63-26x32-699,700 | 140,000 | 1958 | Sold for scrap (Damaged in wreck) |
| 601 | 0-10-2 | S7 | Baldwin | 61907 | 1936 | 1949 | 61-28x32-422,000 | 90,900 | 1959 | Ex Union R.R. 301 — Scrapped |
| 602 | 0-10-2 | S7 | Baldwin | 61908 | 1936 | 1949 | 61-28x32-422,000 | 90,900 | 1958 | Ex Union R.R. 302 — Scrapped |
| 603 | 0-10-2 | S7 | Baldwin | 61909 | 1936 | 1949 | 61-28x32-422,000 | 90,900 | 1961 | Ex Union R.R. 303 — Returned to Union R.R. for display |
| 604 | 0-10-2 | S7 | Baldwin | 61910 | 1936 | 1949 | 61-28x32-422,000 | 90,900 | 1963 | Ex Union R.R. 304 — Scrapped |
| 605 | 0-10-2 | S7 | Baldwin | 61911 | 1936 | 1949 | 61-28x32-422,000 | 90,900 | 1958 | Ex Union R.R. 305 — Scrapped |
| 606 | 0-10-2 | S7 | Baldwin | 62059 | 1937 | 1949 | 61-28x32-422,000 | 90,900 | 1959 | Ex Union R.R. 306 — Scrapped |
| 607 | 0-10-2 | S7 | Baldwin | 62060 | 1937 | 1949 | 61-28x32-422,000 | 90,900 | 1958 | Ex Union R.R. 307 — Scrapped |
| 608 | 0-10-2 | S7 | Baldwin | 62061 | 1937 | 1949 | 61-28x32-422,000 | 90,900 | 1959 | Ex Union R.R. 308 — Scrapped |
| 609 | 0-10-2 | S7 | Baldwin | 62062 | 1937 | 1949 | 61-28x32-422,000 | 90,900 | 1959 | Ex Union R.R. 309 — Scrapped |
| 700 | 2-10-4 | E4 | Alco | 68891 | 1937 | 1951 | 64-31x32-520,000 | 96,700 | 1961 | Ex B&LE 621 — Scrapped |
| 701 | 2-10-4 | E4 | Alco | 68892 | 1937 | 1951 | 64-31x32-520,000 | 96,700 | 1961 | Ex B&LE 622 — Scrapped |
| 702 | 2-10-4 | E4 | Alco | 68893 | 1937 | 1951 | 64-31x32-520,000 | 96,700 | 1961 | Ex B&LE 623 — Scrapped |
| 703 | 2-10-4 | E4 | Alco | 68894 | 1937 | 1951 | 64-31x32-520,000 | 96,700 | 1961 | Ex B&LE 624 — Scrapped |
| 704 | 2-10-4 | E4 | Alco | 68895 | 1937 | 1951 | 64-31x32-520,000 | 96,700 | 1961 | Ex B&LE 625 — Scrapped |
| 705 | 2-10-4 | E4 | Alco | 68896 | 1937 | 1951 | 64-31x32-520,000 | 96,700 | 1961 | Ex B&LE 626 — Scrapped |
| 706 | 2-10-4 | E4 | Alco | 68897 | 1937 | 1951 | 64-31x32-520,000 | 96,700 | 1961 | Ex B&LE 627 — Scrapped |
| 707 | 2-10-4 | E4 | Alco | 68898 | 1937 | 1951 | 64-31x32-520,000 | 96,700 | 1961 | Ex B&LE 628 — Scrapped |
| 708 | 2-10-4 | E4 | Alco | 68899 | 1937 | 1951 | 64-31x32-520,000 | 96,700 | 1961 | Ex B&LE 629 — Scrapped |
| 709 | 2-10-4 | E4 | Alco | 68900 | 1937 | 1951 | 64-31x32-520,000 | 96,700 | 1961 | Ex B&LE 630 — Scrapped |
| 710 | 2-10-4 | E5 | Baldwin | 64150 | 1941 | 1951 | 64-31x32-519,740 | 96,700 | 1961 | Ex B&LE 631 — Scrapped |
| 711 | 2-10-4 | E5 | Baldwin | 64154 | 1941 | 1951 | 64-31x32-519,740 | 96,700 | 1961 | Ex B&LE 635 — Scrapped |
| 712 | 2-10-4 | E6 | Baldwin | 64578 | 1942 | 1951 | 64-31x32-524,382 | 90,900 | 1961 | Ex B&LE 637 — Scrapped |
| 713 | 2-10-4 | E7 | Baldwin | 64718 | 1943 | 1951 | 64-31x32-523,600 | 90,900 | 1961 | Ex B&LE 638 — Scrapped |
| 714 | 2-10-4 | E7 | Baldwin | 64721 | 1943 | 1951 | 64-31x32-523,600 | 90,900 | 1961 | Ex B&LE 641 — Scrapped |
| 715 | 2-10-4 | E7 | Baldwin | 70059 | 1943 | 1951 | 64-31x32-523,600 | 90,900 | 1961 | Ex B&LE 645 — Scrapped |
| 716 | 2-10-4 | E7 | Baldwin | 70060 | 1943 | 1951 | 64-31x32-523,600 | 90,900 | 1961 | Ex B&LE 646 — Scrapped |
| 717 | 2-10-4 | E7 | Baldwin | 70061 | 1943 | 1951 | 64-31x32-523,600 | 90,900 | 1961 | Ex B&LE 647 — Scrapped |
| 1312 | 2-8-2 | N4 | Alco | 64742 | 1923 | 1948 | 63-28x30-333,000 | 63,467 | 1958 | Ex EJ&E 746 — Scrapped |
| 1313 | 2-8-2 | N4 | Alco | 64743 | 1923 | 1948 | 63-28x30-333,000 | 63,467 | 1961 | Ex EJ&E 747 — Scrapped |
| 1314 | 2-8-2 | N4 | Alco | 64744 | 1923 | 1948 | 63-28x30-333,000 | 63,467 | 1961 | Ex EJ&E 748 — Scrapped |
| 1315 | 2-8-2 | N4 | Alco | 64745 | 1923 | 1948 | 63-28x30-333,000 | 63,467 | 1958 | Ex EJ&E 749 — Scrapped |
| 1316 | 2-8-2 | N4 | Alco | 64746 | 1923 | 1948 | 63-28x30-333,000 | 63,467 | 1959 | Ex EJ&E 750 — Scrapped |
| 1317 | 2-8-2 | N4 | Alco | 64747 | 1923 | 1948 | 63-28x30-333,000 | 63,467 | 1959 | Ex EJ&E 751 — Scrapped |
| 1318 | 2-8-2 | N4 | Alco | 64748 | 1923 | 1948 | 63-28x30-333,000 | 63,467 | 1959 | Ex EJ&E 752 — Scrapped |
| 1319 | 2-8-2 | N4 | Alco | 64749 | 1923 | 1948 | 63-28x30-333,000 | 63,467 | 1959 | Ex EJ&E 753 — Scrapped |
| 1320 | 2-8-2 | N4 | Alco | 64750 | 1923 | 1948 | 63-28x30-333,000 | 63,467 | 1958 | Ex EJ&E 754 — Scrapped |
| 1321 | 2-8-2 | N4 | Alco | 64751 | 1923 | 1948 | 63-28x30-333,000 | 63,467 | 1959 | Ex EJ&E 755 — Scrapped |
| 1322 | 2-8-2 | N5 | Lima | 6695 | 1923 | 1948 | 63-28x30-333,000 | 63,467 | 1958 | Ex EJ&E 756 — Scrapped |
| 1323 | 2-8-2 | N5 | Lima | 6695 | 1923 | 1948 | 63-28x30-333,000 | 63,467 | 1961 | Ex EJ&E 757 — Scrapped |
| 1324 | 2-8-2 | N5 | Lima | 6695 | 1923 | 1948 | 63-28x30-333,000 | 63,467 | 1959 | Ex EJ&E 758 — Scrapped |
| 1325 | 2-8-2 | N5 | Lima | 6695 | 1923 | 1948 | 63-28x30-333,000 | 63,467 | 1958 | Ex EJ&E 759 — Scrapped |
| 1326 | 2-8-2 | N6 | Baldwin | 61076 | 1929 | 1948 | 63-28x30-333,000 | 63,467 | 1958 | Ex EJ&E 761 — Scrapped |
| 1327 | 2-8-2 | N6 | Baldwin | 61077 | 1929 | 1948 | 63-28x30-333,460 | 63,467 | 1961 | Ex EJ&E 762 — Scrapped |
| 1328 | 2-8-2 | N6 | Baldwin | 61078 | 1929 | 1948 | 63-28x30-333,460 | 63,467 | 1958 | Ex EJ&E 763 — Scrapped |
| 1329 | 2-8-2 | N6 | Baldwin | 61079 | 1929 | 1948 | 63-28x30-333,460 | 63,467 | 1958 | Ex EJ&E 764 — Scrapped |
| 1330 | 2-8-2 | N6 | Baldwin | 61080 | 1929 | 1948 | 63-28x30-333,460 | 63,467 | 1962 | Ex EJ&E 765 — At Gary, Indiana |
| 1331 | 2-8-2 | N6 | Baldwin | 61081 | 1929 | 1948 | 63-28x30-333,460 | 63,467 | 1959 | Ex EJ&E 766 — Scrapped |
| 1332 | 2-8-2 | N6 | Baldwin | 61372 | 1930 | 1948 | 63-28x30-333,460 | 63,467 | 1958 | Ex EJ&E 767 — Scrapped |
| 1333 | 2-8-2 | N6 | Baldwin | 61373 | 1930 | 1948 | 63-28x30-333,460 | 63,467 | 1959 | Ex EJ&E 768 — Scrapped |
| 1334 | 2-8-2 | N6 | Baldwin | 61374 | 1930 | 1948 | 63-28x30-333,460 | 63,467 | 1958 | Ex EJ&E 769 — Scrapped |
| 1335 | 2-8-2 | N6 | Baldwin | 61375 | 1930 | 1948 | 63-28x30-333,460 | 63,467 | 1958 | Ex EJ&E 770 — Scrapped |
| 1336 | 2-8-2 | N6 | Baldwin | 61378 | 1930 | 1948 | 63-28x30-333,460 | 63,467 | 1959 | Ex EJ&E 773 — Scrapped |
| 1337 | 2-8-2 | N6 | Baldwin | 61379 | 1930 | 1948 | 63-28x30-333,460 | 63,467 | 1958 | Ex EJ&E 774 — Scrapped |

Bruce E. Meyer

## DIESEL LOCOMOTIVES: DULUTH, MISSABE & IRON RANGE RAILWAY

| Orig. No. | Type & Class | | Builder and Type | | Constr. No. | Date Built | Dimensions Dr.—Wt.—H.P. | Tractive Effort | Date Retired | Final Disposition and Remarks |
|---|---|---|---|---|---|---|---|---|---|---|
| 11 | B-B | DS-1 | Electro-Motive | SW-9 | 17870 | 1953 | 40-246,660-1,200 | 62,000 | 1958 | Electro-Motive |
| 12 | B-B | DS-1 | Electro-Motive | SW-9 | 17871 | 1953 | 40-246,660-1,200 | 62,000 | 1960 | Electro-Motive |
| 13 | B-B | DS-1 | Electro-Motive | SW-9 | 17872 | 1953 | 40-246,660-1,200 | 62,000 | 1963 | Union R.R. |
| 14 | B-B | DS-1 | Electro-Motive | SW-9 | 17873 | 1953 | 40-246,660-1,200 | 62,000 | 1958 | Electro-Motive |
| 15 | B-B | DS-1 | Electro-Motive | SW-9 | 17874 | 1953 | 40-246,660-1,200 | 62,000 | 1963 | Union R.R. |
| 16 | B-B | DS-1 | Electro-Motive | SW-9 | 17875 | 1953 | 40-246,660-1,200 | 62,000 | 1963 | Union R.R. |
| 17 | B-B | DS-1 | Electro-Motive | SW-9 | 17876 | 1953 | 40-246,660-1,200 | 62,000 | 1960 | Electro-Motive |
| 18 | B-B | DS-1 | Electro-Motive | SW-9 | 17877 | 1953 | 40-246,660-1,200 | 62,000 | 1960 | Electro-Motive |
| 19 | B-B | DS-1 | Electro-Motive | SW-9 | 17878 | 1953 | 40-246,660-1,200 | 62,000 | 1963 | Union R.R. |
| 20 | B-B | DS-1 | Electro-Motive | SW-9 | 17879 | 1953 | 40-246,660-1,200 | 62,000 | 1960 | Electro-Motive |
| 21 | B-B | DS-1 | Electro-Motive | SW-9 | 17880 | 1953 | 40-246,660-1,200 | 62,000 | 1960 | Electro-Motive |
| 22 | B-B | DS-1 | Electro-Motive | SW-9 | 17881 | 1953 | 40-246,660-1,200 | 62,000 | 1960 | Electro-Motive |
| 23 | B-B | DS-1 | Electro-Motive | SW-9 | 17882 | 1953 | 40-246,660-1,200 | 62,000 | 1963 | Union R.R. |
| 24 | B-B | DS-1 | Electro-Motive | SW-9 | 17883 | 1953 | 40-246,660-1,200 | 62,000 | 1962 | Chicago Short Line |
| 25 | B-B | DS-1 | Electro-Motive | SW-9 | 17884 | 1953 | 40-246,660-1,200 | 62,000 | 1962 | Chicago Short Line |
| 50 | C-C | RS-5 | Alco | DL-600-B | 81756 | 1959 | 40-387,000-2,400 | 96,750 | 1964 | Bessemer & Lake Erie 881 to Cartier |
| 51 | C-C | RS-5 | Alco | DL-600-B | 81757 | 1959 | 40-387,000-2,400 | 96,750 | 1964 | Bessemer & Lake Erie 882 to Cartier |
| 52 | C-C | RS-5 | Alco | DL-600-B | 81758 | 1959 | 40-387,000-2,400 | 96,750 | 1964 | Bessemer & Lake Erie 883 to Cartier |
| 53 | C-C | RS-5 | Alco | DL-600-B | 81759 | 1959 | 40-387,000-2,400 | 96,750 | 1964 | Bessemer & Lake Erie 884 to Cartier |
| 54 | C-C | RS-5 | Alco | DL-600-B | 81760 | 1959 | 40-387,000-2,400 | 96,750 | 1964 | Bessemer & Lake Erie 885 to Cartier |
| 55 | C-C | RS-5 | Alco | DL-600-B | 81761 | 1959 | 40-387,000-2,400 | 96,750 | 1964 | Bessemer & Lake Erie 886 to Cartier |
| 101 | C-C | RS-1 | Electro-Motive | SD-9-R | 21727 | 1956 | 40-387,000-1,750 | 96,750 | 1965 | Bessemer & Lake Erie 826 |
| 102 | C-C | RS-1 | Electro-Motive | SD-9-R | 21728 | 1956 | 40-387,000-1,750 | 96,750 | 1965 | Bessemer & Lake Erie 827 |
| 103 | C-C | RS-1 | Electro-Motive | SD-9-R | 21729 | 1956 | 40-387,000-1,750 | 96,750 | 1965 | Bessemer & Lake Erie 828 |
| 104 | C-C | RS-1 | Electro-Motive | SD-9-R | 21730 | 1956 | 40-387,000-1,750 | 96,750 | 1965 | Bessemer & Lake Erie 829 |
| 105 | C-C | RS-1 | Electro-Motive | SD-9-R | 21731 | 1956 | 40-387,000-1,750 | 96,750 | 1965 | Leased to Elgin, Joliet & Eastern |
| 106 | C-C | RS-1 | Electro-Motive | SD-9-R | 21732 | 1956 | 40-387,000-1,750 | 96,750 | 1965 | Leased to Bessemer & Lake Erie 826 |
| 107 | C-C | RS-1 | Electro-Motive | SD-9-R | 21733 | 1956 | 40-387,000-1,750 | 96,750 | 1965 | Leased to Bessemer & Lake Erie 830 |
| 108 | C-C | RS-1 | Electro-Motive | SD-9-R | 21734 | 1956 | 40-387,000-1,750 | 96,750 | 1965 | Leased to Elgin, Joliet & Eastern |
| 109 | C-C | RS-1 | Electro-Motive | SD-9-R | 21735 | 1956 | 40-387,000-1,750 | 96,750 | 1965 | Leased to Elgin, Joliet & Eastern |
| 110 | C-C | RS-1 | Electro-Motive | SD-9-R | 20655 | 1955 | 40-387,000-1,750 | 96,750 | 1967 | Leased to B&LE 831 |
| 111 | C-C | RS-2 | Electro-Motive | SD-9-R | 23099 | 1957 | 40-387,000-1,750 | 96,750 | | |
| 112 | C-C | RS-2 | Electro-Motive | SD-9-R | 23100 | 1957 | 40-387,000-1,750 | 96,750 | | |
| 113 | C-C | RS-2 | Electro-Motive | SD-9-R | 23101 | 1957 | 40-387,000-1,750 | 96,750 | 1968 | Leased to B&LE 833 |
| 114 | C-C | RS-2 | Electro-Motive | SD-9-R | 23102 | 1957 | 40-387,000-1,750 | 96,750 | 1968 | Leased to B&LE 834 |
| 115 | C-C | RS-2 | Electro-Motive | SD-9-R | 23103 | 1957 | 40-387,000-1,750 | 96,750 | | |
| 116 | C-C | RS-2 | Electro-Motive | SD-9-R | 23104 | 1957 | 40-387,000-1,750 | 96,750 | | |
| 117 | C-C | RS-2 | Electro-Motive | SD-9-R | 23105 | 1957 | 40-387,000-1,750 | 96,750 | | |
| 118 | C-C | RS-2 | Electro-Motive | SD-9-R | 23106 | 1957 | 40-387,000-1,750 | 96,750 | | |
| 119 | C-C | RS-2 | Electro-Motive | SD-9-R | 23107 | 1957 | 40-387,000-1,750 | 96,750 | | |
| 120 | C-C | RS-2 | Electro-Motive | SD-9-R | 23108 | 1957 | 40-387,000-1,750 | 96,750 | 1972 | |
| 121 | C-C | RS-2 | Electro-Motive | SD-9-R | 23109 | 1957 | 40-387,000-1,750 | 96,750 | 1972 | Leased to EJ&E |
| 122 | C-C | RS-2 | Electro-Motive | SD-9-R | 23110 | 1957 | 40-387,000-1,750 | 96,750 | 1972 | Leased to B&LE |
| 123 | C-C | RS-2 | Electro-Motive | SD-9-R | 23119 | 1957 | 40-387,000-1,750 | 96,750 | 1972 | Leased to B&LE |
| 124 | C-C | RS-2 | Electro-Motive | SD-9-R | 23112 | 1957 | 40-387,000-1,750 | 96,750 | 1972 | |
| 125 | C-C | RS-2 | Electro-Motive | SD-9-R | 23108 | 1957 | 40-387,000-1,750 | 96,750 | | |
| 126 | C-C | RS-2 | Electro-Motive | SD-9-R | 23108 | 1957 | 40-387,000-1,750 | 96,750 | | |
| 127 | C-C | RS-2 | Electro-Motive | SD-9-R | 23108 | 1957 | 40-387,000-1,750 | 96,750 | 1968 | Leased to EJ&E |
| 128 | C-C | RS-2 | Electro-Motive | SD-9-R | 23108 | 1957 | 40-387,000-1,750 | 96,750 | | |
| 129 | C-C | RS-2 | Electro-Motive | SD-9-R | 23108 | 1957 | 40-387,000-1,750 | 96,750 | | Equipped with Steam Boiler |
| 130 | C-C | RS-2 | Electro-Motive | SD-9-R | 23118 | 1957 | 40-387,000-1,750 | 96,750 | | Equipped with steam boiler |
| 131 | C-C | RS-3 | Electro-Motive | SD-9-R | 23911 | 1958 | 40-387,000-1,750 | 96,750 | 1971 | Leased to Bessemer & Lake Erie |
| 132 | C-C | RS-3 | Electro-Motive | SD-9-R | 23912 | 1958 | 40-387,000-1,750 | 96,750 | | |
| 133 | C-C | RS-3 | Electro-Motive | SD-9-R | 23913 | 1958 | 40-387,000-1,750 | 96,750 | 1971 | Leased to EJ&E |
| 134 | C-C | RS-3 | Electro-Motive | SD-9-R | 23914 | 1958 | 40-387,000-1,750 | 96,750 | | |

## DIESEL LOCOMOTIVES: DULUTH, MISSABE & IRON RANGE RAILWAY

| Orig. No. | Type & Class | | Builder and Type | | Constr. No. | Date Built | Dimensions Dr.—Wt.—H.P. | Tractive Effort | Date Retired | Final Disposition and Remarks |
|---|---|---|---|---|---|---|---|---|---|---|
| 135 | C-C | RS-3 | Electro-Motive | SD-9-R | 23915 | 1958 | 40-387,000-1,750 | 96,750 | 1971 | Leased to EJ&E |
| 136 | C-C | RS-3 | Electro-Motive | SD-9-R | 23916 | 1958 | 40-387,000-1,750 | 96,750 | 1964 | Bessemer & Lake Erie 821 |
| 137 | C-C | RS-3 | Electro-Motive | SD-9-R | 23917 | 1958 | 40-387,000-1,750 | 96,750 | | Leased to Bessemer & Lake Erie |
| 138 | C-C | RS-3 | Electro-Motive | SD-9-R | 23918 | 1958 | 40-387,000-1,750 | 96,750 | | |
| 139 | C-C | RS-3 | Electro-Motive | SD-9-R | 23919 | 1958 | 40-387,000-1,750 | 96,750 | | |
| 140 | C-C | RS-3 | Electro-Motive | SD-9-R | 23920 | 1958 | 40-387,000-1,750 | 96,750 | 1964 | Bessemer & Lake Erie 822 |
| 141 | C-C | RS-3 | Electro-Motive | SD-9-R | 23921 | 1958 | 40-387,000-1,750 | 96,750 | 1964 | Bessemer & Lake Erie 823 |
| 142 | C-C | RS-3 | Electro-Motive | SD-9-R | 23922 | 1958 | 40-387,000-1,750 | 96,750 | | |
| 143 | C-C | RS-3 | Electro-Motive | SD-9-R | 23923 | 1958 | 40-387,000-1,750 | 96,750 | | |
| 144 | C-C | RS-3 | Electro-Motive | SD-9-R | 23924 | 1958 | 40-387,000-1,750 | 96,750 | | |
| 145 | C-C | RS-3 | Electro-Motive | SD-9-R | 23925 | 1958 | 40-387,000-1,750 | 96,750 | | |
| 146 | C-C | RS-3 | Electro-Motive | SD-9-R | 23926 | 1958 | 40-387,000-1,750 | 96,750 | 1964 | Bessemer & Lake Erie 824 |
| 147 | C-C | RS-3 | Electro-Motive | SD-9-R | 23927 | 1958 | 40-387,000-1,750 | 96,750 | | Leased to EJ&E |
| 148 | C-C | RS-3 | Electro-Motive | SD-9-R | 23928 | 1958 | 40-387,000-1,750 | 96,750 | 1964 | Bessemer & Lake Erie 825 |
| 149 | C-C | RS-3 | Electro-Motive | SD-9-R | 23929 | 1958 | 40-387,000-1,750 | 96,750 | | |
| 150 | C-C | RS-3 | Electro-Motive | SD-9-R | 23930 | 1958 | 40-387,000-1,750 | 96,750 | | |
| 151 | C-C | RS-3 | Electro-Motive | SD-9-R | 23931 | 1958 | 40-387,000-1,750 | 96,750 | 1971 | Leased to Bessemer & Lake Erie |
| 152 | C-C | RS-3 | Electro-Motive | SD-9-R | 23932 | 1958 | 40-387,000-1,750 | 96,750 | | |
| 153 | C-C | RS-3 | Electro-Motive | SD-9-R | 23933 | 1958 | 40-387,000-1,750 | 96,750 | | Leased to EJ&E |
| 154 | C-C | RS-3 | Electro-Motive | SD-9-R | 23934 | 1958 | 40-387,000-1,750 | 96,750 | 1971 | |
| 155 | C-C | RS-3 | Electro-Motive | SD-9-R | 23935 | 1958 | 40-387,000-1,750 | 96,750 | | |
| 156 | C-C | RS-3 | Electro-Motive | SD-9-R | 23936 | 1958 | 40-387,000-1,750 | 96,750 | | Leased to EJ&E |
| 157 | C-C | RS-3 | Electro-Motive | SD-9-R | 23937 | 1958 | 40-387,000-1,750 | 96,750 | | Leased to EJ&E |
| 158 | C-C | RS-3 | Electro-Motive | SD-9-R | 24487 | 1958 | 40-387,000-1,750 | 96,750 | | Leased to EJ&E |
| 159 | C-C | RS-4 | Electro-Motive | SD-9 | 25259 | 1959 | 40-387,000-1,750 | 96,750 | | Leased to EJ&E |
| 160 | C-C | RS-4 | Electro-Motive | SD-9 | 25260 | 1959 | 40-387,000-1,750 | 96,750 | 1980 | Rebuilt DM&IR — Renumbered 302 |
| 161 | C-C | RS-4 | Electro-Motive | SD-9 | 25261 | 1959 | 40-387,000-1,750 | 96,750 | | |
| 162 | C-C | RS-4 | Electro-Motive | SD-9 | 25262 | 1959 | 40-387,000-1,750 | 96,750 | | |
| 163 | C-C | RS-4 | Electro-Motive | SD-9 | 25263 | 1959 | 40-387,000-1,750 | 96,750 | | Converted to Low Hood — 1972 |
| 164 | C-C | RS-4 | Electro-Motive | SD-9 | 25264 | 1959 | 40-387,000-1,750 | 96,750 | | |
| 165 | C-C | RS-4 | Electro-Motive | SD-9 | 25265 | 1959 | 40-387,000-1,750 | 96,750 | | |
| 166 | C-C | RS-4 | Electro-Motive | SD-9 | 25266 | 1959 | 40-387,000-1,750 | 96,750 | | |
| 167 | C-C | RS-4 | Electro-Motive | SD-9 | 25267 | 1959 | 40-387,000-1,750 | 96,750 | | |
| 168 | C-C | RS-4 | Electro-Motive | SD-9 | 25268 | 1959 | 40-387,000-1,750 | 96,750 | | |
| 169 | C-C | RS-4 | Electro-Motive | SD-9 | 25269 | 1959 | 40-387,000-1,750 | 96,750 | | |
| 170 | C-C | RS-4 | Electro-Motive | SD-9 | 25270 | 1959 | 40-387,000-1,750 | 96,750 | | |
| 171 | C-C | RS-4 | Electro-Motive | SD-9 | 25271 | 1959 | 40-387,000-1,750 | 96,750 | | |
| 172 | C-C | RS-4 | Electro-Motive | SD-9 | 25272 | 1959 | 40-387,000-1,750 | 96,750 | | |
| 173 | C-C | RS-4 | Electro-Motive | SD-9 | 25273 | 1959 | 40-387,000-1,750 | 96,750 | | |
| 174 | C-C | RS-4 | Electro-Motive | SD-9 | 25274 | 1959 | 40-387,000-1,750 | 96,750 | 1979 | Rebuilt DM&IR — Renumbered 301 |
| 175 | C-C | RS-6 | Electro-Motive | SD-18 | 25779 | 1960 | 40-387,000-1,800 | 96,750 | | |
| 176 | C-C | RS-6 | Electro-Motive | SD-18 | 25780 | 1960 | 40-387,000-1,800 | 96,750 | | |
| 177 | C-C | RS-6 | Electro-Motive | SD-18 | 25781 | 1960 | 40-387,000-1,800 | 96,750 | | |
| 178 | C-C | RS-6 | Electro-Motive | SD-18 | 25782 | 1960 | 40-387,000-1,800 | 96,750 | | |
| 179 | C-C | RS-6 | Electro-Motive | SD-18 | 25783 | 1960 | 40-387,000-1,800 | 96,750 | | |
| 180 | C-C | RS-6 | Electro-Motive | SD-18 | 25784 | 1960 | 40-387,000-1,800 | 96,750 | | |
| 181 | C-C | RS-6 | Electro-Motive | SD-18 | 25785 | 1960 | 40-387,000-1,800 | 96,750 | | |
| 182 | C-C | RS-6 | Electro-Motive | SD-18 | 25786 | 1960 | 40-387,000-1,800 | 96,750 | | |
| 183 | C-C | RS-6 | Electro-Motive | SD-18 | 25787 | 1960 | 40-387,000-1,800 | 96,750 | | |
| 184 | C-C | RS-6 | Electro-Motive | SD-18 | 25788 | 1960 | 40-387,000-1,800 | 96,750 | | |
| 185 | C-C | RS-6 | Electro-Motive | SD-18 | 25789 | 1960 | 40-387,000-1,800 | 96,750 | | |
| 186 | C-C | RS-6 | Electro-Motive | SD-18 | 25790 | 1960 | 40-387,000-1,800 | 96,750 | | Converted to Low Hood — 1971 |
| 187 | C-C | RS-6 | Electro-Motive | SD-18 | 25791 | 1960 | 40-387,000-1,800 | 96,750 | | |
| 188 | C-C | RS-6 | Electro-Motive | SD-18 | 25792 | 1960 | 40-387,000-1,800 | 96,750 | | |
| 189 | C-C | RS-6 | Electro-Motive | SD-18 | 25793 | 1960 | 40-387,000-1,800 | 96,750 | | |
| 190 | C-C | RS-6 | Electro-Motive | SD-18 | 25794 | 1960 | 40-387,000-1,800 | 96,750 | | |

## DIESEL LOCOMOTIVES: DULUTH, MISSABE & IRON RANGE RAILWAY

| Orig. No. | Type & Class | | Builder and Type | | Constr. No. | Date Built | Dimensions Dr.—Wt.—H.P. | Tractive Effort | Date Retired | Final Disposition and Remarks |
|---|---|---|---|---|---|---|---|---|---|---|
| 191 | C-C | RS-6 | Electro-Motive | SD-18 | 25795 | 1960 | 40-387,000-1,800 | 96,750 | | |
| 192 | C-C | RS-6 | Electro-Motive | SD-18 | 25796 | 1960 | 40-387,000-1,800 | 96,750 | | |
| 193 | C-C | RS-6 | Electro-Motive | SD-18 | 25797 | 1960 | 40-387,000-1,800 | 96,750 | | |
| 201 | C-C | RS-7 | Electro-Motive | SD-38 | 37069 | 1971 | 40-387,000-2,000 | 96,750 | | |
| 202 | C-C | RS-7 | Electro-Motive | SD-38 | 37070 | 1971 | 40-387,000-2,000 | 96,750 | | |
| 203 | C-C | RS-7 | Electro-Motive | SD-38 | 37071 | 1971 | 40-387,000-2,000 | 96,750 | | |
| 204 | C-C | RS-7 | Electro-Motive | SD-38 | 37072 | 1971 | 40-387,000-2,000 | 96,750 | | |
| 205 | C-C | RS-7 | Electro-Motive | SD-38 | 37073 | 1971 | 40-387,000-2,000 | 96,750 | | |
| 206 | C-C | RS-7 | Electro-Motive | SD-38 | 37074 | 1971 | 40-387,000-2,000 | 96,750 | | |
| 207 | C-C | RS-7 | Electro-Motive | SD-38 | 37075 | 1971 | 40-387,000-2,000 | 96,750 | | |
| 208 | C-C | RS-7 | Electro-Motive | SD-38 | 37076 | 1971 | 40-387,000-2,000 | 96,750 | | |
| 209 | C-C | RS-8 | Electro-Motive | SD-38 | 74649-1 | 1975 | 40-387,000-2,000 | 96,750 | 1980 | Leased to Bessemer & Lake Erie |
| 210 | C-C | RS-8 | Electro-Motive | SD-38 | 74649-2 | 1975 | 40-387,000-2,000 | 96,750 | | |
| 211 | C-C | RS-8 | Electro-Motive | SD-38 | 74649-3 | 1975 | 40-387,000-2,000 | 96,750 | | |
| 212 | C-C | RS-8 | Electro-Motive | SD-38 | 74649-4 | 1975 | 40-387,000-2,000 | 96,750 | | |
| 213 | C-C | RS-8 | Electro-Motive | SD-38 | 74649-5 | 1975 | 40-387,000-2,000 | 96,750 | | |
| 301* | C-C | | Electro-Motive | SD-38 | 25260 | 1959 | 40-387,000-1,750 | 96,750 | | Orig. No. 174 rebuilt by DM&IR 1979 |
| 302* | C-C | | Electro-Motive | SD-38 | 25274 | 1959 | 40-387,000-1,750 | 96,750 | | Orig. No. 160 rebuilt by DM&IR 1980 |
| 900 | C-C | RS-9 | Alco | | 3440-1 | 1966 | 40-394,000-3,000 | 98,500 | 1976 | From UP '73; Leased, DM&IR to Cartier |
| 901 | C-C | RS-9 | Alco | | 3440-2 | 1966 | 40-394,000-3,000 | 98,500 | 1976 | From UP '73; Leased, DM&IR to Cartier |
| 902 | C-C | RS-9 | Alco | | 3440-3 | 1966 | 40-394,000-3,000 | 98,500 | 1976 | From UP '73; Leased, DM&IR to Cartier |
| 903 | C-C | RS-9 | Alco | | 3440-4 | 1966 | 40-394,000-3,000 | 98,500 | 1976 | From UP '73; Leased, DM&IR to Cartier |
| 904 | C-C | RS-9 | Alco | | 3440-5 | 1966 | 40-394,000-3,000 | 98,500 | 1976 | From UP '73; Leased, DM&IR to Cartier |
| 905 | C-C | RS-9 | Alco | | 3440-6 | 1966 | 40-394,000-3,000 | 98,500 | 1974 | From UP '73; Leased, DM&IR to Cartier |
| 906 | C-C | RS-9 | Alco | | 3440-7 | 1966 | 40-394,000-3,000 | 98,500 | 1974 | From UP '73; Leased, DM&IR to Cartier |
| 907 | C-C | RS-9 | Alco | | 3440-8 | 1966 | 40-394,000-3,000 | 98,500 | 1976 | From UP '73; Leased, DM&IR to Cartier |
| 908 | C-C | RS-9 | Alco | | 3440-9 | 1966 | 40-394,000-3,000 | 98,500 | 1974 | From UP '73; Leased, DM&IR to Cartier |
| 909 | C-C | RS-9 | Alco | | 3440-10 | 1966 | 40-394,000-3,000 | 98,500 | 1976 | From UP '73; Leased, DM&IR to Cartier |

*New number after rebuilding. No company classification assigned.

A trio of SD-9's leads an ore train at Iron Junction, May 26, 1961.

DM&IR collection

## SELF-PROPELLED RAIL CARS

| No. | Railroad | Builder | Date Built | Remarks |
|---|---|---|---|---|
| MC-1 | D&IR | Barney & Smith | 1907 | Remodeled from combine car No. 19 by D&IR in 1926. Equipped with two Red Seal Continental 104-hp, 6-cylinder gas engines. Seating capacity: 36 persons. Used on Western Mesaba Branch between Allen Junction and Virginia. |
| M-55 | DM&N | Ohio Falls Car Co. | 1901 | Remodeled during 1927 from coach No. 55. Equipped with two Red Seal Continental 70-hp, 6-cylinder gas engines. Seating capacity: 64 persons. Used for Proctor roundhouse jitney service. |
| W-56 | DM&IR | Twin City Rapid Transit Co. | 1914 | Remodeled from Duluth Street Railway trolley car in 1939. Equipped with General Motors 160-hp diesel engine and generator by DM&IR. Seating capacity: 36 persons. Used for Proctor roundhouse jitney service. This motor car replaced M-55. Ex Dul. St. Ry. No. 268. |
| M-108 | DM&N | American Car & Foundry | 1908 | Remodeled during 1928 from combine car No. 108. Equipped with two Red Seal Continental 104-hp, 6-cylinder gas engines. Seating capacity: 30 persons. Used on Alborn Branch. |
| RDC-1 | DM&IR | Budd Co. | 1953 | Rail Diesel Car - type RDC-3. Equipped with two 275-hp model 61801RA General Motors diesels. Builders No. 5701. Seating capacity: 48 persons. Sold to the Northern Pacific Railway (now Burlington Northern). |

DM&IR RDC-3 No. 1.                                                        DM&IR collection

# DULUTH, MISSABE & IRON RANGE RAILWAY
## Locomotives Owned

| | Class RS-2 (5) | |
|---|---|---|
| 121 | Leased EJ&E | 9-17-72 |
| 122 | Leased B&LE | 7-03-71 |
| 123 | Leased B&LE | 7-03-71 |
| 129 | | |
| 130 | | |

| | Class RS-3 (23) | |
|---|---|---|
| 131 | Leased B&LE | 6-29-71 |
| 132 | | |
| 133 | Leased EJ&E | 1-19-71 |
| 134 | | |
| 135 | Leased EJ&E | 10-27-71 |
| 137 | Leased B&LE | 6-29-71 |
| 138 | | |
| 139 | | |
| 142 | | |
| 143 | | |
| 144 | | |
| 145 | | |
| 147 | Leased EJ&E | 10-27-71 |
| 149 | | |
| 150 | | |
| 151 | Leased B&LE | 7- 2-71 |
| 152 | | |
| 153 | | |
| 154 | Leased EJ&E | 10-27-71 |
| 155 | | |
| 156 | | |
| 157 | | |
| 158 | | |

| Class RS-4 (14) | |
|---|---|
| 159 | 167 |
| 161 | 168 |
| 162 | 169 |
| 163 | 170 |
| 164 | 171 |
| 165 | 172 |
| 166 | 173 |

| Class RS-6 (19) | |
|---|---|
| 175 | 185 |
| 176 | 186 |
| 177 | 187 |
| 178 | 188 |
| 179 | 189 |
| 180 | 190 |
| 181 | 191 |
| 182 | 192 |
| 183 | 193 |
| 184 | |

| Class RS-7 (8) | |
|---|---|
| 201 | 205 |
| 202 | 206 |
| 203 | 207 |
| 204 | 208 |

| | Class RS-8 (5) | |
|---|---|---|
| 209 | | |
| 210 | Leased B&LE | 3-28-80 |
| 211 | | |
| 212 | | |
| 213 | | |

| | Class RS-9 (10) | |
|---|---|---|
| 900 | Leased Cartier | 4- 5-76 |
| 901 | Leased Cartier | 3-24-76 |
| 902 | Leased Cartier | 4- 5-76 |
| 903 | Leased Cartier | 3-24-76 |
| 904 | Leased Cartier | 4- 5-76 |
| 905 | Leased Cartier | 4-10-74 |
| 906 | Leased Cartier | 4-10-74 |
| 907 | Leased Cartier | 3-24-76 |
| 908 | Leased Cartier | 4-10-74 |
| 909 | Leased Cartier | 4- 5-76 |

| Old Class (2) | |
|---|---|
| 301 | (Old 174) |
| 302 | (Old 160) |

TOTAL DIESELS: 86

Note: Diesels listed as leased are those on long term lease: 20
short term lease: 1#
21#

Office of Chief Mechanical Officer / Proctor, Minnesota / March 25, 1981

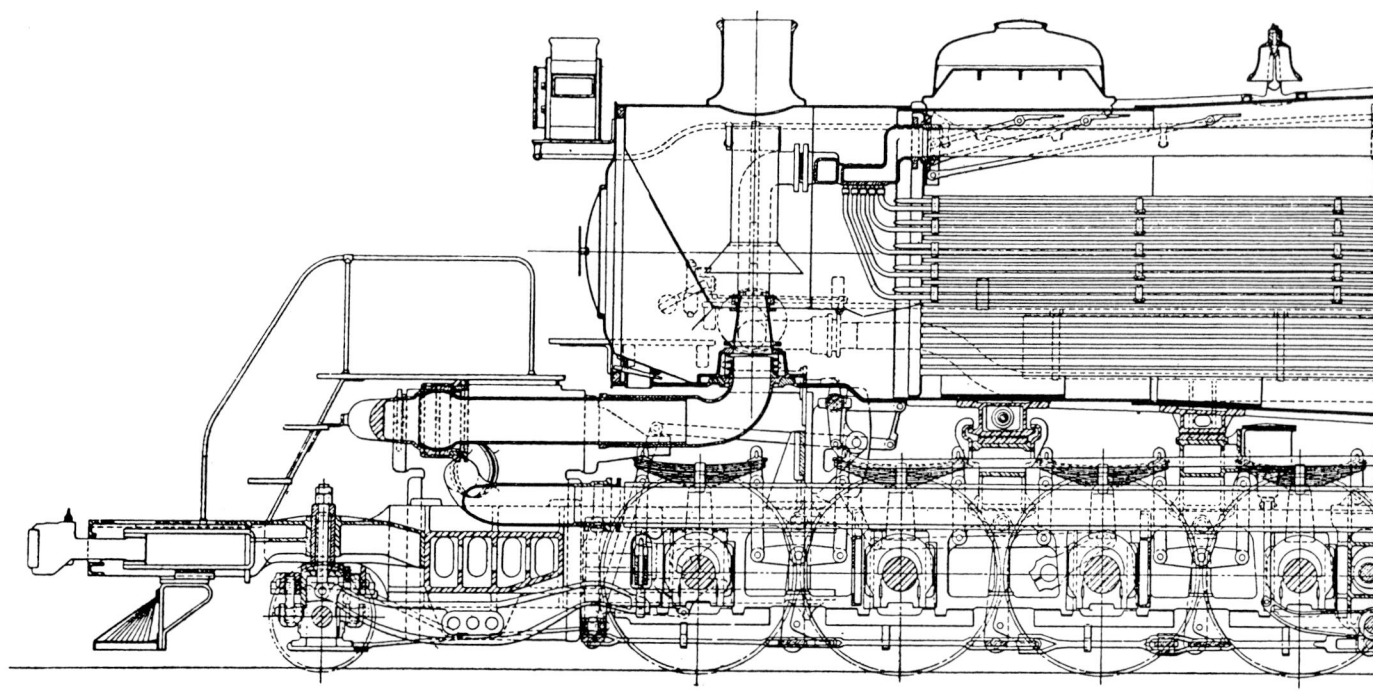

## A

Adolph, Mn. **100-101**, 119
Agate Bay 11
Allen Junction 15, 114, 173
Allouez 27, 108
American Steel & Wire Corp. 62
Amundsen, Louis (Engineer) 14, 117
Armour, P.D. (meat-packer) 21

## B

Baldwin (Locomotive Works) 11-12, 15-16, 50, 79, 84, 94, 107-108, 110, 112, 118 (diesel), 158
Balkan Mining Co. 296
Barco Manufacturing Co. **159**
Bessemer & Lake Erie 79, 118
Bijold, Walter "Mose" (Engineer) 119
Biwabik, Mn. 15, 20, 27, 53, 81, 84, 110, 113, 118, 136, Depot **189**, 225, Yards **242**
Bohannon, George W. 111
Brimson (Depot) **188**
Budd Car No.1 **202-203**, 175
Business Cars
  "Missabe" **29**, 194, 200, "Olivette" **186**, "Minnesota" **186**, "Northland" **180, 268-269**

## C

Carlson, Charles Edwin 111
Cartier Ry. (Quebec) 244-245, 256
Cazenovia Southern 28, 34
Chandler Mine 15
Chesapeake & Ohio R.R. 117
Chicago, Ill. 16, 112
Chicago & Eastern Illinois 15
Chicago & Northwestern 34, 111
Cloquet River bridge 119
Coaling Towers **283-284**
Coffin Feedwater Heater 81, **83, 89, 94-95**, 109-110
Coleraine, Mn. **69**, 119, Junction **161**
Cooke Locomotive Works (Alco) 39

## D

DC&S 4-6-0 No.15 **36**
Deer Park R.R. 173
Denver & Rio Grande 29, 111, 117
Denver & Rio Grande Western 225, 2-8-2 No.1205 **232**, 4-8-2 No.1552 **232**
Depots **188-189**
Detroit Caro & Sandusky 36
Dickson Locomotive Works (Alco) 39

314

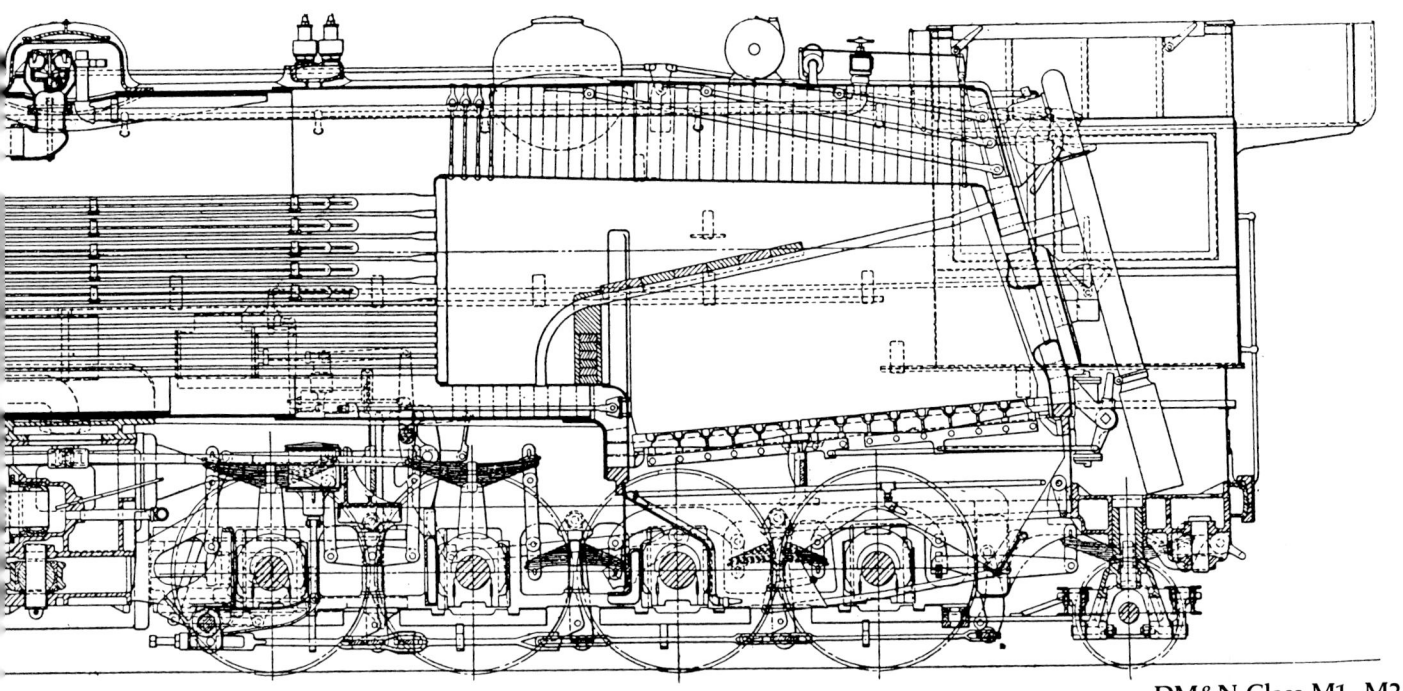

**DM&N Class M1, M2**

Diesel Facilities **285**
Duluth, Mn. 11-12, 15, 24, 27, 29, 32,
    Ore Docks **32-33**, 114-115, Union Depot **32**, 47,
    60, 70, 78, 86, 93, 107-108, 113, 118, 120, 124,
    148, 151, **65-66**
Duluth & Northern Minn. Ry. 47, 75
Duluth Street Ry. 15
Duluth & Winnipeg (CPR) 27

# E

East Mesaba Branch 43-44
Eddystone, Pa. (Baldwin) 112
El Paso & Northeastern 16
Elesco Feedwater Heaters 81, **90-91**, 93, 95, **105**,
    108, 111, 120
Elgin, Joliet & Eastern 243
Ely, Mn. 15, 142, 173
Electro Motive Division 119, 243
Endion 86, 93
Endion Roundhouse **280**
Eveleth, Mn. 289
Eveleth Branch 144

# F

Fairbanks, Mn. 152
Fayal Main **20**, Yard 114, 117

Fire Tug "Torrent" **42**

# G

Gas Motor Car No.55 **200**
Grand Trunk (Ry.) 107
Great Northern Ry. 15, 107-109
    Mallet No.2008 **109**, 119, 144
    FT's (diesels) **162**, 243, F-units **247**
G.N. Power Co. 107
Greatsinger, J.L. (Pres. D&IR R.R.) 16

# H

Hanna Ore Mining Co. 294
Hanna Stoker 111
Head of the Lakes 112
Hibbing, Mn. 32, 96, 118, 174-175
High Grade Yard 119
Highland, Mn. 114, 157
Hull Rust Yard (Hibbing) **167**
Hinsdale (Depot) **188**

# I

Illinois Steel Co. 12
Indiana, Illinois & Iowa R.R. 39
Iron Junction, Mn. 27, , 70, **282**

315

Here's a view of massive Missabe iron ore dock No. 6 at Duluth. Pittsburgh Steamship Company's ore boat "Mataafa" is filling her hold with ore. This dock, built of concrete and steel, stands 84 feet above the water. It is 2304 feet long and has a total storage capacity of 153,000 gross tons.

Author's collection

# L

Lake Superior 11, 107
Lake Superior Museum of Transportation 118, 148
LeMassena, Robert A. 111
Leonidas Hill 115
Lima Locomotive Works 78-79, 88

Locomotives
  4-4-0 (American type) D&IR No.1 and 2 12; No.1 **16, 18**; No.2 **17**; No. 23 **175**; No. 24 **21**; No.99 **25, 27,** 173

  4-6-0 (Ten-wheeler) D&IR Class M 173; No.101 **176-177**; No.102 **177**; DM&N 29; No.7, No.9 **30**; No.31 **31**; No.19, No.20, No.22 **35**; No.17 **34**; No.5 **36**; No.21 **37**; No.30 **37**; DM&N Class F 173-174; No.17,19 **190**; No.30 **190**; No.100,101 **191**; No.102 **194**

  4-6-2 (Pacific) D&IR Class A No.107-110 173; No.1107,175 **178**, 180-181; No.400 **195**; No.401 **196**; No.402 **198-199**; D&IR No.110 **182**

  4-8-0 (Twelve-wheeler) D&IR No.68 15-16; No.60 **22**; No.66 **23**; No.67 **23**; No.69 **24**; No.83 **24,** 25, 39

  Switchers 207-208; 0-4-0 D&IR No.4 **17, 20, 209**; No.14 **20, 209**; 0-6-0 D&IR No.27 **210**; DM&N No.31 56, **211**; No.57 **212**; MD&W No.8 **212**; 0-6-0 D&IR No.27 **210**; DM&N No.31,56 **211**; No.57 **212**; MD&W No.8 **212**; No.59,61,64 **213**; 0-8-0 No.87 **206**; DM&N No.81 **215**; No.82,83,84 **216**; O.I.M. No.401 **219**; No.86 **219**; 0-10-0 DM&N No.90,91, 92 **220**; No.91,93 **221**; No.93 **222-223**

  2-8-0 (Consolidation) D&IR No.8 11; No.28-33 15; No.7,9 and 10 18; No.12 **19**; No.51 **21**, 29; No.46 **38**; DM&N No.300 **31-32,** 39-40; D&IR No.141 40, **41**; No.38 **41-42**; No.37 **42**; No.45 **43**; No.49 **43-44**; No.50 **45**; No.52 **46**; No.152 **46**; No.53 **47**; No.54 **47**; No.191 **49**; No.197 **49**; No.92 **50**; No.196 **50**; No.208 **51**; No.1200 and 1201 **51**; No.1209 **52**; No.1212 **52**; No.1213 **53** (DM&IR); No.216 **54**; No.1214 **54**; No.1217 **55**; No.1218 **56** (DM&IR); D&IR No.1223 **57**; DM&N No.301 **58**; No.302 **59**; No.306 **60-61**; DM&IR No.307 **62**; No.308 **62**; DM&N No.309,310 **62**; No.311 **63**; No.309,311 **63**; No.315 **65**; O.I.M. No.513 **64**; DM&N No.325 **68**; No.327 **68**; No.324 **68**; No.328 **69**; No.332 **70**; D&NE No.28 **71**; DM&N No.333 **72**; MN&S No.404,405 **73**; DM&IR No.335 **74**; DM&N No.340 **75**; No.348 **76**; D&NE No.27 **76**; DM&N No.305 **303**; DM&N No.346,347,350 77, 79, 107

  2-8-2 (Mikados) DM&IR No.1304 78, 79, 81; No.1303 **81**; D&IR No.300,301 **82**; No.1300,1301 **83**; D&IR No.302 **84**; DM&IR No.1303 **84**; D&IR No.304 **85**; DM&IR No.1304 **85, 86**; D&IR No.305 **88**; DM&IR No.1305 **88**; D&IR No.306,307 **89**; No.309 **90**; No.310,311 **91**; DM&IR No.1310 **92**; No.1311 **93**, 110; Ex-EJ&E **225**; No.1336 **205**; No.756,1313,1321 **226**; No.765,1320 **227**

  2-10-2 79-80 DM&N No.500 **94**; DM&IR No.500,503 **95**; DM&N No.504, 505 **96, 98**; No.506 **98**; No.507 **97 99**; No.509 **100**; DM&IR No.508 **100-101**; No.510 **102**; No.512,514 **103**; No.514 **104**; No.513 **105**

  2-10-4 (Ex-B&LE Texas types) 225, 118; No.625 **233**; No.706 **233**; No.707 **234-235**; No.715 **237**; No.709 **238**; No.714 **239**; No.717 **240**; No.711 **241**; No.700,714 **241**

  2-8-8-2, 2-8-8-4 (Articulateds and Mallets) 107-118 DM&N No.201 **109**, 116; No.210 **109**; "Madam Queen" 110; No.200 **120-121**; No.201 **122**; No.203 **123**; No.204 **123-124**; No.205 **125**; No.206 **126**; No.207 **127-128**; No.208 **129**; No.209 **130**; No.210 **131-133**; No.211 **134-137**

  (Yellowstones) 81; No.230 **106**, 111-119; No.220-221 **138-139**; No.221 **140**; No.222 **140,** 143; No.223 **143**; No.224 **144**; No.225 **144-145,** 148; No.226 **146-147**; No.227 **149-151**; No.228 **154-155**; No.230 **150,152-153**; No.231 **156**; No.231 and 232 **157,** 160-161; No.233 **162**; No.234 **156**; No.235 **162**; No.235 **166,** 164; No.237 **168-169**; No.224 **162-163**

Locomotives—Mining **289-296**

Locomotives—Porter **289-290**

Locomotives—Postwar 118, 225
  Union Ry 0-10-2 No.601 **224**; No.607 **228, 231**; No.604,605,606 **229**; No.605 **230**

Locomotive—Rosters **297-311**

Locomotives—Diesel 118, 243-245
  Alco 118; Ex-Union Ry **247**; DL600 Demo unit **256**; No.50 **256**; No.54,55 **257**; Ex-UP No.909 **253**; EMD SW-9 **248**; No.12,14,15 **249**; SD9 No.32 **140,250-251**; No.158 **252**; No.171 **253**; No.177,178 **255**; No.129,130 **261**; No.129 **268-269**; No.110 **271**; No.58 **265**; Misc. SD9's **242, 243 260**; Rebuilt SD9's No.301 **266**

  Shops **267** (see Diesel Facilities) SD38-2's No.204,208 **262-263**; No.202 **264**; Fairbanks-Morse "Trainmasters" 243, **258-259**; GN F Units **247, 253**; 1000 HP Diesel Switcher (Alco) **295**; RDC Cars **202-203,** 310

Loraine Steel Co. 207

317

## M

Mahoning Ore Co.  290
Maps
    D&IR 10;  DM&N 26;  DM&IR 304
Mail Car No.10  **183**
Marshall Field  21
Meagher, P., Mining Co.  207
Merritt Brothers  27
Mesabi Iron Co.  293
Mesabi Range  27, 29, 39, 107, 117
Mill, Darius Ogden  21
Minnesota, Dakota & Western  207
Minnesota Iron Co.  12
Mitchell, Mn.  53
Mountain Iron  27;  Depot **189**
Motor Car No.M-108  **201**

## N

New York Construction Co.  27
New York Central Moguls  27
Norfolk & Western  110, 117-118
Northern Pacific  27, 117

## O

Oliver Iron Mining Co.  65, 207
    Mine 291;  0-8-0 **293**
Owens, Thomas (Supt. D&IR)  12

## P

Parlor Car No.27 **187**
Passenger Cars  **185**
Pennsylvania Railroad  40
Pennsylvania Steel Co.  11
Philadelphia, Pa.  11, 111
Pioneer Mine (Ely)  45
Pitkin, A.J.  16
Pittsburgh Locomotive Works  27, 29-40, 65, 207
"Pork City Hill"  48
Proctor, Mn.  29, 31, 35-36, 40, 54-55, 57-60, 68, 73, 75, 79, 94-96, 99-100, 107-108, 110, 118-119, 122-127, 129, 131-132, 134, 139, 144, 147, 155-158;
    Ore Scales **157, 162,** 167, 207, 225, 243;
    Backshops 110, **270-271, 276-279**
Pullman Co.  111

## Q

Quebec, Cartier Ry. (U.S. Steel Sub.)  118

## R

Rainy Junction Yard  114
Rust Crusher Yard (Hibbing)  96
Rogers Locomotive Works  207
Rolling Stock  **288, 289**

## S

Saginaw, Mn.  144, 152, 160
St. Louis River  107
St. Paul & Duluth  15
Schenectady
    (Locomotive Works)  15-16, 22, 207-208
Self-propelled Cars  **200-201**
Shop Motor Car W-56  **201**
Soudan, Mn.  12
Southern Pacific R.R.  15
Sparta, Mn.  135-136
Standard Stokers  108, **159**
Steelton Yard  **74**
Stone, Ella G. (Company Tug)  11
Stony Brook Junction  27
Sullivan, Patrick M.
    (Road Foreman of Engines; also DM&IR Supt.
    of Motive Power and Cars)  113, 174
Superior, Wisc.  27
Superior National Forest  53

## T

Taconite Junction  119
Tennessee Pass (D&RGW)  117
Tower, Mn.  11-12, 15, 56
Tower, Charlemagne, Jr.  11, 13
Truman, Harry S  243
Two Harbors, Mn.  11-12, 15, 18, 20, 40, 42, 46, 48, 50, 78-80, 82, 88-89, 91, 110, 112-118, 142, 148; Depot **189**, 243-244; Yard **170**, 173, 207, 225; Backshops **273-275**; Roundhouse **22, 273**

## U

Union Pacific R.R.  112, 117, 244
USRA (United States RR Administration)
    100, 102, 111
US Steel Corp.  39, 59

## V

Van Hoven, Paul H.  117
Vermilion Range  11-12, 117
Virginia, Mn.  48, 52, 57, 104; Enginehouse **281**

## W

Waldo (Summit)  117
Wales Branch  55-56, 243
Western Pacific R.R.  111, 117

Westinghouse AirBrake  159
Wheeling & Lake Erie  225
Wolf (Contractor-D&IR)  11
Wolf, Mn.  27, 136
Wood, Lowell  118
World's Fair (Chicago)  15
World War II  40, 117
Worthington Feedwater Heater  111
Wyeman, Mn.  148

Frank A. King

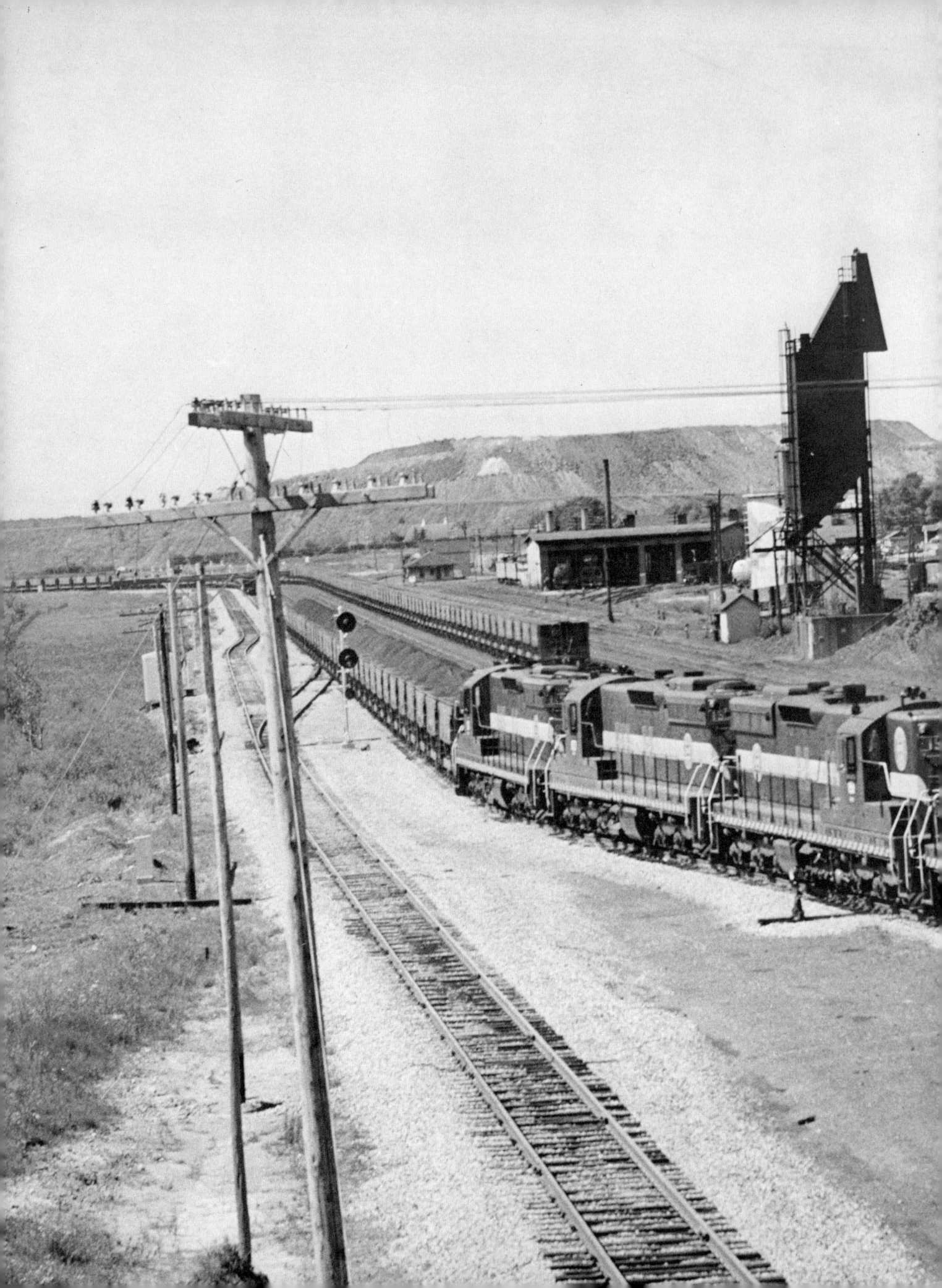